ABRAHAM AND SARAH –

ABRAHAM AND SARAH – HEIRS TOGETHER

Roger Lewis

The Christadelphian
404 Shaftmoor Lane, Hall Green, Birmingham B28 8SZ, UK
2014

First published 2014

ISBN 978 0 85189 289 4 (print edition)
ISBN 978 0 85189 290 0 (electronic edition)

Printed and bound in Malta by
Gutenberg Press Limited

CONTENTS

FOREWORD

NO married couple in Scripture is given quite the same attention as Abraham and Sarah. Many aspects of their marriage are open to scrutiny, and even the most intimate facets of their life together are set out for extensive examination. All this is for good reason.

The journeys they undertook together, both physical and spiritual, were to test their faith in the extreme. Called upon to leave country, kindred and family they responded without hesitation, beginning their physical journey without question or complaint. By the time their spiritual journey was complete they had experienced considerable emotional stress over the delayed birth of the promised son, attempted to bring human solutions to matters divine, and had displayed moments of weakness which resonate with today's reader. Ultimately they were given the unique privilege and greatest trial of sharing in the Almighty's most beneficent act, that of offering up an only begotten son. To reach such a stage of spiritual maturity requires a lifetime of experience and challenge, and of careful attention to the things of heaven. Few attain this, even after years of effort, but in the example of Abraham and Sarah, all children of faith are presented with very human examples of high endeavour on which their own lives of faithfulness can be based.

This book is offered in the hope that others will appreciate afresh the joys and sorrows of the account of Abraham and Sarah, gaining new insights into passages that have become familiar. It is also hoped that today's spiritual children may begin to understand the emotions and feelings of this faithful couple, who, through adversity and blessing, grew in grace until they were fully persuaded that what God had promised He was able also to perform. If sons and daughters by grace could capture but a part of Abraham and Sarah's faith, hope and love, their own journeys to the land of promise would be filled with greater satisfaction and reward.

Andrew Bramhill
Birmingham
November 2014

PROLOGUE

THE Bible was written to be read aloud. The oracles of God were given in many parts, and many ways, but chiefly for the benefit of those that have an ear to hear "what the Spirit saith". The instructions of the Torah were read in the hearing of the congregation, who assembled that they might listen to the Levites. The songs of the psalmists were sung in the presence of the faithful who stood before the house of God. The prophets thundered their denunciations in the cities of Israel and Judah, and their audience knew that the word of God had been spoken to them. The parables of Christ were taught to the multitudes, which heard his words and loved his doctrine. In the ecclesias of God, the writings of the apostles were circulated and read aloud for the edifying of the saints. For most generations of the people of God, their knowledge of the truth was founded upon what they had heard, rather than what they had read. To hear, to know, to love, to obey, was the simple fourfold maxim for spiritual life.

This book has been written from a similar perspective. The writer would urge the reader therefore to read this writing aloud with passion and with care. For when the story is read aloud, the force and vigour of word and thought, of sound and idea, will be savoured properly.

Planted deep within us all is a love of stories, and the telling of them by the storyteller. We are drawn to certain characters, and are touched by experiences in their lives, for which we feel affinity or understanding. The Bible is filled with such accounts of the people of God, and the hand of the Almighty at work in their lives. These narratives are not the fictions of imagination, but the true and honest stories of real men and women

1

whose lives were recorded by the Spirit,[1] that others might learn.

That which follows is just such a story, for this book seeks to enter into the life and times of the Bible's most illustrious couple, and tell the tale of their marriage together. It is a story that ought to be told, because it has the warrant of Scripture to authenticate it. Here is a record of drama and woe, of faith and fear, of triumph and despair, but most of all of struggle and growth in spiritual things. There is no account to match it in Holy Scripture. No other marriage is recorded with such breadth of circumstance, or in such intimacy of detail. No other marriage is referenced in Scripture as often as this one, and this for reasons, which by and by we shall know, but only when the final chapter is turned and the tale is told. Then we shall appreciate, that from beginning to end, there is something uniquely special about this couple.

A work of fiction would try to embellish the record with imaginary people and imagined events. This is not the purpose or intention of this book. Instead, it seeks to trace the Scriptural diary of their life, and to reflect upon the events recorded. At the same time however the writer has sought to enter into the heart of each episode, to see the surrounding countryside and know the seasons, to picture the household at work in daily toil and hear the flocks of the fold, to know the spirit and mind of this man and woman who walked before God in the hills and valleys of Palestine. Yet even these reflections are carefully measured, for comment is only made on those episodes actually recorded, or on events which although not mentioned, occurred with certainty or reasonable probability. Where a matter seems in doubt

---

1 'Spirit' here is used in the sense of the overshadowing of God in the writing of the holy oracles (2 Peter 1:20,21). Despite the fact that amanuenses were used, they all "spake as they were moved by the Holy Spirit", and in this way were but the instruments to record such matters and events as the Spirit thought necessary for our salvation.

or requires expansion, chapter footnotes and appendices give greater detail.

The writer is acutely aware of his own mistakes in life, of shortcomings in word and thought and deed. He is also mindful of failings in his own personal discipleship, which have fallen short of the divine ideal, and for which he has needed to seek forgiveness. And yet sin, faced, confessed and forsaken is the very stuff of which this story is made. This couple were imbued with the same fleshly infirmities that plague and distress us day by day, as we wrestle with our nature, and face the consequences of our sinful tendencies. Far from being above and beyond us, their story unfolds to reveal a man and a woman beset with all the issues of daily life with which we ourselves struggle, their very circumstances so similar at their heart to ours, that we can take comfort from their lives and encouragement from their story.

For in truth the marriage of Abraham and Sarah brought together two wonderful individuals, who were at once both illustrious and imperfect. Abraham was a man sought after for his faithful valour,[2] known for his deep integrity of purpose,[3] and noted for his warm hospitality.[4] Yet the same man was to be admonished for his use of deceit,[5] and corrected for his fleshly thinking.[6] He was a man of extraordinary faith,[7] yet wrestled with the weakness of his fear.[8] His wife was no different. For Sarah was admired for her exceptional beauty,[9] commended for her genuine submissiveness,[10] and mentioned for her spiritual insight.[11] Yet this very

---

2 Genesis 14:14,15.
3 Genesis 14:22,23.
4 Genesis 18:3-5.
5 Genesis 12:18,19.
6 Genesis 21:11,12.
7 Genesis 22:16,17.
8 Genesis 20:11,12.
9 Genesis 12:14,15.
10 Genesis 18:12.
11 Genesis 21:9,10.

3

woman was to be rebuked for her incredulity,[12] and chided for her extremity of passion.[13] She was a woman of enormous perception,[14] yet struggled with the strength of her feelings.[15] The writing of the Spirit portrayed them both with characteristic frankness, unmerciful in this respect that their personal weaknesses were left on view, to emphasise that it was God working in them to make them what they were. They might indeed be special, but they were not exempt from fear, from folly or from failure. They were real people with real problems, and yet because of this we can feel closer to them both.

There have been learned dissertations produced upon the patriarchal time, which categorise their faults in the language of this age. Terms such as dysfunctional families, abusive relationships, gender issues, disenfranchised minorities are not uncommon. The writer is uneasy about such writing for two reasons. The first is that such terms are all the expressions of academic humanism, the current *lingua franca* of worldly wisdom. But they are not the breathings of the Spirit. Men and women who love the word will seek to use a style of language that is harmonious with the utterances of the Spirit, even in the contemplation of the failings of others. Moreover, such thoughts do not always do justice to Abraham and Sarah. Whatever their faults, and they are recorded for us, this man is described in Scripture as the "Friend of God", and his wife (by extension) as the "mother of us all". We should take great care therefore before describing their faults in the pejorative language of fleshly experts, or imputing evil motive and intention when the divine writ itself does not so do. Where Scripture plainly suggests a failure in faith, then we should be guided by its own description. Bible terms are not only best when describing deficiencies, but also best when describing how to overcome them. Spiritual life is linked to spiritual

12 Genesis 18:14,15.
13 Genesis 16:5,6.
14 Genesis 21:6,7.
15 Genesis 18:11,12.

thought, and spiritual thought is linked to spiritual language. When the depth and quality of spiritual language is lost, so also is the profundity of spiritual thought it describes. To express both our weaknesses and our aspirations in the exalted dialect of the word is, for our community, a great *desideratum* of the age.

Abraham and Sarah, despite their weaknesses, both had decisive characters, refreshing in their strength and clarity of purpose. There are many who in their marriages blandly follow the way of sameness, and aspire only to the ordinary and the mundane. Here was a couple who, inspired by the call of God, responded with all their heart and soul, following His command wherever it might lead them. The result of this passionate commitment to God's way, was a marriage that reached astounding spiritual heights with hearts and minds entwined together in mutual understanding of divine principles, a marriage which would become the benchmark and standard of those that followed.

So important was their story, that the Spirit moved the pens of several ready writers, who spoke and wrote upon the lessons of their life together. In this they were unique among the patriarchs, for Isaac and Rebekah appear only once as a couple in the New Testament, Jacob and Leah never, nor Joseph and Asenath. From the exodus to the monarchy, there were other faithful couples, yet these are not mentioned in the New Testament. We do not hear of Amram and Jochebed, or of Moses and Zipporah. Boaz and Ruth do not appear, or Elkanah and Hannah. Illustrious kings married special wives, and yet even in their greatness failed to receive a mention together in the writings of the apostolic age. We search in vain for a mention of David and Bathsheba for they do not appear; there is not one reference to Solomon and Pharaoh's daughter, or to Hezekiah and Hephzibah.

Yet this couple grace the pages of gospel and epistle time and time again, standing together in a special way that sets them apart. The final vision of Scripture reveals the consummation of a promise that began in

Hebron, when the angel appeared and spoke to this man and his wife.[16] Genesis and Revelation are thus bound together by a golden theme that begins with Abraham and Sarah, and ends with all nations rejoicing as their spiritual seed, in fellowship with God. The entire world their offspring! What manner of people are these two?

The years of the life of Abraham were one hundred and seventy-five. Not all of these were spent wandering in the hills of Canaan, for he was already seventy-five when he first entered the land. Apart from the notable record of his faithful obedience to the call of God,[17] we know but little of these first seventy-five years. And yet the end of the patriarch is like his beginning. For aside from the famous incident of his obedient faithfulness to the command of God,[18] we know but little of his last seventy-five years. It is as if both these epochs of time pass from the holy oracles in relative obscurity. But in the middle, the very middle of his life, are twenty-five years of vital personal history upon which it was the sovereign pleasure of God to focus with almost exclusive intensity.

Almost all of these episodes concern the man and his wife. The events of these years must be charged with significance, for they are selected as representative of their marriage and life together as a whole. They show above all things the development of their faith through the circumstances of their times. These two remarkable people matched each other stride for stride, yet each developed in their own way according to their several abilities. Brothers and sisters alike will learn much from the diary of these two.

---

16 Revelation 21:1-3. The famous promise that 'God would be their God and that they would be his people' reverberates down through the entire Scriptural record, and reaches its climax in the Apocalypse with the whole world in covenant fellowship with the Deity. But the kernel of this promise began with Abraham and Sarah, from whom God's people would spring (cp. Genesis 17:5-8,15,16).

17 Genesis 12:1-5.

18 Genesis 22:1-5.

It will be our privilege to journey with them. We shall not accompany them as unaffected bystanders, or as merely curious onlookers. For their record is the code book for our own accounts of faith, our own stories of trial, our own lives of growth. Let the journey begin.

1

EMBARKING ON THE JOURNEY OF FAITH TOGETHER
(Genesis 11:27 – 12:9)

HIGH in the mountains of Armenia, not far from the snow-clad slopes of Ararat, a river began its odyssey. From the foundation of the world, it had been one of the four heads into which the ancient river of God had been parted, and more than once it would find prominence in the purpose of God's dealing with His people. Fed by the snows of these heights, the great Euphrates flowed dark and strong through wild mountains, and across tablelands, determined on emptying itself into the Mediterranean. Defeated in its aim however, by the noble risings of other mountain ramparts, the river at last turned eastwards and inland, and began its stately traverse across the hills and valleys of Mesopotamia. As it travelled, it was swollen in size by the mighty confluence of other rushing streams that poured their waters into its channel, yielding to its primacy. Only the Tigris, flowing further east, would match this Euphratean tide, as together they watered the 'land of the two rivers'.[1]

In Ur of the Chaldees

Although the river meandered in places, its general direction was purposeful and unchanging. It swept south-east across the plain, sinking by successive stages through alluvial flats and across clay pans until at last, depleted by the draw of irrigation and the drain of marsh, it ended with its final embouchure into the Persian Gulf. Along its length great cities arose, and these were nourished by its blessings. Mari, Babylon, Borsippa, Erech, Larsa, Ur, all these were watered by the mighty stream.

---

1 The meaning of the word 'Mesopotamia'.

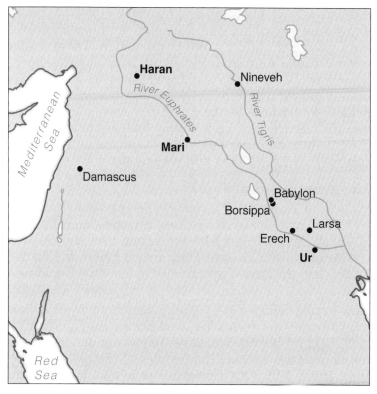

But Ur was the last before the sea was reached, and this proximity was the key to its importance and power. The city boasted two harbours, with the river encircling the town. Ships from the Persian Gulf brought their wares upriver to Ur. Diorite and alabaster, gold and copper, ivory and hardwoods, the exotic and the rare all found their way into the trading houses of Ur, and from thence northward with the merchants who energetically plied their trade and their craft upon the waters of the river, and thereby to the river towns. The treasures of Egypt, of Ethiopia and of India were all moved across the plain by such river vessels, and much of it began its journey in Ur.

The city of Ur was organised as a state. Under the guidance of its laws, commerce and industry were regulated. Town planning organised the layout of streets and paths, plumbing and drainage, and architectural laws governed building and construction. There was a state religion administered by an official priesthood, which presided over the worship of the moon-god Nanna, in the ziggurat temple of Ur. Education was promoted and politics flourished. Writing and the arts, mathematics and the sciences were all notable features of society, for the inhabitants of Ur enjoyed a standard of living and culture that was refined and prosperous.

The generations of Terah

"And Terah lived seventy years, and begat Abram, Nahor, and Haran. Now these are the generations of Terah: Terah begat Abram, Nahor, and Haran; and Haran begat Lot. And Haran died before his father Terah in the land of his nativity, in Ur of the Chaldees."

(Genesis 11:26-28)

Now in this civilized yet pagan place, there dwelt a man whose name was Terah. He lived among the inhabitants of Ur, and yet he was a stranger in their midst, for he did not share their origin. The peoples of the plain sprang from Ham,[2] but with Terah it was not so. Instead, the blood of Shem ran in his veins, for he was descended from Noah through that line. He was separated by enormous distance from Shem, and was removed from him to the eighth generation, yet one day his own son would meet and converse with his illustrious progenitor.[3]

Terah's own marriage was fruitful in raising up three sons, upon whom the future and destiny of the house

---

2   The kingdoms of the land of Shinar were founded by Nimrod, who (through the line of Cush) was of Hamitic not Semitic origin (Genesis 10:6-12).

3   Based upon the suggestion that the Melchizedek of Genesis 14:18-20 who conversed with Abraham, was in fact Shem. Not only is this a chronological possibility, but also sets Shem as the great patriarchal head of the true worship in Salem in direct opposition to the rival system of worship established by Nimrod in Babylon. Abraham's exodus from the one centre to the other is highly significant in the context of his call to the true worship of God.

depended. The genealogy would carefully list them as Abram, Nahor and Haran, although this was not the order of their birth. For Abram was Terah's youngest son, far younger than his firstborn, a child verily of Terah's old age.[4] Yet for all that, the record spoke true in placing Abram first, for he would become Terah's most famous son and the focus of the story to follow.

The record of Terah's family however, would begin, not with Abram, but with the firstborn son. Haran, the eldest, had already married, and had fathered one son and two fine daughters. His branch of the family seemed secure, but one day in the prime of his manhood, he died. Terah, old yet hale, was a grief stricken witness of his son's tragic death,[5] which was doubtless premature.[6]

The shock of his son's demise was a solemn reminder to Terah of his own mortality, and to Abram, on later reflection, that the truth does not always reach and touch whole families. Haran's death also left his children without guidance and support. Moved therefore by this sorrow shared, the family drew together within its own ranks. Abram and Nahor, Haran's younger brothers, married their nieces[7] to help preserve their brother's line, and provide for his fatherless daughters.

So Haran died exactly where he had been born. Despite his firstborn status, he had made no spiritual progress. He was a man without promise and without change, without response and without growth. His whole life was encompassed therefore, within the span of just one place. For as he lived, so thus he died, and where he lived, so there he died.

Entering the record of Scripture together

"And Abram and Nahor took them wives: the name of Abram's wife was Sarai; and the name of Nahor's

---

4   See Appendix 1, "When did Terah beget Abram?"
5   The phrase in Genesis 11:28 – 'died before Terah' means literally 'before the face of', or 'in the presence of' Terah (cp. NASB).
6   Haran's death well before his father's certainly implies this.
7   See Appendix 2, "Who was Iscah?"

wife, Milcah, the daughter of Haran, the father of Milcah, and the father of Iscah. But Sarai was barren; she had no child." (Genesis 11:29,30)

In Abram, however, there would be seen another example of a younger son who showed greater faithfulness, and who rose to greater spiritual heights than the firstborn.[8] Yet his spiritual success would not be his alone, but would be shared by his heart's companion. For no sooner does he appear in the narrative, than his wife appears alongside him. They would be inseparably bound in the record from this moment forth. The unfolding story would chronicle their triumphs and their tragedies, as hand in hand they walked together before God. The Spirit would reveal their motives, and the providential hand of the Father upon them. They would eventually come to understand by experience the meaning of His work in their lives. By the time, however, this realization had borne its precious fruit, they would know both exaltation of spirit and depth of despair. Through such means, Ail Shaddai would mould their characters for His glory, as they eventually learned to have faith in Him.

For the development of this spirit of faith did not come at once, it happened gradually; it grew in stages. It developed through experience, and was formed through trial. And the trial that came upon them was not just the burden and care of daily difficulties, but the pressing anxiety of a personal sorrow that overshadowed their relationship. Every marriage has its maturing trial, and this couple was no exception. The particular grief of Abram and Sarai was that their marriage was childless. Their union as husband and wife had begun with all the joyous expectation and excited hope that is shared by every newly-wed couple. Within the sanctity of their marriage bond they rejoiced in the prospect of offspring, and in the blessing of their firstborn son. For the birth

---

8 The theme of a younger brother who was more faithful than the firstborn is a pervasive story in the Old Testament record. Consider Cain / Seth, Japheth / Shem, Haran / Abram, Ishmael / Isaac, Esau / Jacob, Reuben / Joseph, Manasseh / Ephraim etc.

of this child, fondly awaited, would be at once the seal of their early fruitfulness, and the earnest of a richer harvest to come.

When, at first, no child was conceived, they accepted this as part of the uncertainty that shrouded the mystery of childbearing. But as days and months, and cycles and seasons passed, cheerful patience gave way to unease, and unease brought forth the cruel pain of fear. It was a trial that would haunt them for years, for decades, until the last vestige of human hope had been wrung out of them. And the tragedy of this barrenness was made the more sorrowful by repeated assurances, which avowed the ownership of the land to their seed ... their seed ... their seed. Every chapter in their life would vibrate with the story of the seed, and the pain of a marriage unable to produce that seed.[9] Truly this was a burden of unbelievable magnitude.

Yet this childless couple, dwelling in Ur of the Chaldees, were to be the very foundation of a new family, through whom God's purpose would now be advanced. Of course, a miracle would be needed to accomplish this, the miracle of divine interposition in their lives. Only the Father's hand would be mighty enough to bring forth fruit out of barrenness, and such fruit as would 'fill the face of the world'.

When the God of glory appeared

"And Terah took Abram his son, and Lot the son of Haran his son's son, and Sarai his daughter in law, his son, Abram's wife; and they went forth with them from Ur of the Chaldees, to go into the land of Canaan; and they came unto Haran and dwelt there."

(Genesis 11:31)

At the moment then of His sovereign choice, the Lord intervened in their lives, and to them came the call that would forever change their lives. It was a moment to be recounted and celebrated throughout the subsequent

---

9   Genesis 11:30; 15:2; 16:1,2; 17:17; 18:12,13.

history of Israel,[10] for the call of God had come to this particular man, and despite his idolatrous background, he had responded in faith, and experienced the guiding hand of God upon his travels. But it was the very spirit of Abram to reach out and include others,[11] and before long he had gathered his family into the promise as well. Terah his father responded, and as patriarchal head of the household, led the family forth[12] on this first stage of the journey of faith.[13]

---

10 Genesis 15:7; Joshua 24:2,3; Nehemiah 9:7,8; Acts 7:2,3; Hebrews 11:8.

11 Genesis 12:5; 14:13; 21:32.

12 This is the most satisfactory explanation to reconcile the statement of Terah's initiative in Genesis 11:31, with the scriptural account of Abraham receiving God's call (cp. Genesis 15:7; Nehemiah 9:7,8; Acts 7:2,3 etc.). There are other explanations, but they fall short in various ways.

   • One suggestion is that the call came to all the family including Terah, who responded in moving at least as far as Haran. But this view fails to give proper weight to the Scriptures quoted, which clearly indicate Abraham as the primary recipient of the call.

   • Another suggestion is that the call came only to Abraham, but that Terah decided on migration for his own private reason, and that Abraham simply joined his father in response to the call. But this view fails to account for the statement of Genesis 31:53, and the action of Abraham in 24:4, which suggests that the rest of the family were at least partial worshippers of God, and therefore had similarly moved in response to the divine call.

   • An even more recent view suggests that Abraham followed his father to Haran in contravention of the call he had received from God, and that his action was not really the response of faith, but of subservience to the domination of his father. Any view, however, that ignores the possibility of harmonizing Scriptural records, and is content instead to imply that they may be contradictory, is to be repudiated. When Paul states categorically that Abraham responded in faith to God's gracious call – and this in the chapter of faith's responses – then it is Biblcally unsound to suggest that it was not so.

13 The very description of the beginning of their pilgrimage in Genesis 11:31 indicates that Haran was only a preliminary station, the first stage of a journey that would ultimately lead to the land of Canaan.

Yet not all the family would respond. Then, as now, the call of the truth parted households asunder. Abram's brother Nahor remained behind in Ur, at least for the present, and Sarah therefore likewise was deprived of the company of her sister.[14] In the subsequent story of their pilgrimage of faith, these two brothers and these two sisters would never meet again, although the generation of their children which followed, would, in the providence of God, be brought together in a strange and wondrous way.

Although their final destination was the land of Canaan, lying almost due west of Ur, Abram and Sarai did not yet know this.[15] This first call bade them to separate from the past, but did not reveal the location of the future. In its very imprecision it demanded the finest of responses, a faith that impelled forward despite continuing uncertainties. In any event a journey in the direction of Canaan was impossible. Westwards of Ur there stood an endless barricade of arid desert steppes that forbad access to soldier, to merchant and to traveller alike. Terah's eye turned northward upon the highway that marched in sympathy with the channel of the Euphrates, and decided to travel in this direction.

The riband of the river

Thus it was that Abram and Sarai found themselves, together with the rest of Terah's entourage, following the coursings of the river as it swung north-westward,

---

14 There is certainly no mention of Nahor, Abraham's brother, identified in Genesis 11:27,29 as travelling with them in the account of verse 31. The silence of the record may be taken as inferring that Nahor remained in Ur after Abraham had left. He evidently migrated to Haran later however, as his family is seen to be resident in that city (24:10; 27:43).

15 The command of Genesis 12:1, which came to Abraham in Haran (as well as in Ur: Acts 7:2,3) implied a destination as yet not fully known. Hebrews 11:8 supports this notion, and the comment of Genesis 11:31, written in retrospect, does not negate this. Part of the magnificence of Abraham's faith lay in his unhesitating obedience to begin an uncertain future in journeying to an unknown land.

guiding them around the vast curve of the Fertile Crescent itself. Both of them would be tested in their faith in different ways, as the journey unfolded. Abram, striding ahead with the men, had his mind fixed on matters of route and terrain, of distance and time. He grappled with problems of pasturage[16] and water, with organizing encampment and security. Sarai, travelling with the women, found her mind filled with questions of quantity and measure, of order and portion. She sought to solve problems of duties and provisions, with arranging equipment and storage. Both would need to put their trust in the God of glory who had called them. This new nomadic life, foraging along the riverbanks, would be a vastly different one from the settled luxury of Ur. The divine interposition in their lives demanded dramatic change from the very outset, and it is a mark of their faith that they responded.

Much of the Euphrates is navigable, and at times when the terrain grew difficult or tortuous, the family travelled by river. With their broad sails unfurled, the narrow river craft skimmed the water's surface, hastening the family onwards. As the journey progressed, they passed by the mighty cities that were the beginning of Nimrod's kingdom including famed Babel itself, already a legend of notoriety. For it was here that God had shown His displeasure at the vaunting ambition of man and his desire for pre-eminence.

Still visible was the tower of pride, which jutted forlornly skywards, its monumental architecture firmly rooted in the plain, but with its topmost edifice pathetically short of the heavens it aspired to reach unto. Here was the symbol of a rival system of religion. Here, evident in Babel's ziggurat, was dreadful testimony to man's worship of himself. Even at this time, the priests of Nimrod sought to bind men's hearts and minds to another way. The people of the plain, among whom Abram and Sarai now journeyed, were steeped in this false worship,

---

16 It is likely that Abram, even though a city dweller, would have taken some animals, if only for food.

a worship that allured through mystery and intrigue. Abram looked, but passed by. His calling was to the true worship of God, and his separation as a pilgrim set him apart from this system of man's own devising.[17]

Even now the spirit of faith in this man and woman of Ur would never allow them to remain in this plain of wickedness. Both the cities of Shinar and the towns of Asshur would be left behind, as the household moved beyond the land of Nimrod where only darkness shone. The river moved decisively to the west, and after several weeks of travel the great city of Mari was reached. Here was the largest castle in the ancient world. Mari was a prosperous centre of commerce, a peaceful place of comfortable and ordered life, with regulations and customs to ensure that culture and religion were preserved. It was another Ur, and perhaps for this very reason the sojourners did not stay. The stream continued, and so did they. For another two hundred miles they traced its course, the shining riband of the river their daily guide as they learned the meaning of pilgrim life, perpetual strangers on an endless journey.

At rest in Haran

Yet soon there was to come a pause, for even now they had reached the juncture with the River Balikh, a tributary of the Euphrates whose waters fell from the mountains of Armenia. Just a few days north, according to their sources, lay a flourishing city in a place where important caravan trails met, a meeting place where news could be obtained of travellers from other parts. The city was in the centre of the fertile land of Padan

---

17 There is a dramatic contrast in the following two passages which tells the story of this moment: "And they said, Go to, *let us build us a city* and a tower, whose top may reach unto heaven; and *let us make us a name*, lest we be scattered abroad upon the face of the whole earth" (Genesis 11:4). "By faith Abraham, when he was called to go out into a place which he should after receive for an inheritance, obeyed; and he went out, not knowing whither he went ... for he looked for *a city* which hath foundations *whose builder and maker is God*" (Hebrews 11:8-10).

Aram, and was a good site for their journey to be broken for a season. Whatever travel might yet lie ahead, they would for the present stop here, in Haran. The first great stage of their journey was over.[18]

Terah was glad of the opportunity to settle for at least a little while. Countless weeks of marching lay between them and the land of their nativity, and he had felt the creak of old bones on this long passage. It would be good to rest, to enjoy a time of established existence again, to savour stillness and quiet … He did not yet know it, but his journey was over. He would never leave this place, and others of his family who reached this point would likewise travel no further. Of those who did, there would be none who would travel the road as far as Abram and Sarai. The unfolding of this story would reveal a man and a woman who were remarkably different from their relatives. From the very beginning, faith at work in their lives separated them to a different mode of thinking and action.[19] Yet faith at least had brought them all thus far. And years later, when Abram was searching for a suitable bride for his only begotten son, he would find her here, in this very place, among those of his family who still resided in Haran, the city of Nahor.[20]

The foundation promise

The Lord was to make wondrous promises to Abram. Successive manifestations of faith would lead to further revelations, but here at the beginning of their journey was the granting of the foundation promise itself.[21] The words were few but great:

---

18 Genesis 11:31 (cp. Jerusalem Bible, NASB).

19 Abraham had one brother (Haran) who died in Ur, symbolic of no response to the truth. His other brother (Nahor) responded, but only after delay, and would not leave Haran, symbolic of an initial response, but no fruit of real repentance in baptism. Sarah had a sister (Milcah) who likewise made only a half-hearted endeavour, and a brother (Lot) who made a commitment to the truth, but who, when left to his own resources fell into worldly company.

20 Genesis 24:4; 27:43; 29:4.

21 See Appendix 3, "What was the foundation promise?"

18

"I will make of thee a great nation, and I will bless thee, and make thy name great; and thou shalt be a blessing: and I will bless them that bless thee, and curse him that curseth thee: and in thee shall all families of the earth be blessed."   (Genesis 12:2,3)

Breathtaking in the magnitude of the assurances it gave, it opened with a series of special blessings to Abram himself, blessings that would exalt his name through all the earth. Built upon these pledges of personal greatness and influence were further levels of fulfilment, which only time and the unfolding of God's purpose would reveal. But even in its primary sense, the promise was huge, so extensive, so far-reaching as to make Abram the most important person to tread the earth in his day. Beyond his day, the promise would grow larger again, expanding and expanding until at the last it would gather into its embrace every living person in the whole earth. There had never been a promise like this one, and in certain ways it would never be equalled again. All this was vouchsafed to one man, in the wisdom of God.

But it centred on one crucial feature upon which every part depended. It all awaited the seed, the promised seed, the longed for seed. Until this special child came, the promise would remain latent but lifeless. Only with the birth of the seed could the wonder of the promise be unlocked, and for the child to be born it must first be conceived in the womb. Abram knew with humble certainty of his own part in the promise. He had not yet understood that his wife was inextricably bound to the promise as well, for she, and she alone, was to be the bearer of the child. Yet how could he know this? His wife, dear companion as she was, still remained barren, and that after many years of marriage. Abram felt with reasonable certainty, that however this child might come into the world, it would not be through his Sarai.

The promise made to this one man, however, was also to be fulfilled through this one woman. Her involvement was vital. When, by and by, their true seed finally walked

19

among men, his teaching would establish the thought that Sarai's part in the fulfilment of the promise was every whit as important as Abram's.[22] They were, as always, bound together in this most marvellous of God's promises to them.

The separation of faith

But first there must be the obedience of faith, as together they began this journey. This would be their story. Their faith would take them into the land, support them through their private diary of joys and tragedies, bringing them at last to the final triumph of utter conviction in God, and thus to the miraculous birth of their son. When faith and fulfilment were finally joined, the story was finished which began in Ur of the Chaldees.

"Get thee out of thy *country*, and from thy *kindred*, and from thy father's *house*, unto a land that I will shew thee." (Genesis 12:1)

The first step was made complete in the journey to Haran that they might 'leave their *country*'. This second step away from Haran would mean that they must 'leave their *kindred*'. Later, the final separation from Lot would cause them to 'leave their father's *house*'. So different would their lives be under God's providence, that their family associations would only bring the constraint of unbelief. Better then for faith to separate them to a new life and a new household whose spirit matched theirs. Messiah would know the same truth in his own life, and would remember Abram and Sarai's experience:

"But Jesus said unto them, a prophet is not without honour, but in his own *country*, and among his own *kin*, and in his own *house* ... And he marvelled because of their unbelief." (Mark 6:4-6)

And into the land of Canaan they came

"So Abram departed, as the LORD had spoken unto him; and Lot went with him: and Abram was seventy and five years old when he departed out of Haran.

---

22 See Chapter 9, "Encouraging the children of faith together".

And Abram took Sarai his wife, and Lot his brother's son, and all their substance that they had gathered, and the souls that they had gotten in Haran; and they went forth to go into the land of Canaan; and into the land of Canaan they came." (Genesis 12:4,5)

When the call came, Abram responded. There was no hesitation or delay. Indeed, they had been waiting for this next summons. Yet this time there were more than just the two of them. Their sojourn in Haran had been long enough for Abram to prosper, and a gradual enlargement of flocks and herds was matched by an increase in his household. When Abram moved this second time therefore, there came with him a whole encampment, a travelling tribe who looked to him as their leader and chieftain, and who shared his spiritual values. Abram's spirit was seen in his servants, for those he met he touched with the excitement of his faith.[23]

Sarai, in like manner, was a wise and spiritual woman in the administration of her servants. But how desperately she longed to be a loving mother also, to clasp her own babe to her bosom, to dandle her own son upon her knees. When therefore this next part of their journey began, the mistress of the household stepped out with a glad and hopeful heart. For might not a new beginning in a new land bring with it the possibility of new life for her that had been called 'the barren one'? Sarai gave a little skip of happiness, and Abram smiled at her joy.

Providence also smiled with favour on their journey, for their travellings were blessed with safe passage. Their pilgrimage began with baptism as the entire household crossed over Euphrates with their master, and the legend of Abram the Hebrew was born.[24] These 'crossers over'

---

23 So often those who had dealings with Abraham ended up in covenant relationship with him (Genesis 12:5; 14:13; 21:32).

24 This title appended to Abram appeared to be indicative of his status as a unique and special individual, marked out from this transforming moment in his life. Cp. Genesis 14:13 and 1 Samuel 13:7 where his faithless descendants showed the opposite spirit, and 'hebrewed' back over Jordan.

then struck westward, moving along the natural corridor that lay beneath the Taurus Mountains, and that linked the Euphrates valley with the Mediterranean. Here there was sufficient pasture to sustain the flocks of passing caravans, and Abram was glad to see his animals well provided for. They had a long way to travel as yet. Reaching the Orontes River they turned southwards to follow its journey upstream. Unlike the Euphrates however, which had at times borne their family in the merchant boats that plied its waters, the Orontes was largely unnavigable. Besides, his burgeoning household and herds made river passage impractical. They would continue to travel on the land, marching along the valley as it ascended slowly to the plateau country.

Between the two great mountain ranges of Lebanon and Anti Lebanon, the valley along which they travelled narrowed to form a deep but fertile cleft of rich grazing land. Abram was drawn inexorably southwards, the land itself providing successive signposts to the patriarch. The continuing fertility that greeted him at each stage told him – 'this is the way, walk ye in it', and he was thankful to do so. Crossing beyond the watershed from where the Orontes flows north and the Litani falls south, the household of faith slipped between a break in the mountain heights, and descended into Damascus. Here the plain was so abundantly watered as to make Damascus an oasis of green, with abundant crops and luxuriant verdure. It was a good place to rest, for man and beast to be refreshed, and for the household to restore its supplies. Flocks could only be driven day by day for a certain period. Then a time of respite was needed, to recruit their energies for the next stage. Damascus then, became such a resting place. No heavenly message was forthcoming, however, to tell Abram and Sarai that this was their final destination. So after a period of peaceful sojourning, their journey began again. Yet their visit here was marked in history, for ever since the Damascenes would speak of Abram's stay among them, and acknowledge him with the deepest respect as a man of great renown.[25]

One young man in particular would remember with gratitude the appearance of these travellers in their midst. For he, like others from Haran and elsewhere, fell under the influence of this godly couple, and gladly accepted an invitation to join their household. Even they did not then appreciate how deeply faithful this young man would become, or how close they would grow to him. But this new found retainer would show that even a Gentile could walk in the steps of faith, and become a spiritual offspring of the patriarch, a true son in the faith.[26] When they left Damascus to travel south again, Eliezer travelled with them. He observed their procedures for the movement of the camp with a keen eye, and was impressed with the speed and efficiency of the household. Yet even so, there were some things that could be improved. When opportunity arose, he would speak with his master Abram.

The wondrous promise of a son

"And Abram passed through the land unto the place of Sichem, unto the plain of Moreh. And the Canaanite was then in the land. And the LORD appeared unto Abram, and said, Unto thy seed will I give this land: and there builded he an altar unto the LORD, who appeared unto him." (Genesis 12:6,7)

Their journey took them beneath the blue heights and snow-capped peaks of Hermon, the northern guardian of the land. Crossing Jordan below the waters of Merom, they began a steady march down the length of the land of Canaan. The heart of the land lies in the mountains of the central plateau. Here they came upon the valley

---

25 Josephus records that even in his day the name of Abram was famous in Damascus, and that there was a village named – 'the Habitation of Abram' (Flavius Josephus, *Antiquities of the Jews,* Book 1, chapter 7.2).

26 So trusted a retainer indeed in manifesting his master's spirit, that Abram was willing to declare him his *de jure* son and heir (Genesis 15:2,3).

where Shechem would later nestle between the broad shoulders of Ebal and Gerizim. Rich black soil and an abundance of fountain springs helped to fill the valley with a profusion of gardens and orchards all bursting with fruitfulness. Into this scene of verdant loveliness stepped the man and his wife, their delighted gaze resting upon these many signs of heaven's blessings of fertility and growth. On the valley floor there grew a prominent oak, surrounded by its offspring. This grove of trees[27] with spreading foliage for shade and shelter positively invited repose, and Abram was prompt to call a halt right here. The tents would be pitched beneath this leafy canopy, the flocks would settle within the shade, a brook betokened water aplenty.

It was here in this place of fruitfulness that this second promise was given. The promise was brief yet full. For it used with wondrous clarity the one word not used in God's earlier promise, yet the one thing that lay implicit in all that had been promised. Now, at last, there fell from the lips of the angel[28] the word that this couple fervently desired to hear, "Unto thy *seed* have I given this land".

Abram beamed and Sarai cried. It was for them both a word of heart-rending joy. And the promise moreover was unconditional in its certainty. When Abram built an altar to offer the sacrifice of dedication, his mind was not just on the promise of the land, but also on the son who would be given the land, his boy, and, if they had understood the angel aright, Sarai's child. A fervent prayer of gratitude ascended with the smoke, as Abram and Sarai stood together in thanksgiving on that day.

---

27 The word "plain" is *elown* in Genesis 12:6 indicating an oak, and possibly an oak grove given the fertility of the area (cp. Greens, RSV, etc.). A grove of such trees providing spreading foliage for shade would be a natural place for encampment, to stop and pitch tent.

28 For, of course, the divine manifestation that communicated with Abram on successive occasions was not the Father Himself, but His angelic representative, and on most occasions was probably Michael (Genesis 12:1,3; Exodus 23:20-22).

"And he removed from thence unto a mountain on the east of Beth-el, and pitched his tent, having Beth-el on the west, and Hai on the east: and there he builded an altar unto the LORD, and called upon the name of the LORD. And Abram journeyed, going on still toward the south."   (Genesis 12:8,9)

But as to when and how the promise might be fulfilled, the details as yet were not clear. In fact there were obstacles. The gardens and orchards that had so delighted their eye, were evidence that the land was already inhabited, and therefore could not be claimed by Abram or his seed. Numerous settlements testified to the fact of the Canaanite's presence in the land. A profane race that dwelt under the divine curse,[29] these people did not share Abram's faith, and the man of God learned that, for the moment, he was still a stranger in the land.

Removing from thence, he came by stages to a mountain east of Bethel, and there another altar proclaimed his loyalty to the Lord amidst those who knew Him not. His special petitions to the Father doubtless asked for guidance on how he might live a life of faithfulness, surrounded as he was by the unfaithful.

Once again the encampment travelled south. Abram did not yet know the full extent of the land promised to his seed,[30] so his southwards drift was not an attempt to explore the limits of this territory. Yet there was purpose in his movement. In the nomadic existence that they now led, it was normal to graze their animals until the land was bare, and then to move on in search of fresh pasturage. Southwards therefore now, but eventually by a continuous circling motion, old grazing grounds would be revisited once the good earth was renewed, and the herb and grass of the field had regrown.

---

29 Genesis 9:25.

30 This detail would not be revealed until he entered into covenant relationship with God (Genesis 15:18).

And there was perhaps another reason. Abram was restless in spirit,[31] and seemed undecided as to where he might settle, especially with the Canaanites present in the land, a people avaricious in trade and immoral in behaviour. His wanderings were not aimless however, for he kept to the central mountain route, and followed this into the Negev. These regions were sparsely settled, and thus provided extensive pasturage. But their chief attraction lay in the fact that the main centres of the Canaanites lay instead to the north and in the valleys, far away from the patriarchal tent.[32] Abram was thus free to dwell apart as a separate people. Indeed his altars were a declaration that he and his household worshipped a different God, and led a different life. In the south country therefore he found room to live and room to worship, and was content to have it so.

---

31 The narrative indicates this. Genesis 12:6, "passed through"; 12:8, "removed from thence"; 12:9, "journeyed, going on still" (cp. margin).

32 *McMillan Bible Atlas*, Carta Edition. See notes to Map 27 – Jacob's travels in the land of Canaan.

2

ENCOUNTERING TROUBLE AND TESTING TOGETHER
(Genesis 12:10 – 13:18)

THE onset of famine came as a surprise. Having arrived in 'the land of promise', they did not expect such a time of trial, nor that the land should fail them. But it did.[1] Abram's flocks began to suffer, and he knew that unless they moved, all could be lost. The very proximity of Egypt seemed to be a sign, and Abram perhaps had heard how the Nile's annual inundations guaranteed the crops of Egypt, even in a time of drought elsewhere. He could travel by the way of Shur, or take the coastal route of the way of the Philistines. Either would bring him to the 'granary of the ancient world', to grain and provender, and to Egypt therefore they would go. The journey was not easy. The way was not especially difficult, but it was a sore trial to witness the death of oxen and sheep which, emaciated and exhausted, collapsed on the route. It was a relief to draw near Egypt at last.

A concerned man and a comely woman

Not given to boldness or rashness, Abram was by nature a cautious man. In his dealings with others therefore, he had the foresight to anticipate difficulties before they arose, and to make wise provision to deal with them. There was a difficulty with his wife. She was beautiful, remarkably beautiful. And in what did this beauty consist? Surely it was a compound substance. It was formed by some strange alchemy between sparkling eyes and gracious speech, between tender warmth and graceful tread, produced by some secret chemistry between decisive movement and restful stillness,

---

1 Genesis 12:10 states that there was not only famine, but a grievous one at that.

27

between laughing wit and thoughtful silence. The result of this pleasing fusion in Sarai was a woman who at sixty-five[2] was still wondrously attractive.[3]

Abraham realised that entering as they now were into a new and unknown region, would bring again the challenge of his wife's appearance. Sarai's loveliness would be manifest to all, and Abram was certain it would be noticed. He had lived with her for many years, and was not unaware of the admiring glances cast in her direction by the men of many different places. Even there they had seen enough to know. Here in the land of dark skinned Hamites, the comparative fairness of Sarai, openly displayed and beautifully evident, was bound to arouse attention. It was that attention which deeply concerned Abram, because with it came danger. Drawing Sarai aside before they crossed into Egypt, he outlined his concerns and proposed his solution.

"Behold now, I know that thou art a fair woman to look upon: therefore it shall come to pass, when the Egyptians shall see thee, that they shall say, This is his wife: and they will kill me, but they will save thee alive. Say, I pray thee, thou art my sister: that it may be well with me for thy sake; and my soul shall live because of thee." (Genesis 12:11-13)

The contrivance of fleshly fear

This was not a hasty solution concocted on the border. For even before their journey into Canaan, Abram had requested and she had consented to the arrangement now to be used. Travelling through strange lands with different customs and despotic rulers demanded prudence. In perilous situations therefore, they would act as brother and sister, at least until local circumstances became clear.[4] Nor was Abram's plan simply centred on his own preservation; it was perhaps the best strategy to

---

2   Abraham was 75 when he entered the land (Genesis 12:4), and Sarai was 10 years younger than he (17:17).

3   Genesis 12:11.

4   Genesis 20:13.

safeguard Sarai also. For if she was the sister of a visiting chieftain, and became the unwilling but determined focus of attention from some Egyptian nobleman, certain formalities would have to be observed. If marriage were contemplated, it would be Abram's permission and approval that would need to be sought. In such a case there would be time for Abram and Sarai to leave the area, and move on.[5]

It was a careful solution that bore all the hallmarks of careful thought, and all the subtleties of careful design. But for all its reasoned carefulness, it was grievously wrong. Its wrongness lay in the source of its inspiration, for this was not the outcome of spiritual thinking but the contrivance of fear. It was a plan that sprang from the exigency of his situation, but it recognised no spiritual dimension to the problem. His thinking was wrong on several counts. The land from whence he had but recently come had been promised as a possession to his seed.[6] And given that his seed had neither been born nor even conceived, it was impossible for him to lose his life at this time. This was the real power of the promise that God would make of him a great nation.

His solution apparently solved his problem, but in reality it greatly increased the danger for Sarai, for it involved the withdrawal of his protection as a husband. In moving the threat away from himself, Abram jeopardized her position as the bearer of the promised seed. His action showed his lack of appreciation for the part she would play in the fulfilment of the promise, and his inability to see the real danger that could follow. Moved by fear, he was moreover prejudging the character and standard of the Egyptians in an unfair light, and his assessment subsequently proved to be completely wrong.

---

5   It would seem that Abram's fears were not groundless. There is in the British museum, an Egyptian papyrus dated after Abram which relates how a Pharaoh on the advice of his counsellors sent armies to take away a man's wife by force, and then to murder her husband.

6   Genesis 12:7.

The crowning irony of this fleshly plan was that in his concern about their lack of honour and integrity, Abram himself was prepared to resort to the use of deceit. It is true that he and Sarai were related, but not perhaps in quite the way he proposed. And whatever was the exact nature of their family connection, their public statement was a lie, because it was uttered with the intention to deceive.

No word of prayer seemed to pass the lips of Abram in coming to this decision.[7] The Father's guidance had not been sought. But the Father was about to test this scheme, and discover its foundation. Abram's prescience concerning Sarai was confirmed, for her fair beauty was not only seen but also discussed in the highest quarters of Egyptian nobility, reaching the ears of the royal chamberlains. Discreet enquiries had elicited her single status, travelling as she was under the care of her older 'brother'. And thus was set in motion a series of events which revealed to Abram the appalling weakness of his plan, and the folly of depending on self.

Taken into Pharaoh's household

"And it came to pass, that, when Abram was come into Egypt, the Egyptians beheld the woman that she was very fair. The princes also of Pharaoh saw her, and commended her before Pharaoh: and the woman was taken into Pharaoh's house." (Genesis 12:14,15)

It was the swiftness of the thing that surprised. For one day, one fateful day, Abram received an unexpected visitation from the princes of Pharaoh. Their message, simple and succinct, fell like a thunderbolt. 'It would please Pharaoh well for Sarai, your sister, to join the royal household. We are commanded to bring her'. So there it was. No warning, no time, no room for prevarication.[8]

---

7   Genesis 12:8, 13:4 and 13:18 certainly imply other occasions where Abram sought God's guidance, but not so at the commencement of this episode.

8   Genesis 12:15: the word "taken" implies the decisive action of Pharaoh, irrespective of Abram's wishes or feelings. Covering a

Called by a breathless maidservant who came running with the message, Sarai appeared and walked towards Abram. She saw the princes, felt Abram's tension and looked swiftly to him hoping for some clue as to his feelings or intentions. But his eyes were downcast, avoiding her. 'You must ask her yourself' he said, and their request was now repeated for Sarai's benefit. She, likewise, was dumbstruck. Giving Abram a last glance of appeal she was startled to receive in return a look of naked desperation. He was indeed in an impossible situation. He could raise no demur as a brother, and was powerless to refuse this royal request unless he was prepared to declare as a husband. But to do this was to acknowledge deceit, and cause Pharaoh loss of face, and what outcome might that procure but death for either or both of them. His eyes conveyed not faith, but fear, and something more besides. His look reminded her of their agreement, and sought for her submission to it. Now came the test of that pledge. His life depended on what she might say in that next moment. In an instant she knew his need, and what she would do. Without hesitation, for even a pause could prove fatal, she turned to face the princes. Bowing low she acceded to their request. Her firm and gracious voice surprised even Sarai herself in its steadiness. 'I am honoured to accept. But there is much to arrange, my possessions and garments to prepare, I will need time'.

'You need bring nothing' came the reply, 'the palace will provide all that you might need, but you are to return with us'. No chance then for fresh plans now, no opportunity for escape. They were completely caught, thoroughly entangled in their own device. Sarai took leave of her 'brother', and was gone. Outwardly calm, the thud of her heart and the terrible shaking of her limbs told otherwise. The journey to the palace was but a dream, she would afterwards have no recollection of

---

wide range of meanings including to snatch, acquire, carry off, seize – the Hebrew root (in the passive *Hophal*) conveys the meaning of being taken against one's will.

the route they travelled or the streets they walked. In a moment of time the palace stood before them.

A holy woman who trusted in God

When Sarai entered Pharaoh's house, she was taken immediately to the chambers of the women. But these were not the womenfolk of Pharaoh's menservants. Nor were they the maidservants of the palace who toiled in the royal kitchens or gardens. The women of these chambers were reserved for the king and his attentions alone. Here then Sarai met the other residents of the household. There were many of them, all beautiful, elegant, vibrant, sad. For in these rooms, behind the laughing chatter, the bathings and anointings, the whispered secrets, the sumptuous food and gorgeous apparel, there lay an indefinable air of wistful sorrow and constriction. When a woman entered this household there would be no escape, no other life. The silken threads of royal protocol enmeshed her forever within the harem. Free to roam their private courtyards, she accepted the inevitability of imprisonment for life. And if this was the world in which she was constrained to live, if purpose and meaning were only found within the confines of the harem walls, then the great object of private discussion and even more of private thought, was to compare the relative merits of each member of the golden circle.

Into this strange and scented world Sarai came. Her senses told her without seeing that this process of comparison had begun. She was conscious of eyes beneath lowered lashes that studied her deportment, appraised her form, gazed upon her fairness and assessed her prospects. There was danger here from more than one quarter, and the enormity of her predicament burst upon her. Sarai turned the problem over and over in her mind, but could see no solution. Unable to talk with Abram, unknown within the palace, unwilling to confide with any other woman, she felt an unutterable loneliness in facing this crisis. Yet this loneliness bore fruit. It caused Sarai to turn to the only one from whom help could come.

32

From her first sleepless night within these walls, she besought God in prayer. Her petitions were so focused and intense, that her mind was pierced with the pain of her grief, her pleadings so urgent and desperate that her body shook. Her importunities left her exhausted, but at peace. She would trust in God. There was no other course. And borne aloft with the tender solicitude of angelic care, these cries of a faithful woman were heard in heaven above. Even as she prayed, the divine providence was shaping the means for her complete deliverance. God was not unmindful of the anguish of his daughter. Had she but known it, her life was sacrosanct, her virtue safe from the very moment she had trodden over the threshold of Pharaoh's house. In God's good time she would yet be the bearer of the promised seed, and her womanhood was under the divine guardianship ere that day should dawn.

He who searches all hearts knows our prayers of course, before we even utter them. He does not require us to pray so that He might comprehend our need, but rather that in prayer we might come to understand our own need, and how deep and real it is. And all response to prayer, in whatever form it comes, is based first on our appreciation that we acknowledge fully, unreservedly, that our lives and times are in His hands. Effectual fervent prayer is the privilege of all God's servants who pray earnestly in time of desperate need, and Sarai was about to learn that her own prayers offered in this spirit would avail much indeed.[9]

The triumph of Sarai's submission

There may have been purification rites that kept her from Pharaoh until now.[10] But a more dramatic event showed Sarai clearly that God knew of her plight.[11]

---

9   James 5:16.

10 Esther 2:9,12.

11 Genesis 12:17 records, "And the LORD plagued ... *because of Sarai*", and by implication therefore, primarily because of her prayers rather than Abram's. It was the divine response to *her* faith.

"And the Lᴏʀᴅ plagued Pharaoh and his house with great plagues because of Sarai Abram's wife."

(Genesis 12:17)

The laughter and noise had ceased from the chambers of the women.[12] Both the beauties of the harem and the maidservants who waited on them were alike smitten and fearful. Only one woman appeared untouched amidst the atmosphere of pestilence. Sarai, serene and strong, was alone in her wellness, strangely immune to the all-pervading affliction. Kept beyond the reach of the plague, Sarai knew immediately that the matter was of God, and she felt the trembling weakness of relief. Her pleadings had been heard and mightily answered. From this time forth she would always be aware of the power of prayer and the reality of God's watchful care. Whatever entreaties Abram might have offered, the Lord had answered her prayers, and for her sake. It was an earnest of the promise that still seemed fresh in its newness – "I will curse him that curseth thee". To Sarai, no less than Abram, did this promise of divine protection hold true.

But this singular exemption, which told Sarai so surely of God's intervention, told Pharaoh with equal certainty of her connection with the problem. 'Who is this woman'? 'Why', came the answer, 'she is the sister of the Hebrew chieftain recently come'. But had he not observed due protocol in obtaining this woman? And had he not blessed the man with handsome gifts? Why then this calamity, and how exactly was this woman involved? Strange circumstances these, for a woman to move freely among the stricken with no trace of fever or plague. By what power was she shielded? What unseen hand protected her? Pharaoh pondered. There was need for caution here until the thing could be unravelled, for that there was a tangle was certain.

---

12 Given that 'the house' has reference to the royal harem, the plague may well have been a physical affliction among the womenfolk. Yet Sarai remained unaffected.

Brought before Pharaoh, and faced with his skilful yet courteous probing, Sarai resolved to speak the truth. Emboldened by evidence of the divine hand, and encouraged by the demeanour of the king, she told the whole with candour and simplicity. Where guile had failed, honesty now succeeded. But more than anything else this was the triumph of her submission. Sarai's astonishing spirit had rescued her family. Through it, Sarai delivered herself, her husband and her household.[13]

Abram's folly and failure

These had been terrible days for Abram. His household had grown in number, yet bereft of his wife it was empty. At night the loneliness of the tent reminded him of his dreadful failure as a husband, and of Sarai's present danger. There, kneeling or prostrate within the sanctuary of the curtains, in the one place where he could be truly private, he implored heaven for guidance out of this hopeless predicament, wept tears of remorse and shame, and trembled with a worry that shook his frame like an ague.

Awaking each morrow, the fear would return which fitful sleep could only ever briefly assuage. Yet for the present, until a way became clear, the façade would continue. Pulling aside the tent flap each morning, he stepped outside as Abram the chieftain, and the day's duties began. The round of daily tasks, constant and pressing, helped deaden the mind to other concerns. Looking to the state of his flocks and herds, and knowing well the needs of his household, was a charge still to be fulfilled. Its performance each day, however, only reminded Abram that he had, through his weakness and lack of faith, lost the dearest member of his household. It was only with a supreme effort that he was able to master his emotions and accept with apparent pleasure the copious gifts that now flowed from the palace.

---

13 See notes in Chapter 9 on 1 Peter 3 (page 199).

Time and again over the ensuing days and weeks[14] the men of Pharaoh would appear, their faces wreathed in smiles, and bringing 'a gift from our lord, Pharaoh'. Each time Abram would offer the appropriate words of thanks, whilst inwardly his mind recoiled with the horror of his own perfidy. For these were not innocent, unconditional presents, given out of affection for him, they were dowry offerings; they were the price of his wife. Misery of miseries, this wretched deceit. "Say … thou art my sister; that it may be *well* with me for thy sake" he had asked Sarai, and now it had come to pass, for Pharaoh "entreated Abram *well* for her sake".[15] But this was not what Abram had intended, and certainly not what he expected or desired. Yet the circumstances of the moment meant that he found himself unable to refuse, even though he wished to. Only later would he show a clearer faith that declined those gifts where his integrity might be compromised.[16]

Now it seemed that finally these visits had ceased, although Abram was not exactly certain why. His unease was compounded by reports from the royal palace. Word had come that affliction lay upon the household of Pharaoh. There were whisperings of sudden illness, virulent and contagious, that had swept the palace. Was Sarai safe? Was she among the stricken? Was the illness fatal? Was their secret discovered? How many things he needed to know. How helpless was he in his ignorance. If only the way forward might become clear, but what path should he tread in the meantime?

An angry Pharaoh and a just rebuke

"And Pharaoh called Abram, and said, What is this that thou hast done unto me? Why didst thou not tell me

---

14 Genesis 12:16 in Rotherham's *Emphasised Bible* implies some passage of time for the accumulation of the gifts which flowed from Pharaoh – "and with Abram dealt he well for her sake, *so that he came to have* flocks and herds".

15 Genesis 12:13,16.

16 Genesis 14:22,23.

that she was thy wife? Why saidst thou, She is my sister? so I might have taken her to me to wife: now therefore behold thy wife, take her, and go thy way."

(Genesis 12:18,19)

His daily round was at length interrupted, and this again by palace visitors. When Abram saw Pharaoh's men his heart sank. Gone now were the gracious smiles that accompanied each successive gift. The men who stood empty-handed before him were grim faced and abrupt – 'Pharaoh calleth for thee'. Their stance plainly showed that he was to go with them, immediately, and flanked by this unsmiling guard, he was marched out of his encampment. Abram's journey to the palace retraced the route that Sarai had taken. He followed her footsteps, and felt her fear.

The palace was forbidding in its majesty. Imposing steps formed a broad ascent and led the eye upwards to the entrance. There, like standing sentinels in rank, massive stone columns rose in uniform splendour to hold aloft a giant stone pediment. The stupendous magnitude of these portals proclaimed that within was a dwelling place for not just a man, but one who was a god to his people. Abram stepped between the pillars and beneath the portico, and entered the palace. The sudden dimming of the light matched his own increasingly sombre mood. Through chamber and court, Abram was marched at last into the royal presence of he who was in very truth the ruler of all Egypt. Resplendent on his throne, attended by his vizier and surrounded by his court officials, Pharaoh awaited his approach and the customary obeisance that belonged to the lord of the lotus kingdom. As Abram bowed low, arose and looked toward the throne, he beheld in Pharaoh a stern and angry man, and could taste the nausea of fear. A silence, palpable and frightening, enveloped him. Finally Pharaoh spoke.

"What is this"? "Why didst thou not"? "Why saidst thou"? Abram was challenged with a barrage of indignant questions, and rightly so. How sharp the sting when we receive a merited rebuke from those in the world, who,

37

lacking our Scriptural insight and spiritual standard have nevertheless behaved themselves more nobly and justly than we in a matter of principle. Pharaoh's questions tried Abram at the bar of Gentile justice, and even there found him lacking. Honesty, even in extenuating circumstances, is a godly virtue, but there are moments of trial that can call every principle into question. Abram's faith had faltered at this moment in his own life, but under an extremity that few of us will ever be called upon to match. Out of his lapse and subsequent recovery however, he would learn a valuable lesson. Abram would not only learn that he needed to hold fast to the way of truth, but that dishonest behaviour brings the truth itself into disrepute. Honesty of principle and practice is a characteristic of those who are true strangers and sojourners among the Gentiles.[17]

'As for Sarai', expostulated Pharaoh, 'so might I have taken her to me to wife'. His mind had not been on a casual liaison, but rather the offer of genuine marriage. What a precarious situation was this? Into what jeopardy did this place the 'bearer of the seed'? Thankfully Pharaoh, although ignorant of the truth, had sufficient integrity to repudiate an adulterous union. He rebuked Abram not only for deception, but because that deception had almost led to further sin. He had brought the truth into disrepute through deceit, and was now taught a lesson in honesty. Pharaoh's point-by-point examination of Abram's position did not allow an answer. Indeed there was none. Alone and ashamed he stood for sentence, his bowed silence the witness of his guilt, the charges unanswerable, his case indefensible. Given Pharaoh's sovereign right to try the case, what might his judgement be? Death had no doubt been decreed

---

17 Romans 12:17; 2 Corinthians 8:21; 1 Thessalonians 4:12; 1 Timothy 2:1,2; 1 Peter 2:9-12. Interestingly, Peter's terms – "strangers" and "pilgrims" are identical to those in the LXX of Genesis 23:4 concerning Abraham towards the end of his life. Perhaps this is an indication that the final encomium from Abraham's contemporaries affirmed that he was indeed a man of honesty.

for much lesser offences than his, and his, moreover, had called in question the moral integrity of the man enthroned before him. Yet what words were these that Abram now heard – "behold thy wife, take her". Royal mercy, unexpected and certainly undeserved, filled his heart with thankfulness and humility. He felt justly reproved, yet graciously released as a debtor forgiven. Where now his doubts in the power of God to rescue from danger?

Not for Abram to know that Pharaoh's judgement was tempered with caution and not a little fear. Beneath the royal robes, the royal body was itself afflicted.[18] He urgently needed to rid his household of whatever curse had befallen it through Sarai's presence there. If in reuniting her to Abram he could restore his household to health, yet appear to have judged with authority and power, then his standing as ruler would be enhanced. And if in returning the man's wife he could shame and reprove him, then it would help expedite his departure from Egypt without delay. Pharaoh was an astute man, and judged to a nicety how the matter might best be handled. So his extension of mercy helped to create a spirit of humble embarrassment in Abram, before making demand for his exodus. And if Abram's chagrin before Pharaoh was not enough, there was burning shame to come with what followed. "Now therefore behold thy wife". A group of Pharaoh's men advanced then parted, and from their midst, moving with the graceful step he knew so well, there came – his wife, but no, another woman, his Sarai, yet no, a stranger attired in Egyptian linen, adorned with Egyptian amulet, anointed with Egyptian paint.

As he saw the fold of harem robe about her body, and caught the elusive scent of harem oil upon her person, he realised with a fresh stab of fear what peril he had placed her in. How could he have deserted her in this way? What had he been thinking? What terrors had she

---

18 Note the expression – "and the LORD plagued *Pharaoh* and his house with plagues" (Genesis 12:17).

faced through his cowardly abandonment? "Behold thy wife". How little did he deserve her, and how deeply did he know it. Sarai walked towards him, and Abram found himself engulfed in a tumult of bittersweet emotions. Excited thankfulness at seeing her again jostled with shock and horror at her appearance. Unutterable gladness for her safety mingled with shame and misery at his own cowardice. Wondrous joy at receiving her back competed with sharp anxiety about her feelings now for him.

It was almost too much to bear to look at her directly. What might her eyes reveal? Accusation or forgiveness? Hurt or love? Pain or understanding? Oh what infinite complexities of thought and feeling can be woven into a single moment of time.

Dismissal and departure from the land of darkness

Pharaoh's words of dismissal, stern and abrupt, curtailed the moment. Sarai stood now at his side. "Behold thy wife, take her, and go thy way." There was no time now for words of recrimination or reconciliation. There was not even time for an awkward embrace. Time simply to bow out of the royal presence with seemly haste.

The journey back to their encampment offered no chance for talk. Pharaoh's men walked with them.[19] The call of Abram brought retainers running, as he issued rapid instructions for the break up of the camp. Sharp-witted servants saw their mistress safely returned, heard the brusque urgency of their master's voice, observed the presence of the royal guard, and knew that safety for all depended on speed. In seconds the household was a bustle of activity.

Strong youths pulled up the heavy stakes and cords and the dwellings of Abram sank into flatness. Children

---

19 The narrative certainly implies that Pharaoh's judgement was to be expedited without delay, and doubtless Abram was anxious to comply. "Take her, and go thy way ... and they sent him away" (Genesis 12:19,20).

ran over the last billowings of the curtains and trod them into obedience. Women packed utensils, folded the tents, stored food. Men began the lading of the camels, and the strapping of leather bags onto braying asses. Boys scurried off to round up their precious flocks, while girls mothered the babies and scolded the little ones. Amidst the shoutings and calls, the bleatings and cries, Sarai slipped quietly back into the sanctuary of her own household. She felt the warm comfort of her own folk, and was soothed by the practiced routine of departure which now surrounded her. There would be time alone with Abram later. For now she would immerse herself in the tasks brought to her for decision and approval. Abram likewise moved among his people, conferring, directing, nodding in agreement, delivering new orders, and in a short time the jumbled welter of noise and person was resolved into order and harmony. The entire household was ready to leave and, departing with surprising swiftness, they left their place of sojourn in Egypt. A bare expanse of sand and scuffled soil was the only visible sign that Abram and Sarai had been in that place, a silent witness to the turmoil of this moment in their marriage.

All circumstances in life end with this little patch. The crisis comes, we wrestle with principle and practice, the moment ends, our lives move on, and naught but the empty spot remains. Yet what we have done there, and why we have done so, is forever written in the book of account. On each successive page in the record of our lives, we have opportunity to write but once. How vital then that every episode be written up with care, and that each circumstance we face be handled in accordance with divine principles. In the providence and wisdom of God, this particular episode had finally come full circle.

"The princes also of Pharaoh saw her, and commended *her* before Pharaoh: and the woman (*ishshah*) was *taken into* Pharaoh's house."

(Genesis 12:15)

41

"And Pharaoh commanded his men concerning *him*: and they *sent him away*, and his wife (*ishshah*) and all that he had." (verse 20)

Even the courtesy of the escort that Pharaoh provided, had as its real objective the guarantee that Abram was beyond Egypt's borders and gone for good. Pharaoh need not have been concerned. Abram had long since realised his mistake in coming to Egypt,[20] and he would never return again.[21] With every step away from the land of sin and darkness, his feet grew lighter, yet his tread more firm. And there walking by his side was his beloved and faithful wife, who had shown a more resolute spirit of faith than he in this episode. One day Abram would be known to his people as 'the father of the faithful'. But his faith had not yet reached that fulness of maturity. When it did, he would also know with glad certainty and heightened appreciation that this remarkable woman who trod the road with him was indeed 'the mother of the faithful', his equal and his counterpart.

Engaging in the blessing of restoration together

The time for Abram and Sarai's reconciliation finally came. Whether on the evening of their departure, or after crossing the border, or when they reached the place near Bethel again, we cannot tell. But at some moment this husband and this wife found the opportunity for personal reconciliation and healing prayer.[22] Beyond question he had erred grievously. But although he was

---

20 It is at least a mark of his faith that he never intended to stay in Egypt. Cp. the temporary term "to *sojourn* there" (Genesis 12:10) with the more permanent expression, "*dwelled* in the land" (13:12) once he had returned.

21 Certainly there is no record in the Scripture of him doing so.

22 We are not told this specifically, but the record is eloquent of Abram's deep desire to recover himself to his earlier state of faithfulness. Every phrase in Genesis 13:3,4 indicates his absolute determination to learn from this episode and rise up again. Back to Bethel, back to his place of worship, back to his altar, back to prayer. It is a reasonable inference that 'back to oneness with his wife' was also an imperative which Abram would feel compelled to accomplish, and that the responsibility for this lay with him.

not a man of natural courage, he was a man of spiritual faith, and he did possess that essential quality which would render reconciliation possible. Humility of spirit and contriteness of heart are not easy virtues for men in particular to manifest. Abram could and he did.[23]

So at the right moment they withdrew to the relative isolation of the chieftain's tent, which lay, as always, a little apart. As the curtain flap of goat's hair fell, they were at last alone. Within the tent, a single flame fed from an oil lamp cast a steady glow across the room. The light shone clear on Abram's face, but drew harsh lines of charcoal shadow across his brow, which was wrinkled with worry. He felt the responsibility and the need to speak first in this strangely awkward moment, but his mind was bereft of the proper words to say. Sarai turned towards him, the light illumined her countenance, and the message of her eyes well nigh broke his heart in wonder and shame. This was the moment, and Abram took it. There is nothing that open and honest and gentle discussion cannot solve, when both husband and wife are committed absolutely to the greatness of God's purpose in their lives. No matter how hard the matter, hearts attuned to God will find a way. And when the talking was ended, they knelt together in prayer.[24] Abram's tongue was loosed and flowed with unabated fervour to the Father, for confirmation of all they had shared in this discussion. Even Sarai, accustomed to his prayers, was moved by the impassioned cry of her husband that now poured forth. His contrite pleadings to the Father were at the same time his confession to her, and she understood this in the wisdom of her womanhood. Firstly then, praise to Almighty God for delivering them both from the brink of despair, that they might learn to trust in Him, and be sensitive to His providential care. Then Abram's

---

23 Genesis 13:9; 18:2,3,27.

24 Certainly the record indicates that when back in the land, Abram was anxious to converse with the Father in prayer. The phrase "called upon the name of the LORD" (Genesis 13:4) indicates his desire for God's help in all the circumstances of his life (including marriage), for such is the spirit of this importunity.

frank confession for the collapse of his faith, which had led to this time of distress. Petition followed for strength to start anew, and to help with resolution for greater faithfulness in future. Finally, the words of entreaty for the divine blessing that they might be restored together in trust, and reunited in love. The tremble in his voice gave eloquent proof to his wife of his desperate yearning for this.

As Abram prayed heavenward for them both, Sarai felt the peace and contentment of a rupture healed, of harmony restored. There was comfort and security in being again at one. She had needed him to show headship in seeking reconciliation, and to show this leadership in humility. She was thankful for the atoning power of his prayer. They could move on. The episode would not be forgotten, for they never are, but its lessons could be learned and their marriage would grow and deepen as a consequence. Together they would learn that faith could overcome trial and help them now to begin afresh. The life of faith is not immune from failure, from folly or from fear, but our subsequent response is so vital for the blessing of God's forgiveness and renewal. The contrite heart that trembles before Him, and that bows before His word, is the spirit that God delights in, for it leads, after repentance, to spiritual growth.

And Abram was very rich

"And Abram was very rich in cattle, in silver, and in gold … And Lot also, which went with Abram, had flocks, and herds, and tents. And the land was not able to bear them, that they might dwell together: for their substance was great, so that they could not dwell together." (Genesis 13:2,5,6)

Events in life can so often bring unexpected consequences. One of the results of this journey into Egypt was that Abram returned with an enlargement of his household and property. The excursion had enriched him materially, but at considerable cost to his marriage and spiritual walk before God. The very increase of his cattle soon led to a controversy with Lot, whose own holdings were substantial. Their combined wealth (measured as it was by the size of their flocks and herds) could not be sustained by the land where they dwelt together. Their very possessions precluded proximity. Already there had been friction between the two camps, with rival herdsmen jealously seeking and claiming the best grazing for their master.[25] And they were not alone in competing for the grass and herb of the field, for the Canaanites who had been in the land before Abram removed to Egypt, were still there in the land after his return.[26] Perhaps there had been no need to leave at all! The life of both person and beast had been preserved in the land of Canaan throughout the famine. And if the life of the Canaanite was preserved, then how much more the household of faith, who lived under God's watchful eye? Abram needed to ponder the extent of the divine hand in all the circumstances of his life, both temporal and spiritual.[27]

The controversy of the moment might have widened, but for a wise course of action initiated by Abram, who sought to preserve the family relationship whilst separating physically so that each might move to grazing grounds sufficient for their needs. Despite his seniority, Abram graciously gave Lot the choice, and Lot chose unwisely. He saw the fertility of the plain of Jordan, and its suitability to sustain his growing enterprise. But he did not see the wickedness of the inhabitants of the plain or consider the effect on his household in spiritual things. He chose and moved away, and in departing, Abram and Sarai had now finally left behind 'their father's house'. It would seem that Abram had learned what Lot had not. The journey into Egypt, and his encounter there, had borne fruit through painful experience.[28] His decision

---

25 Genesis 13:7.

26 Genesis 12:6; 13:7.

27 Psalm 33:18-22.

28 Genesis 13:1 indicates that Abram retraced his steps into "the south" or in other words, to the very place where he had been before this whole episode occurred (12:9). He wanted to begin

was based on what would be best for the truth, for his family and for his own faith, and so it was that he chose the mountains of Judaea and dwelt apart on high, whilst Lot languished in the valley below.

And as if to signify that God was well pleased with their choice, the angel of God came again with an expansion of the promise. It reaffirmed the blessing of the land to their seed, and that forever, but it also made clear the joyous truth that he, Abram the Hebrew, would inherit the land of the promise as well. Abram felt deeply conscious of this renewal of promise that followed his fall. How unworthy he was, and how well did he know it. And yet was not this heaven's endorsement of his subsequent spirit of repentance, and of their restoration together? God does not provide unconditional promises to unrighteous men. Despite his mistake and despite his sin, he was in covenant relationship with the Lord, and this latest blessing was the proof.

"And the Lord said unto Abram, after that Lot was separated from him, Lift up now thine eyes, and look from the place where thou art northward, and southward, and eastward, and westward: for all the land which thou seest, to thee will I give it, and to thy seed for ever. And I will make thy seed as the dust of the earth."　　　　　　　　　　(Genesis 13:14-16)

Hebron's height and a new home

Abram did indeed look in every direction, but he walked south. From his vantage point in the mountains of Judaea nigh unto Bethel, the eye could see as far south as a singular height. Upon that elevation was the ancient town of Hebron, and Abram trod upon all the land between to show his confidence in the promise of God.[29] Just as there was a mark of faith in Abram's decision to

---

afresh, and with a better spirit, and his behaviour in these subsequent events as they unfold is proof of this.

29 The very act of treading on the land was an act of faith in the promise. Israel itself would later be asked to demonstrate Abram's spirit in claiming their inheritance (Joshua 1:2,3).

remain alone in the mountains, so now there was faith in the walk of the patriarch toward this height.

They had encountered trouble and testing indeed on this journey to Egypt and back, but they had done so together, which is the secret of all strong marriages. There had been a rupture of love and trust in this episode, but they had endured. They were alone now, but together in their faithfulness. They walked by themselves, but also with their God. They had truly come to Hebron – the place of union,[30] and here in this new resting place the man and his wife were united again in fellowship with each other, and with the Lord, unto whom another altar was reared that they might offer their sacrifices of praise and prayers of thanksgiving. Hebron would be their new home and here, therefore, they would worship and pray unto the Lord who so evidently was at work in their lives.[31]

There was an oak in Shechem under which they had first dwelt in the land. There was a mighty oak here in Hebron as well.[32] Under its canopy the tabernacle of Abram and Sarai was now pitched. Here in this place, so much of the story of their life would be unfolded, as together they lived and learned and loved the principles of the God of glory who had called them both to this new life of faith in Him.

---

30 Hebron is from *habar* – to be joined, united, coupled, have fellowship with. A derived word, *habaret*, meaning companion, is used as a synonym for a wife (Malachi 2:14), indicating the close relationship that *habar* expresses. The name of the place to which they had now come was eloquent of the restoration to unity between Abram and Sarai.

31 Proverbs 24:15,16.

32 In Genesis 13:18 the word "plain" indicates an oak or terebinth tree, as in 12:6. For many generations a venerable terebinth was shown in Hebron as being Abram's tree.

3

ENDURING THE DISTRESS OF BARRENNESS TOGETHER
(Genesis 16:1-16)

WITHIN a tent a woman wept. Visible in the sky above was the celestial orb of the night, a heavy yellow ball, that hung in stately stillness, established for a sign and a season, a day and a year.[1] The tears that fell from the bowed form were not in a sense new, for she had shed them a thousand times before. She was not by nature lachrymose; in fact her character was one of considerable fortitude and spiritual strength. Yet the particular matter over which she wept affected her so deeply that even the slightest thing could sometimes begin her tears afresh – the softness of a new lamb nuzzling its dam, the unfolding of a blue hyacinth on Hebron's hills, the call of the turtledove which sounded so like the gurgling of a child, even the moon above in its heaviness. The tent was Abram's, and the woman was Sarai.

The bitterness of a barren womb

> "Now Sarai Abram's wife bare him no children: and she had an handmaid, an Egyptian, whose name was Hagar." (Genesis 16:1)

Since the encampment had first settled in Hebron, she had gazed upon the new moon over six-score times. Each time that first sliver of silver had appeared in the inky blackness of Mamre's night, she had marked the beginning of a new month that brought new hope and fresh yearning as the manner of women came upon her.[2] Each time she wished so desperately for that miraculous yet infinitesimal beginning of conception, which the birth

---

1 Genesis 1:14.
2 Genesis 18:11.

of the new moon heralded in its slenderness.[3] Each time the moon waxed to the abundance of its promise, she felt pain and grief and disappointment that her empty womb was the very antithesis of the moon's final splendour, plump in its fullness, replete in its roundness. It was as if the heavens mocked her.

Every godly woman wanted to bear a godly seed. But Sarai's desire was not just to bear children to Abram, but to produce the child of the angel's repeated assurances.[4] This was the seed on whom the promises of God rested, and she had not been able to bear him. The angel had said with certainty that the son to come would be Abram's own, but it seemed to Sarai that he would not be hers. She felt that the burden lay with her, and that she had let her husband down. So huge had the matter of her barrenness become in her mind, so intense the pressure of her inability to bear, that now it affected her attitude to everything. She felt that this was her responsibility, and that she had failed. She had prayed to the Father about her barrenness, and certainly desired His blessing. Her prayers had been frequent and fervent, as God was witness, yet He had never answered her. If there was to be fruit of the union between her and Abram, then why could not God grant them a child, just one, just one precious son? It was not as if they would neglect the child. He would be raised with love and care in the nurture and admonition of the Lord. He would be taught the greatness of the truth and the virtues of faith and obedience. If a son, a seed was needful that God's own promise to them might be fulfilled, then why did He not bless them with this son? Why this delay, this intolerable delay, which chafed her spirit so bitterly? What had she

---

3 Indeed, the waxing and waning of the moon in the heavens is adduced (for the unfailing regularity of its monthly cycle) as a faithful witness (Psalm 89:37).

4 Already the promise had come on three occasions, and each time it was contingent upon the appearance of the seed (Genesis 12:7; 13:15,16; 15:18). The emotional burden of this on Sarai must have been considerable.

done or not done, that heaven remained closed to her entreaties?

She had asked herself these questions on countless occasions, and still did not know the answers. There was only one thing that she knew with certainty, and that was this, that despite her prayers, she was barren, as barren as she had been when they first left Ur.[5] Perhaps this was, after all, the Father's reply. Perhaps it was His way that she should remain so. Perhaps it was His purpose that she should be restrained from bearing.

In truth, however, the Father had not restrained her at all. When Sarai's faith came to blossom and bud in unreserved certainty of the Father's mighty power, then likewise her womb would quicken to nourish a child for Abram. There was no shortening of the Lord's hand that He could not at this moment send His angel with the touch that could heal and empower. But He waited for a faith that Sarai, lost in the labyrinth of her own fear, had not yet found. He waited for her to believe that He could provide what she herself could not, that her inadequacy, her weakness, her deficiency were no match for the all-surpassing greatness of His power and love.

But Sarai could wait no longer. It was enough. If heaven would not answer and open her womb, then she would provide another way for the promise to be fulfilled. This was to be her initiative.[6] Sarai was to take over the leadership of the family with disastrous results. For in her agitation of mind, she was about to assume not just the headship of Abram, but the responsibility of God Himself. She believed that God was unable or unwilling to fulfil the promise through her, and that she must needs therefore find another way. And there was in the customs of the day a practice that might serve her need.

---

5 Genesis 11:30.

6 The emphasis of the record indicates this. Genesis 16:1,2 states – "Now *Sarai* Abram's wife bare him no children: and *she* had an handmaid ... and *Sarai* said unto Abram ..."

A handmaid called Hagar

When a married woman found that she was barren, it was permissible for her to provide a slave-wife for her husband. The children of the union would be accepted by the first wife as her own, and would be considered as true sons and daughters. She knew how the burden of being childless weighed on Abram's mind,[7] for they had discussed the matter often enough. But Abram's feelings were as nothing compared with hers. This lack of an heir was a desolation to her soul. Being utterly bereft of a child was not just a sorrow to be quietly borne, the fretting anxiety of it extinguished her very spirit; she was smothered, stifled, enveloped in its pain. She was alive yet dead. She felt the crushing weight of this empty void. Even her husband could not enter into the feelings she had, for they lay deep within the essence of her womanhood.[8]

She then, needed to resolve this thing, and best that she suggest this course of action to Abram, rather than he to her. After all, what was needed was not just the way forward, but also the means. Abram might agree in principle, but only she could solve the practical dilemma of who this slave-wife might be.

Now among her retinue of servants was a young woman whom Sarai thought might be suitable. Hagar was one of her handmaidens that had served her now for over ten years.[9] She was of a good countenance, albeit in quite a different way from Sarai, and this was not without purpose. She was eager to serve yet generally of a docile disposition, and her servant mentality should

---

7 As witnessed by Abram's heartfelt cry in Genesis 15:2-4.

8 Compare the agonised spirit of the woman of Shunem in 2 Kings 4:14-16,27,28, and this in a passage filled with allusions to the story of Abram and Sarai.

9 It would seem that Hagar had joined the household as a result of the journey to Egypt. Genesis 12:16 states, "and he entreated Abram well for her sake: and he had ... *maidservants*". If this was the moment of her addition to Abram's retinue, then she had indeed served Sarai for the ten years indicated in 16:3.

keep her within the bounds of her proper position. She was young and healthy, but lacked the maturity and assurance of her mistress. Lastly, her thinking would never match Sarai's in spiritual things, and for this reason it was unlikely that Abram would ever develop an affinity of mind with her. She was in short an excellent choice for the purpose Sarai had in mind. A woman who could bear a strong and comely child for them, but who, most certainly, was not a soulmate who might supplant her mistress in the heart of her lord.

That I may be builded by her

"And Sarai said unto Abram, Behold now, the LORD hath restrained me from bearing: I pray thee, go in unto my maid; it may be that I may obtain children by her." (Genesis 16:2)

Sarai turned the matter over and over in her mind. Each time she became more reconciled to the idea, and more certain that her choice of Hagar was prudent and sensible. The time had come to speak with Abram, to suggest what he could not suggest, and to convince him that this arrangement was still really working with the Almighty. She chose her moment with care. For one evening as dusk fell, they sat outside the tent door and observed the quiet bustle of the encampment as it prepared for the hours of darkness and sleep. A knot of children sped past giggling merrily, intent on evading capture by the determined maidservant who followed pursuing, equally intent upon delivering them safely to their beds. Abram chuckled, and then smiled the wistful smile of a childless man.

"Behold now" said Sarai, seeing her chance, "the LORD hath restrained me from bearing: I pray thee, go in unto my maid; it may be that I may obtain children by her". As Abram looked at her in astonishment she pressed on with her explanation, her voice low and pleading, her eyes expressive of her need for him to listen carefully and understand. They never wavered from searching his face as she spoke, and in turn Abram read in her face the earnest conviction of a woman who believed in the truth of what she said.

Sarai's suggestion placed Abram in a quandary. His immediate reaction was to feel distinctly uneasy about the possible consequences of this arrangement should they move ahead. He was not at all sure that Sarai realised how things might turn as time unfolded. And what of divine principle? They had heard the story of Adam and Eve being recounted, and knew that the divine ideal of marriage from the beginning had been one man, one woman, committed for life through weal or woe. Such singleness of union was surely still the best basis for the bringing forth of a godly seed. Yet he was aware that her proposal had social acceptance in their day, and that legal provision was made for it.

Abram smiled wryly as he thought upon the matter. Years before he had let her down, and she had ended up in association with another man. Now she sought his support that he might have association with another woman! What strange circling of circumstances was this, that led them to this reversal?

He understood completely Sarai's desire to build their household,[10] but how could a woman from another land and another life provide suitable stones for the building?

Then again, he realised how dangerously overwrought his wife was about this present distress. More than once he had found her weeping inconsolably and he knew that this grief affected her health, her equanimity of mind, and her relationship with him. He could not simply reject her suggestion out of hand. In fact her assessment of their situation was completely true. God had indicated that he, Abram, would father the child, but how could they be sure that Sarai would bear it? He wanted her to

---

10 Houses were *built* with stones – *eben*. Households were *built* with sons – *ben*. The desire for offspring as stones to *build* the household may reach back to the 'seed of the woman' promise in Genesis 3:15. Sarai's description of a child by Hagar, so that she might be "*builded* by her" echoes this strong scriptural theme (Deuteronomy 25:5-10; Psalm 127:1-3; Hebrews 3:3-6).

of course, they had always longed for this fruit of their marriage. Yet just as he believed that the bringing forth of children was a blessing from God, so he was bound to recognise that barrenness, or the withholding of the fruit of the womb, was also of God. Sarai's whole argument was that her barrenness was indeed of the Father, and that they finally needed to accept this and move on. How could he suggest that she was wrong, when all the evidence of their marriage for the last forty years or more proved her point to be true?

Abram was hesitant and uncertain, but recognised the look of pleading in her eyes. He knew what this meant to his wife, and he understood what it had cost her even to make this suggestion. Perhaps after all she was right, perhaps the absence of a response from heaven was so that they might seek another way. Certainly he did not want to let her down again when she sorely needed his sympathy and help. 'I agree', he said, 'for your sake Sarai, I will do this thing'.[11]

And Sarai gave Hagar to her husband Abram

"And Abram hearkened to the voice of Sarai. And Sarai Abram's wife took Hagar her maid the Egyptian, after Abram had dwelt ten years in the land of Canaan, and gave her to her husband Abram to be his wife." (Genesis 16:2,3)

It was on the morrow that Sarai gave Hagar to Abram. She presented her handmaid, and withdrew out of earshot. She knew that Abram needed to be alone with Hagar for the conversation that would follow. She could see them both, yet was distant enough to not intrude, and tactfully beyond hearing's range. Hagar stood before Abram in the meekness of submission. As Abram looked upon her, she returned his gaze shyly and bowed low in deference. She was aware of the honour being extended to her in this arrangement, and was sufficiently shrewd to conduct herself with a decorum that would please both her mistress and the master. 'Are you willing, Hagar,

---

11 Genesis 16:2 records that "Abram hearkened to the voice of Sarai".

to become my concubine?"[12] he asked, and received in return her assent. There were, of course, matters to be considered, for with her acceptance of Abram's offer her position and duties in the household would change. Abram explained these changes carefully for in this, as in all his dealings, he would conduct himself with integrity and fairness.

No dowry or marriage ceremony was necessary to formalize the taking of a concubine. But in this case, Hagar was expressly chosen to build the house of Abram and Sarai, and the master gave orders for a feast to be prepared that the household might rejoice. The time to laugh and the time to dance had come, and the voice of melody was heard around the surrounding hills of the Judaean plateau. When the feast day and its celebrations were ended, Abram, with a curiously awkward gesture of the hand, bade Hagar to step within his domain as lord of the encampment. As Hagar stooped to enter Abram's tent, Sarai stifled a sob, drew breath sharply, and turned away that she might not see Abram enter also. She had not until this moment realised the distress she would feel, and she knew not as yet how greatly that distress would be multiplied, as this chapter in their lives unfolded.

It was, of course, Sarai's desire that her house might be builded through Hagar bearing a son to Abram. The birth of a son would cement their marriage, establish their family, and provide the means for the promise to be fulfilled. And perhaps even more than her own desire, she wanted this to be so for Abram's sake. If Hagar could supply her lack, then she might rest content with her husband again. Alas, alas that it was not to be. Everything that Sarai wished for in this arrangement would remain unfulfilled. A child was born by and by, but the lad who sprang from Hagar's line would never be the promised seed. God in heaven would not acknowledge this boy as the channel of His blessing. For Abram's sake,

---

12 For in the final reckoning of Scripture, she is deemed to be Abram's bondwoman and concubine, not his wife (Genesis 21:12; 25:6).

He would preserve the child and build him as a nation, but never to be that people of whom the proclamation had been made – "I will make of thee a great nation ... and thou shalt be a blessing".[13]

Ishmael's birth did in measure establish Abram's family, but it did not establish Sarai's as she hoped. The child would always be his birth mother's, and would manifest his mother's spirit. Ishmael was no son of Sarai as he grew. And Sarai's marriage to her lord, far from being nourished by the birth of this child, was cruelly hurt to the piercing of her soul with a sword.

It had been painful enough to surrender her man into the arms of another woman. She had only borne it because of her love for him, and her grim determination that the promise should be fulfilled. But in her urgent haste to advance the promise of God, she had not pondered carefully enough the consequences that might ensue. For until this moment, the household had simply known and accepted that Abram and Sarai were together childless. It was a communal sorrow they all shared, that the family tree of their lord and mistress still lacked a scion. But with Hagar now in the blossom of expectancy, it was clear to everyone that Abram could produce an heir. Sarai could tell from stolen glances and whispered asides that all now knew the problem lay with her. Her own contrivings had proved it, had shown beyond doubt that she was barren indeed, the sole reason for this tree without a branch. Whatever inadequacy she had felt before, had now been magnified an hundredfold.

An handmaid that is heir to her mistress

"And he went in unto Hagar, and she conceived: and when she saw that she had conceived, her mistress was despised in her eyes." (Genesis 16:4)

It was so difficult to maintain her composure and her calm when she sensed the eyes of all upon her. Worse was to come, for as soon as Hagar had conceived her docile

---

13 Genesis 12:2.

spirit underwent a startling change. Hagar the humble was transformed into Hagar the haughty. All the arts at her disposal were now employed to show her disdain for the mistress she served.

Her walk was slower, and her steps more careful, as if to show that now she walked for two, slowest of all when passing her mistress. When she knew that Sarai was watching, she would stand and straighten in such a way that her gentle swelling was seen and on occasions she stood with her hands on her hips as if to cradle her precious burden and keep it safe. She began to decline her more burdensome tasks on the basis that her condition would not allow it, and that nor would Abram. And the expressions of her face were calculated to cut Sarai to the quick. Her looks were mysterious, challenging, enigmatic, brazen, and all with a knowing smile that hinted at secrets she possessed, but which were not shared by Sarai.

But hardest of all was the change in Abram's behaviour. He was still the same in his affection for her, she was bound to acknowledge that, and yet he was no longer the same man in other ways. He was embarrassed to speak with Hagar in her presence, yet he was obviously eager to know of her welfare. There was a new and strange look in his eye, slightly guilty yet somehow pleased, the gleam of an expectant father, aware of his virility, and rejoicing in the prospect of a child. Yet he never seemed to share that joy with her. When they were alone, his references to Hagar were studied and careful, yet whenever Hagar was present he was all attention and care and fussing concern. And Hagar rewarded every little act of solicitude he showed with a swift smile for him, and a slow smile to her. It suddenly dawned upon Sarai with an unpleasant shock that Hagar was no longer her servant but her rival, and a determined one at that.[14]

---

14 Among the unbearable things which greatly disquiet the earth is "an handmaid that is heir to her mistress" (Proverbs 30:23). The terms "handmaid" and "mistress" are identical to those found in Genesis 16:1,4 and the proverb may well have the story of Sarai and Hagar as its basis.

Already then, the matter was unfolding in a way which Sarai had not foreseen. She had hoped for the sweetness of a family, but the fruits of her actions were already bitter to the taste. The trouble was that decisions had been made which could not now be reversed. There was a lesson here for both of them to learn. Any problem, when allowed to overwhelm us, can cloud our judgement and affect our temperament. Those problems that rule the heart as well as the head disturb our balance the most. Rational thought and Scriptural reasoning are abandoned, because of emotion and feeling. It was a mistake to be guided by her own anxious thoughts. The mind of the flesh can never be trusted to produce the thinking of the spirit.

This couple, momentarily diverted by the burden of their woe, had not yet understood the need to wait patiently upon the Lord.[15] God, who knoweth the thoughts of each heart, would fulfil His words when both He and they were ready. He had promised; He would perform, and they would through faith and patience inherit the promises. But patience needed to have her maturing work, until their confidence in Him was absolute. Patience meant standing back from their problem to see it from a spiritual perspective. Patience meant taking the time to try and appreciate the Father's purpose in the matter. Patience meant understanding fully the law of consequences that would inexorably, relentlessly, follow whatever choice they might make. Only now were the consequences becoming apparent, as the circumstances within the family became more and more entangled.

The wisdom of a soft answer

It was an impossible situation, and soon enough the strain between husband and wife grew into a moment of confrontation. Some especially spiteful act on Hagar's part brought Sarai to Abram's tent. The urgent jerking

---

15 But it is a mark of their wonderful faith that in the end, they did manifest patience, and were rewarded by God (Hebrew 6:11-15).

open of the tent flap told Abram that something was amiss, and when he looked up and saw her the signs were certainly ominous. Sarai stood with arms akimbo and lip aquiver, with bosom heaving and dark eyes flashing, her whole person trembling indignantly. He waited for the expected speech to come, and come it did, a veritable torrent of pent-up feelings, jumbled thoughts and urgent words. Abram had been married for long enough to know what to do. When a woman has bottled feelings, she will also have bottled words. Now that the bottle was open, she would speak until it was empty and he must hear the outpourings of her heart, till all the words were finished. Only then could they begin to deal with the matter. Abram listened.

"My wrong be upon thee: I have given my maid into thy bosom; and when she saw that she had conceived, I was despised in her eyes: the LORD judge between me and thee." (Genesis 16:5)

"My wrong be upon thee" expostulated Sarai, wishing to impress upon Abram the gravity of the problem and the need for him to listen. "I have given my maid into thy bosom; and when she saw that she had conceived, I was despised in her eyes." Here then was the crux of the matter. Sarai was aware, cruelly aware that her plan had gone astray. Upset to the point of distraction, she sought a response from Abram by blaming him for the entire episode. Her words were passionate, emotive, and unreasonable. It was true in one sense, that Abram had not shown spiritual headship in the matter. He should have encouraged Sarai to wait in patience for the fulfilment of the promise, in God's own good time. He should not have allowed spiritual thinking to be overborne by personal feeling. But to lay all blame at his door for something that had been of her making was both unkind and unfair. But she was not finished yet. As her speech came to an end, she uttered the strongest thing she could think of to provoke a response: "The LORD judge between me and thee." Abram blinked. To invoke the Name of God in judgement was very serious, and quite extreme. And were they so far apart that God must now decide between them? These were strong words indeed, and might have aroused the ire of a lesser man.

Thankfully, Abram was a husband of discernment and sensitivity. He knew that there are times when all argument is futile, that there are some debates that cannot be won. He knew that there are occasions, when a woman's emotions are stirred, that whatever a husband might say will still be wrong. And, astute man that he was, he also knew how to read the real message of her words, to understand not what she said but what she meant. His ears had heard the vital clue, hidden in her forceful remonstrance – "I have given my maid into thy bosom".[16] These were not the words of a scheming or angry woman, but the language of a badly frightened wife, who now felt insecure in her marriage. Sarai's deepest fear was not that she was despised in Hagar's eyes, but whether she might be despised in Abram's. She had lost confidence in the security of their relationship. She knew her reasons for giving Hagar, but now she felt unsure of his reasons for taking Hagar. There was a rupture of trust here, and however it had come about, Abram needed to heal the breach. His reply, measured and thoughtful, was a model of marriage diplomacy and tact:

> "But Abram said unto Sarai, Behold, thy maid is in thy hand; do to her as it pleaseth thee."
>
> (Genesis 16:6)

"Behold, thy maid is in thy hand." He did not seek to defend Hagar, or even to mention her by name, for that would be too personal given this fragile moment. His description of her as Sarai's maid, and not his wife, was designed to reassure Sarai concerning her rightful status as the wife of his covenant. Even his choice of words to allow Sarai to deal with the matter were selected with

---

16 A tender term, used in Luke 16:22 to convey the delights of the kingdom age. It indicates here the intimate relationship between Abram and Hagar that now existed, albeit with the consent and approval of Sarai.

delicacy and care, for Hagar was to be left in "her hand", and not in "his bosom". Leaving her in charge of this issue was not a matter of indifference on Abram's part. Instead, he showed his confidence and trust in Sarai to handle the matter on behalf of them both. Yet in this gentle reply, Abram sought to guide Sarai in the spirit of her dealings. "Do to her that which is good in thine eyes."[17] It was a reminder that her actions needed to be just and fair, irrespective of her depth of feeling.

Abram's voice, deep and calm and reasonable, soothed her troubled soul. A soft answer had won far more than the hasty spirit that strives.[18] The breach that had come through mutual foolishness was healed, and their marriage relationship restored. They would live through the consequences of their actions, as every couple must do, but at least they would face them together.

Hagar's flight to freedom

The woman who stepped forth from Abram's tent was happier than the one who had entered it. Sarai walked again in the comfort and security of her husband's love, and with an assurance of bearing that proclaimed her to be the mistress of the household. With a purposeful gleam in her eye she called for Hagar. It was time to put matters right. The bearer of Abram's child was to learn that she was still but a handmaid to Sarai, and not her rival. She had sought to replace her mistress and to become the pre-eminent wife, but she had overstepped her station. She would never do so again. Sarai was stern but just in the humbling and chastening of her servant.[19]

---

17 Cp. 1 Chronicles 21:23, Zechariah 11:12, etc. where the same expression is used, and which evidently refers to that which is fair, or right, or appropriate.

18 Proverbs 15:1, Ecclesiastes 7:9 and Ephesians 4:26 are all illustrative of the wonderful benefits of self-control and mastery of emotions within our personal dealings, and especially within the marriage bond.

19 The term – "dealt hardly" is *anah*, which means to humble or afflict or punish. Since the range of meanings includes 'afflicting' *one's own soul* on the Day of Atonement (Leviticus 23:27; Isaiah

Through the giving of orders, and by the assignment of menial tasks, Hagar was rebuked. Sarai might have erred in making her suggestion to begin with, but that did not justify Hagar's wilful and presumptive spirit. Sarai's actions unequivocally declared that she was Abram's wife, and the entire household knew that Hagar had been put in her place.

It was a bitter blow to Hagar's pride. Now that she had experienced a taste of higher things, she was no longer content with her servant status. She resented her punishment, she resented the need to submit to the authority of another, and she was not prepared to remain subservient to Sarai. So one day, when certain duties brought her to the perimeter of the encampment, she fled. Her speed of travel was not great, for she was with child, but her movements were deliberate in heading south to Beersheba. Beyond Beersheba, about a day's journey, the road turned to strike south-west in the wilderness of Shur. It was an arid and desolate land, but Hagar was glad to be there. For her march was not simply an escape into the wilderness. This road on which she travelled was the highway to Egypt, and she was going home. She was never a spiritual member of Abram's household, far less the companion of his mind. Her thinking was Egyptian, pagan, profane, and the direction of her feet told where her heart lay.

Back in the encampment, all was astir. Abram, doubtless, had sent forth retainers to scour the hills around Hebron in search of Sarai's wayward maid. They could not find her. And meanwhile, several days to the south, the object of their attention was doubtless smiling with satisfaction at her success in eluding her pursuers. Hagar, true to her nature and to her name, had fled.[20]

58:5), and of 'chastening' *oneself* before God (Daniel 10:12) it is evident that the term does not necessarily imply cruelty or oppression. It would seem that Sarai did indeed punish Hagar, but later events would vindicate the rightness of Sarai's actions.

20 Hagar – means 'flight'.

The angelic watcher in the wilderness

But Hagar walked in ignorance of one who saw her every move. A watcher, from the holy ones of Ail, was following her steps. His purpose was to speak with the fleeing one before her discovery by any of Abram's servants. There were certain matters to be impressed upon Hagar before she returned to the household. Hagar trod the desert path, in blissful ignorance of the angelic being that watched her with the piercing eyes of the spirit. Many others since have likewise walked in ways that reveal they are quite unconscious of the ministering spirits who have been nearby, and who see and know. The angel who watched on this occasion was unhurried, for the woman was unaware. He waited for the time to manifest himself, and soon the opportunity he sought was presented. Hagar had reached a water well that lay on the wilderness highway. The little oasis of green and shade, and the prospect of water to slake the thirst were too attractive to pass by. So, secure in her present progress, she decided to rest awhile. Her defences were down for there was no sign of anyone present, and she was certain that none were following. She drank, and sat under a tree to restore her tired limbs. The landscape in front of her shimmered in the desert heat, and the distant horizon receded and advanced through the waves of heated air. It was while she sat at rest that a man suddenly appeared before her. One moment the wilderness lay open and empty, the next he was there. Before she could think, and before she could move, the man had spoken.

> "And the angel of the LORD found her by a fountain of water in the wilderness, by the fountain in the way to Shur. And he said, Hagar, Sarai's maid, whence camest thou? And whither wilt thou go?"
>
> (Genesis 16:7,8)

His words shocked and dismayed her. The man was a perfect stranger, yet he knew everything about her with an intimacy of detail that frightened. With a few brief words he had laid her bare. He knew her name and her status, her immediate past circumstances and her present intention. What was there that he did not know, this unknown yet insightful visitor? Hagar answered with the honesty of fear. There was no point in pretending with one who knew too much already. "I flee from the face of my mistress Sarai". This much at least was true. Of course, the question of whether she was right in doing so remained as yet unanswered, at least until the angel spoke again. Yet before the angel breathed another word, Hagar knew with simple certainty what his reply would be. For in describing her as Sarai's maid and not as Abram's wife, the angel had already pronounced judgement in the matter. It was a declaration that Sarai was right in her insistence on their respective positions. Hagar waited with pained resignation for the words which she felt sure would now come. They did. "Return to thy mistress", was the stern command of the angel, "and submit thyself under her hands".[21] There was to be no escape from responsibility, and Hagar was to face the consequences of her actions.

So also were Abram and Sarai to face the consequences of theirs. It might well have been easier for all concerned for the angel to permit Hagar to escape, and to leave the household in peace. But in the purpose of God she was ordered to return. There was a reason for this. Abram and Sarai were to be chastened by the results of their own actions as we all are in life. If their spirit was right before God, the experience would strengthen their faith and mature their marriage. That chastening might not be joyous, in fact it rarely is, but it would yield the peaceable fruit of righteousness after exercise. And

---

21 The command of Genesis 16:9 indicates that Hagar's behaviour was unacceptable. She needed to return and accept her position, and it is therefore reasonable to assume that Sarai's dealing was not unjust or unrighteous. Especially significant in this context is the fact that the term "submit" is *anah*, the identical word used in verse 6 when Sarai "dealt hardly" with Hagar. The angelic pronouncement for Hagar to return to receive more of the same is a clear endorsement of Sarai's spirit in the matter.

it would engrave the lesson upon their hearts in a way that would never be forgotten.

One of the vital lessons to be learned was that the Almighty grants to every person freedom of choice, but He has attached a terrible legacy to its exercise. The law of consequences is the divinely appointed counterpoise to the doctrine of free will. When the power of the former is finally understood, it will help to circumscribe the proper boundaries of the latter. Simple though this truth is, it can take a lifetime before we finally understand its reality. The law of free will can so easily be translated into the spirit of liberty or licence, which brooks no restraint and recognises no boundaries. Only later, when we experience an outworking of consequences that are relentless, unavoidable, and painful, do we understand that free will is an enormous responsibility, and must always be exercised with thoughtful care and spiritual purpose. The return of Hagar and the birth of her child in the encampment would instruct Abram and Sarai more powerfully than her departure, that all decisions in life bear consequences that must be faced.

The prophecy concerning Ishmael

Hagar then, must return. Yet the angel's edict also implied that Sarai's treatment of Hagar had been just. The counsel to submit to more of the same was based upon its fairness. Abram's words, prudent and kindly in Sarai's ear, had borne fruit. If Hagar went back there would be no miscarriage of justice, although she would need to accept her subordinate role. In one particular matter, however, Hagar was given reassurance that gladdened her heart. Not only would her offspring grow into a multitude, but the child would be indisputably hers. She would carry him, give birth to him, nourish him and name him. The lad would never be Sarai's, and would never build Sarai's family.[22] Hagar was exultant at this news, for she yearned with all her maternal instinct

22 Sarai would despair to learn of this, as her hopes for a child by this means would be extinguished. Only later, in the breathless

to mother the babe as her own. And so she would, for in every sense this child would be his mother's son. In character and temperament, in thought and conduct, the babe was not Abram's child, nor Sarai's, but Hagar's. To the mother then, the child's name was given. Ishmael – God shall hear – was proof that God was aware of her unhappiness.[23] The very promise given to her, that the child was not to be reckoned as Sarai's, was God's response, and incentive enough for Hagar to return to the comfort and safety of Hebron.

"And the angel of the LORD said unto her, Behold, thou art with child, and shalt bear a son, and shalt call his name Ishmael; because the LORD hath heard thy affliction. And he will be a wild man; his hand will be against every man, and every man's hand against him; and he shall dwell in the presence of all his brethren." (Genesis 16:11,12)

The joy of knowing that her son would not be taken from her was tempered by this strange prophecy that followed. The child would not be an easy one to raise. He would prove to be turbulent and contrary, as unteachable and untameable as the wild asses of the desert.[24] His very spirit would set him at odds with others, and they in turn at odds with him. This child of Hagar was emphatically not the true seed. Wherever the true seed went, there would be blessing. Wherever this child went, there would be trouble and controversy. Only in his latter end would there be the prospect of peace and reconciliation, to live in harmony with those who were, after all, his brethren.

---

excitement and wonder of her own child, would she realise that the Father always knows what is best for our development.

23 The term "affliction" *oniy* (Genesis 16:11) indicates unhappiness arising out of many differing circumstances. It is found in Genesis 29:32 (misery from neglect), in 31:42 (hardship through labour), and in 41:52 (trials in exile). Hagar's unhappiness (it must be remembered) was largely self-induced, although she may have suffered real privation in the wilderness, and been nourished by the angel to sustain her on her return journey.

24 The term "wild" (Genesis 16:12) means a 'wild ass', and is translated on every other occasion that way.

The pronouncements of the angel were ended, and Hagar knew that she had received a divine visitation. Awestruck with the knowledge that she had seen, and been seen by, a heavenly being, she gave him the name of Ail Roi in commemoration of their meeting. The name was a revelation of Hagar's mind. The angel who had spoken to her was a manifestation of the Lord. Yet Hagar was not grateful for a covenant God who watches with care, but resentful of a Power who sees to control. She quailed before divine authority, but would never rise to divine principle. She was impressed that she had caught a glimpse of a heavenly messenger, but less inclined to glimpse his heavenly mind. The well of meeting was also given a name that would be a remembrance of their encounter, for it was called Beer Lahai Roi – 'the well of him that liveth and seeth me'. The reality of his watchful eye was enough to turn Hagar's footsteps back. She could not escape, that was clear, and now with certain promises to cheer and comfort her, she bowed to the command and began the homeward trudge, ascending by stages into the rocky summits of the Judaean hills. The air grew cooler, and the flowers and herbs of the mountain slopes appeared to point the way.

And Hagar bare Abram a son

It was the herdsmen who first saw Hagar on the horizon. She drew close enough so that her shape and walk could be recognised, and a lad was dispatched to run back home and tell the news to the master. Onward she came, her shadow slipping ahead of her, but soon her face and features could be made out. The men called out to her, and she came readily enough, and was grateful for some water from their bottle and some cheese from their shepherd's pouch. She ate and drank greedily, for the past few days had yielded but the scant and meagre fare of desert food. Thus fed, the errant wanderer was brought by escort to the patriarch's tent. It was a bedraggled and dusty waif who came to bend the knee before Abram and Sarai. Gone were the imperious looks and high-handed ways. Her spirit was docile again and Hagar, somewhat fearful of her encounter with the angel, was ready to submit and render obedience. After pleading forgiveness and pledging faithfulness, she was led away by the older women that she might be scolded and bathed, examined and rested.

> "And Hagar bare Abram a son: and Abram called his son's name, which Hagar bare, Ishmael. And Abram was fourscore and six years old, when Hagar bare Ishmael to Abram."   (Genesis 16:15,16)

Months passed, and the time came when Hagar travailed in labour. She was delivered of a man child, her firstborn, and the firstborn also of Abram. It was the father who gave name to the child, but the mother who chose it. Hagar had explained the angel's promise to Abram, and her earnest countenance had convinced him of the truth of her account. The child would be called Ishmael – God shall hear – just as the angel had said. Yet tragically the father and mother saw even the name of the boy from different standpoints. For Hagar, the name Ishmael gave assurance that God had heard her woes and would preserve both her and the child. For Abram, the name Ishmael reminded him that God had not forgotten His promises and would fulfil them. There was no unity of thought or purpose here. No marriage relationship can truly prosper when there is no meeting and matching of minds on things divine. There was no affinity here between Abram and this concubine, despite the fact that she had borne his child. Physical relationships make one flesh, but not one spirit. They bring together, yet they do not unite. The child born was Abram's son, but he was not the godly seed promised in God's covenant.

Keturah and her sons

In every age the social habits and practices of the day are accepted by the saints as normal, although they may be far removed from what Almighty God may count as good and reckon as right. In our own age there are many habits and customs that we take for granted, but which bear no resemblance to Biblical practice, either patriarchal or apostolic. We justify them, not because they are Biblical but because they are ubiquitous. And Almighty God in turn makes use of all the circumstances of our lives whether right or wrong to teach us His ways. The patriarch likewise lived his life within the customs of his day. Children were a blessing because they brought the promise of future care. When a father and mother grew old, their children would protect and nourish them. Strong sons would manage the fields and flocks of the family, industrious daughters would provide for their parents, and a couple would pass their later years within the circle of the family bond. Abram had but a short time to father sons before his natural powers waned. These very years marked the end of his opportunity to build branches on his tree. They were not wasted. For soon the shouts and cries of several sturdy lads resounded among the family tents. But none of these younger siblings of Ishmael were sons of Sarai. They were the sons of Abram and Keturah.[25]

Keturah would never cause the trials that Hagar had brought. She was a faithful concubine and contented with her lot. She bore Abram a succession of sons until his quiver was full. She did not seek to move beyond her place, and did not claim a special right for all her little men.[26] She lived within the security of the encampment of the man known as the "Friend of God", and had the happiness of living within a household that worshipped God and walked in His ways. In this respect her lot was blessed. She experienced the support and affection of Abram, and knew him to be a man of integrity and honour. And of all households in the land of Canaan this was the best, the very best to belong to, for it brought both Keturah and her sons into contact with the hope of salvation, a priceless gift that Abram gladly shared with all his family.[27]

---

25 See Appendix 4 – "When were Keturah's children born?"

26 Certainly the record is devoid of any suggestion of friction or tension within the household because of Keturah.

27 Genesis 18:19.

But these boys, together with Ishmael, were the sons of the other women in Abram's life. The story of the concubines was related to the customs of the day, but by the time the story was complete, it had exacted a toll on all the family. Any practice that is a departure from the divine standard will bring the consequence of unexpected trial. This matter was no different. Abram and Sarai would know pain in their marriage because of this. But as with all trial, the spirit and response of God's servants will fundamentally affect the outcome. In the case of this couple it drew them closer, because their lives were truly devoted to the Lord whom they served. A different spirit, however, would have produced a different outcome. The doctrine of free will and the law of consequences are a perpetual cycle in the life of faith. For a choice once made brings its own inevitable consequence, but with it also comes the opportunity to exercise our free will yet again, in choosing how to respond. By such means our faith is matured and our wisdom increased. We all journey in Abram and Sarai's footsteps.

Seven sons were thus born to Abram during this epoch in his life, and not one of them was the child of the promise. That son, the promised seed, was still to come. And when the promised seed finally came, he would be the eighth, and there would truly be a new beginning in the patriarch's life. For this last and special child would be the son of Sarai, the woman of his love, his true and only wife. Almighty God would see to it, and sooner now than either of them realised.

4

EMBRACING THE COVENANT BLESSING TOGETHER
(Genesis 17:1-27)

AS the sun rose over the red ramparts of Moab's mountains, on the other side Jordan, the light of a new dawn crept also across the face of the Judaean hills. In Hebron, the black silhouette of an old oak tree was outlined against a pale pink and mauve sky, ageless in its stately, venerable splendour. The encampment, however, that nestled around and under the mighty tree was not so timeless in appearance. Pathways between tent and fire, and fire and well, and well and field were beaten and worn by the ceaseless rub of countless footsteps, paths that measured the traffic of life now, for more than a score of years. Tent skins, stretched taut with stake and cord, which once were moist and dark, were now faded and frayed. Their spreading expanse still gave protection and shade, but they were bleached to brittleness by the sun of many seasons. Soon they would be needing a new tabernacle. The servants, who rose to tend their daily tasks, were still the old and trusted faces, but the faces were more lined now and the shoulders more stooped. Sarai, still graceful despite her years,[1] was now crowned with a silver mantle, and the patriarchal beard had turned to the white of the blossom on the almond tree.[2]

But let patience have her perfect work

Thirteen years had passed since the birth of Ishmael to Hagar, Sarai's handmaid. The seven sons who had run and climbed, and laughed and cried, were older now. Some of the boys were already at work with the

---

1 She was certainly attractive and graceful enough for Abimelech to take her into his household, a year after this episode (Genesis 20:2).
2 Ecclesiastes 12:5.

herds and flocks, and all of them from eldest to youngest had the burden of some particular responsibility in the household. Ishmael, the oldest, was just beginning to show the first signs of change, with a growing frame, a squarer face, and a deepening voice. The moment comes when the early eager beauty of childhood innocence is marred by the truculence and surliness that so often appears in youth, and recedes in the mercy of God when manhood is finally attained. With Ishmael, however, the spirit of contention would remain, and grow like a canker within him. For the moment he was not especially troublesome, and none of the lads were stubborn or rebellious. Yet Abram and Sarai, having watched them all from infancy, did not feel close to any of them. The cornerstone they yearned for to build their own family, the son who could be the foundation of the household, was not to be seen amongst these. They had learned a valuable lesson from this chapter in their life. Fleshly contrivance is not the answer to the problems of the truth. They had learned, finally, that "the children of the flesh, these are not … the children of the promise".[3]

For even the first child of the promise to come, they would need to trust in Him, and so that their trust might be developed to fulness the Father made use of the experience of delay. It was necessary that they should truly believe in Him because of the great things He would accomplish through them in return. In the divine wisdom therefore, He made them wait until certain years were expired. There was nothing haphazard about the length of the delay. God had in mind the teaching of a profound and powerful truth. For when these vital years of further delay were gone, both Abram and Sarai were so well stricken in age that neither could produce a child.[4] All fleshly hope was extinguished when this moment came. All human possibility was ended. God wished it so.

---

3 Romans 9:8.

4 The testimony of Romans 4:19 is unequivocal on this matter, that both were in the state of 'deadness of body' before this promise of Isaac came.

If a child should now be born to them both, it could only be because of a divinely glorious and miraculous intervention in their lives. They had been brought to the brink of either faith or despair. God had tested them to the utmost, yet not beyond measure. He waited to work a miracle with them, if they would receive it, not just the miracle of a son's birth, but the enactment of a parable that was rich with significance. Abram and Sarai would not in their lifetime understand completely the wondrous things that God would foreshadow through their lives. Enmeshed within the tangle of their own trials, they could but dimly know the greatness of the Father's ways. How oft indeed are all His children unaware of the pattern He weaves through the warp and weft of their own experience? It was nevertheless, the sovereign pleasure of God to exhibit the parable of His own Son in the story of theirs. Unbeknown to the old man and woman who waited with their private dreams, the arrival of their son would portend the coming of another, who also would be begotten "not of blood, nor of the will of the flesh, nor of the will of man, but of God".[5]

Yet even if they did not see the fulness of the Father's plan, they did at least appreciate that their own son could only come through this divinely organised way. This much they saw, and still they believed in the promise of God. Now, herein was a marvellous thing. Despite the fact that all appeared impossible, they had learned at last to wait on God, and appreciate His working in their lives. Their bodies were dead, but their faith was alive. Imperfect perhaps, faltering even, but still alive. Their patience was about to be rewarded. The time had come for another visitation, and the ageless angel came again to the ageing man.

The wondrous power of Ail Shaddai

"And when Abram was ninety years old and nine, the LORD appeared to Abram, and said unto him, I

---

5   John 1:13.

am the Almighty God; walk before me, and be thou
perfect." (Genesis 17:1)

The messenger who came as the Angel of the Name,
was familiar to the patriarch. He had conversed with
this member of the heavenly host before, and his
reappearance now was a cause for excitement. Abram,
waiting in reverence for his opening words, was surprised
and intrigued when they came. For the angel insisted
that he recognise him by a different name, despite their
earlier encounters.[6] Abram's interest and curiosity were
quickened. Almighty God, Ail Shaddai was a title that
spoke of Him who was the nourisher of families, and the
multiplier of seeds. Now why should this mention be
made of a nursing father? Who was there to nurse and
to nourish? What was the angel implying? Could it be
that this had something to do with the promised seed?

The words that followed astounded him even more.
"Walk before me, and be thou upright", said the angel
with firm and measured tone. Abram recognised the
words immediately. Everyone knew the story of the great
flood, for it was the mighty epic of all peoples. And Abram
had heard the story told of famous Noah, the champion of
that earlier age, who in his generation had walked before
God as an upright man. Was the angel then asking him
to emulate this hero from the deluge? But why? And yet,
had not God made a new beginning with this man? And
had not that fresh start been made through his sons?
Could this mean that God now wished to do the same
through him? If only there could be a fulfilment of the
covenant, which God had already pledged with him.
God's covenant had promised him a son, a seed, an heir.
Abram was prepared to make whatever new beginning
the Lord might require, if it could but begin with this
son of the promise. His eyes were fixed with desperate
intensity on the face of the angel, and as he looked he
saw a wondrous sight. For as the angel spake, his noble

---

6 This is the first occurrence of Ail Shaddai, and the context helps
to establish that one of its primary meanings has reference to God
as a nursing father (cp. Genesis 28:3; 35:11).

countenance was made more radiant by the smile on his face. "And I will make my covenant between me and thee, and will multiply thee exceedingly." Ah, what gracious words were these, and graciously spoken.

Here then at last was the moment they had waited for. The pain of threescore years was about to be removed, for the time had come for the covenant to be fulfilled. Abram heard the angel's gracious words, and trembled with the trembling of feeble knees. Even as the angel spake, he fell flat upon the good earth, prostrated in wonder, awe and joy. He had lain thus on the day when the covenant was cut,[7] and he would lie now, on the day when he learned of its certain accomplishment.[8] He felt a painful sense of unworthiness that even now, after all their failures and mistakes, God was still prepared to bless them and be faithful to His covenant. He doubted his own abilities, for life had taught him that, but his faith in Ail Shaddai was complete, for this was the all powerful, all sufficient One, and he believed in Him.

But thy name shall be Abraham

"As for me, behold, my covenant is with thee, and thou shalt be a father of many nations. Neither shall thy name any more be called Abram, but thy name shall be Abraham; for a father of many nations have I made thee." (Genesis 17:4,5)

Thus the angel stood and talked with the man who lay in humility before him. He knew that the man felt inadequate, and sought to comfort and reassure him. "As for me, behold my covenant is with thee", he said. Here then was proof that God's purpose had not altered. Abram might be a weak and sinful man, fearful sometimes and foolish oft, but it was still the sovereign purpose and pleasure of God that he should be the channel of blessing

---

7 Genesis 15:12.

8 Here the word in Genesis 17:2 for 'make' (covenant) is *nathan* referring to its giving or confirming, in contrast to the previous occasion (15:18) when to 'make' the covenant was *karath*, to cut or initiate the covenant.

to others. All God's servants have wondered why the Father has worked through them as instruments for His purpose. They too have felt unworthy of the calling, but thankful like the patriarch that He has been pleased to work in and through them for the glory of His Name.

Not only did the angel's words confirm Abram's blessed role in this covenant promise, but they also gave the guarantee of God's involvement. For here was the assurance that He would fulfil His part through the operation of the Eternal Spirit, in making of Abraham a father. But the fatherhood, which Ail Shaddai had planned, was vastly wider in its scope than Abram had ever, or could ever, imagine. 'Thou shalt be a father of a multitude of nations', came the angel's words. He was to be the father, not just of the son they had been waiting for, and not just of a multitude of sons, but the father of a multitude of nations. The very idea, after years of childlessness, was so stupendous that Abram struggled with the immensity of it all. Yet even as he thought, and lest he should be doubtful, the angel solemnly averred the truth for a second time, 'for a father of a multitude of nations have I made thee'. There was no mistake then in what had been promised, and as a special token that it was true, Abram's name was to be changed to Abraham. His new name commemorated God's part in the promise, for it was God's involvement that empowered Abraham's fatherhood, and God's Name that was now mysteriously surnamed upon his.[9]

God never does anything by halves. Their marriage, touched as it would be by the divine hand, was to be marvellously changed from one that was exceedingly barren, to one that was exceedingly fruitful. Only God can accomplish this transforming miracle, for this was His ancient imperative from the foundation of the world,[10] and His alone the power to fulfil it. He would do so for the advancing of His own purpose in building a people for His own Name. But how grateful Abraham

---

9   See Appendix 6 – "Why were Abram and Sarai's names changed?"
10 Genesis 1:28.

was that the Father's purpose now involved him, so that he might rejoice in this divine blessing, this promise of a multitude of nations that would count their fatherhood through him. In the outworking of this promise, Gentiles would be included,[11] for these nations, these multitudes were related to the patriarch by the operating principle of faith.[12]

Nor were these multitudes to come just ordinary mortals, for Abraham was to breed a royal race. Not just nations were to come forth from him, but rulers of nations; not just kingdoms, but also kings. The royal aristocracy of the age to come[13] would count their descent from this couple, for from them both would spring the generation of the saints who will rule the world.

The finest promise of everlasting fellowship

"And I will establish my covenant between me and thee and thy seed after thee in their generations for an everlasting covenant, to be a God unto thee, and to thy seed after thee. And I will give unto thee, and to thy seed after thee, the land wherein thou art a stranger, all the land of Canaan, for an everlasting possession; and I will be their God." (Genesis 17:7,8)

The promise of God, great as it was in exalting Abraham, was not for the patriarch alone. It was to be sealed as a solemn covenant to future generations of his seed, and thereby accounted as an everlasting covenant in its perpetuity. It promised an everlasting inheritance in the land as only an everlasting covenant can do, and thereby

11 The term "nations" here (Genesis 17:4-6,16) is *goyim*, the standard term used by the Jewish nation to describe Gentiles.

12 The exposition of the apostle concerning those who count Abraham as their father by faith, is based upon this very passage and phrase, "I have made thee a father of many nations" (Romans 4:11-17).

13 This reference to "kings" emanating from both the father and mother of the faithful is the first intimation of a royal family that finds its consummation in the "kings" that reign on the earth when all is fulfilled (Revelation 5:10).

was the patriarch promised a family who would indeed become a great nation.

Abraham could but dimly perceive the magnitude of the promise. He would receive no inheritance in his lifetime, and yet this land of Canaan was so completely his that it would become the lot of his family's inheritance for ever. And if the inheritance was theirs to a thousand generations[14] of the race as an everlasting possession, then surely his family must become an everlasting people? Did God mean that the nation, which sprang from Abraham, would never be extinguished but would remain forever? Or did the promise hint at deeper things that matched an everlasting possession to an everlasting life? There would be time later to ponder all these things in his heart, for now it was enough to listen in awestruck silence to this most splendid of proclamations. The crowning glory of the angel's words was still to come. For the real object in preserving the seed to come was to allow a higher purpose to be fulfilled with them. For "I" said the angel "will make thee exceeding fruitful", and "I will establish my covenant", and "I will give unto thee … the land", and "I will be their God".

This last was the best blessing of all. Other nations would find a path to the Almighty through Abraham the Friend of God. In the fulness of time, all nations of the earth would share the blessing of divine favour through their association with this man. But those counted as the royal seed of Abraham himself were promised this unique and special gift, the exalted privilege of access to the throne of heaven. It would involve a priesthood that God had already consecrated, and whose office He would accept, a priesthood linked with Abraham, for he had already shared a sacrificial meal with its High Priest, Melchizedek. The promise would, of course, find a fulfilment in Abraham's natural descendants throughout their successive mortal generations in the land. It would even reach out to include those natural descendants dwelling in the land in the kingdom of Shiloh, which was

---

14 Psalm 105:8.

to come. But the fulness of the matter was reserved for Abraham's true children.

This covenant of fellowship with God, pledged to Abraham's offspring, was the promise that his spiritual sons and daughters would share the sanctifying association that he himself held with God. Here was the man who walked and talked with Ail Shaddai, as one speaketh with a friend. Why should those who manifested the family likeness, not share also in the intimacy of this close relationship with the Father? To this royal offspring therefore, came this promise of drawing near to God in the spirit of fellowship.

The catalogue of blessings that God would extend by solemn covenant was now complete. It began with the elevation of Abraham to the fatherhood of a multitude that he could scarcely comprehend or number. It ended with the promise that this multitudinous seed, all of them, would enjoy the special privilege of fellowship with God, a fellowship such as no other nation could ever hope to share.

There was, of course, a reason for the particular excellence of these covenant gifts. Although these blessings were to be experienced in Abraham's natural offspring throughout their generations, they were in a higher sense to be realised through the Israel of God. In these promises to Abraham could be seen the overflowing care of God for His own family, the seed of the woman who are the children of God by faith.

The covenant of circumcision

Then came Abraham's part in this covenant promise between Almighty God and His friend. "As for thee" said the angel, and Abraham stood and bowed his head to await the burdens of responsibility that he knew ought rightly to rest upon him in return for God's goodness. God's contribution was abundant in its magnitude. What could be asked of him in return? What could he give that might in any way be adequate in this pledge between unequals? The answer when it came was astounding. In return for God's mercies, copious and complete, Abraham was asked to do one, just one single thing. "As for thee … every man child among you shall be circumcised", came the words of command. Was there nothing else that he must do? Why no. No more than this was asked of him, but no less than this was also expected. The rite of circumcision was God's sole requirement of Abraham, but it was to be sternly and rigorously kept. There were to be no exceptions to this simple yet vital observance. Every male had to comply. It mattered not whether a child was born in the patriarchal camp, or whether they had joined the household by being purchased in the marketplace. The rule applied with equal force to every man child of Abraham's house, and not just for those with him now, but for every subsequent generation of his household. There were to be absolutely no exceptions, for the man child who failed to observe this token of the covenant in his flesh, would be completely cut off, circumcised out of the covenant, by God Himself. The offender was not to feel merely the shame of social banishment. Their lot was far more serious. God intended that they should face the terror of judicial death itself, by which means He would excise them out of the promise.[15]

Yet Abraham was puzzled. Why should the covenant be sealed by such a strange token, and why was it to be observed on pain of death? Here was a covenant that promised him the joy and privilege of fatherhood, and yet the one thing demanded of him by God, this act of circumcision, would make it impossible, at least for the moment, for him to become a father. Why was God so insistent on this rule? If Abraham could not produce the child, then who could? Almost at once Abraham's thoughts soared to the greatness of God's purpose. It was all so breathtakingly, beautifully simple. This was to be God's family, not just Abraham's, a divine family taken from among men, every one of whom would be

---

15 The very expression of judgement in Genesis 17:14 is couched in the language of the circumcision rite itself – "that soul shall be *cut off* from his people".

ultimately begotten by the Spirit. And because it was to be a divine family, God Himself, Ail Shaddai was to be the Father. Now Abraham understood why the promise reached out to embrace a multitude of nations. For if the Lord was to be the Father, then His offspring would be an innumerable company, befitting the operation of the immense creative power of Ail Shaddai, a veritable multitude who would manifest Him. How could it be anything less?

It was true that he, Abraham, might be the producer of the child, but only through the instrumentality and power of God operating upon him. He grasped the lesson God wished him to learn. It was this: that fruitfulness in spiritual things comes from cutting off the flesh. God wanted Abraham to bow before this principle, that the children of God cannot be produced by the natural powers of the flesh.[16] This token of the covenant was to be a perpetual reminder of this truth, and of more than this. For circumcision was not just a disowning of fleshly power and fleshly descent, but a glorious admission that God alone could perform the impossible, that He alone in His sovereign power could triumph where flesh had failed. And had not God already circumcised them both, in effect, through the deadness of their bodies? They were already in a state of total dependence upon Him; they already knew that God alone could accomplish this thing. The man understood. His circumcision was the outward sign of an inward disposition that repudiated the power of the flesh. The secret mark he would carry in his body was but a sign that he was circumcised of heart,[17] and that his faith lay not in any confidence of his own ability, but rather in the inexhaustible power of the living God.

---

16 This is the real force of Stephen's exposition in Acts 7:8 – "And he gave him the covenant of circumcision: and *so* Abraham begat Isaac".

17 Deuteronomy 10:16; Jeremiah 4:4; Romans 2:29.

But Sarah shall her name be

The angel paused and Abraham, his mind whirling with hopes and dreams, strove to collect his thoughts. He was already overcome with the greatness of the covenant promise, and the strange secret of the covenant token. He was about to be overwhelmed:

"As for Sarai thy wife, thou shall not call her name Sarai, but Sarah shall her name be. And I will bless her, and give thee a son also of her ... and she shall be a mother of nations; kings of people shall be of her."

(Genesis 17:15,16)

Abraham gasped with joy. Was his dear Sarai really to be involved? Certainly the angel had spoken so, and with characteristic swiftness Abraham grasped the meaning of the words. For if his name was changed to signify the coming fulfilment of the promise, then what could the change of hers mean, but that she was to be joined with him in the promise. And was not her name to be changed in the same way as his? This promise would come to pass because of the intervention of God in their lives. But how exactly would it happen, and how might He intervene? The words that followed unfolded the full glory of the Father's intentions. "And I will bless her, and give thee a son also of her: yea, I will bless her, and she shall be a mother of nations; kings of people shall be of her". His ears caught and savoured every word, every sound of this heavenly message. These were precious things, and he needed to store them in remembrance to explain it all to Sarai, to Sarah later. Sarah! Her name was to be Sarah. This one who had been his bride and his princess was now to be the queen of others also,[18] the royal progenitor of a royal race brought forth by the blessing of God upon her.

The angel's promise transported Abraham back in time more than thirty years. It had been that long since God had first appeared and spoken with him, yet

---

18 Sarai – 'my princess' is changed to Sarah – 'princess', because now all families of the earth will acknowledge an interest and association with her, not just Abraham and his immediate family.

he remembered it as if it were but yesterday. He would never forget the moment of wonder he felt when the promise had come to bless him. And now, with a mighty leap across this span of time, Elohim had come again and given promise likewise to bless her. Truly, she was his counterpart in the marvels of this day. For she would match him in being the glad recipient of divine power, in the bringing forth of a chosen son, in becoming the multiplier of many nations and in producing a royal offspring, among whom would be counted the Messiah king himself.[19] And all this from her that had been called 'the barren one'. Could there be a more wonderful promise than this!

After all these years of wondering about the part she would play, Abraham was surprised to hear it described in such emphatic and decisive words. Her involvement in this promise was absolute and entire, equal to his in every way. Why had they never seen it with such clarity before? Why had they not understood that God would surely operate by His own standards, established since

---

19 The record is very clear that they were indeed to embrace the covenant blessing together. "My covenant is with thee", was the angelic declaration, but the 'thee' of the promise reached out to include both of them. Note the parallel thoughts expressed concerning the two of them:

Abraham (verses 5,6)	Sarah (verses 15,16)
"Neither shall thy name any more be called Abram, but thy name shall be Abraham"	"As for ... thy wife, thou shalt not call her name Sarai, but Sarah shall her name be"
"for a father of many nations have I made thee"	"and she shall be a mother of nations"
"I will make thee exceeding fruitful"	"I will bless her"
"I will make nations of thee"	"I will ... give thee a son ... of her"
"kings shall come out of thee"	"kings of peoples shall be of her"

the foundation of the world? Was not His rule – one man, one woman and they to seek a godly seed? Well, he knew it now; this truth of God so plain and simple, for there could be nothing plainer than this angelic word. The glad tidings were these, that the promise could only be fulfilled through the birth of a child to them both, a son of Abraham and Sarah. "Between me and thee" had come the oft repeated formula of angelic promise. Now Abraham understood, with glad certainty, that the 'thee' with whom Ail Shaddai would work was both himself and the wife of his covenant. They were inseparably bound together in the hope of its fulfilment. Only in the fulness of time would it become apparent just how vital it was that she match him in this way. Their greater seed would understand, and standing in the land of Abraham about two thousand years later, he would teach that the mother of the true seed was just as important as the father.[20]

As Abraham pondered the matter in his own day however, he thought he knew why they were joined together in the promise. If a miracle was needed to produce this child through him, then it was doubly so through Sarah. God was asking him, nay demanding, that he rise in faith to believe in His power to perform that which was impossible with men, and that he believe it first as the prerequisite for its fulfilment. A man of weaker faith would have stumbled at the foot of this mountain. But Abraham's joyous faith was strong enough to climb it, and to rejoice at the vista beyond.

The laughter of joyous faith

In sheer wonder at God's gracious ways, the man of Mamre sank to his knees and from thence to the ground, prostrated again by the greatness of the promise and the greatness of the Promiser. He laughed aloud, for his amazement was great, and a passer-by might have imagined that his merriment was at some jest or foolish talk. But the Lord knew the character of His servant.

---

20 See Chapter 9 – "Encouraging the children of faith together".

Hesitant and doubtful of his own abilities, he was nevertheless a man of immense faith when it came to the promises of God. When asked to leave both his country and kindred, he departed in faith. When his help was sought in the day of battle, he responded in faith. When brought forth abroad and shown the stars of heaven as a picture of his seed, he surrendered in faith. When later told to offer their only beloved son on whom the promise depended, he obeyed in faith. What God had promised, this man believed, and believed out of a pure heart. It would be no different on this day of great revelations. When asked to believe that God would give to him a son of her in whom his heart delighted, he laughed in simple, certain, joyous faith, and believed that it would be so. Not for nothing was he to be known as the "father of the faithful".

The words that followed were uttered in the spirit of thankful reverie, as a man talks with himself when reflecting on things profound. "Shall a child be born?" he breathed in wonder, as he turned the promise over in his mind. His words were not the queries of doubt or incredulity, for he had prostrated himself in reverence to utter them. These were the amazed yet delighted expressions of a man who believed the promise, but who had not yet plumbed the depths of his own astonished joy and excitement that it would be so. Even as he asked them, he knew with exultant certainty what the reply was. Yet he asked, to savour the sweetness of the answer in his own mind. They were the questions of the fully persuaded man, who had faith in a power greater than his own. The child would be born, of this he had no doubt, and that by the operation of God upon an old couple whose bodies now were as dead.

Loving petition for Ishmael's care

Abraham was not a slow-witted man, and he realised immediately the force of the promise. For if this child to come of Sarah was the channel through whom Abraham would be heir of the world, what might this mean for his firstborn son? A firstborn might not be dispossessed, yet the divine edict seemed to imply this. Abraham's spirit was swift to show care for others, for this had always been his wont, and anxious that Ishmael might be excluded from all blessings of the covenant, he sought reassurance from God. It was a reasonable petition, given that Ishmael's firstborn status seemed about to be superseded by another. Abraham's desire, however, was not that Ishmael might replace the promised seed, but that God might still find some place for him in His purpose. Abraham had already rejoiced to see the day of Sarah's son, for his laughter of delight was evidence that he saw. But here now in his concern for another, he showed why God was pleased to call him near and bless him. For Abraham was a man of compassion as well as a man of faith, a man of thoughtfulness and of care.[21] "O that Ishmael might live before thee", he cried, and the angel nodded in understanding.

> "And God said, Sarah thy wife shall bear thee a son indeed; and thou shalt call his name Isaac: and I will establish my covenant with him for an everlasting covenant, and with his seed after him."

(Genesis 17:19)

"Sarai thy wife shall bear thee a son indeed", said the angel, and it was to his wife that Abraham's attention was gently but firmly directed. She was the focus of this blessing in being the bearer of the child, and all his love and concern would need to be devoted to her in the months to come, and not to others. But this care would be rewarded, for Sarah would truly bear a son "and", said the angel, "thou shalt call his name Isaac". Abraham's eyes filled with tears. God knew their son's name! And if he already had a name, then already in a sense their son was real. 'Isaac' he whispered to himself with trembling voice, testing the sound and picturing the little one to come. It was all so definite and sure and Abraham shook with the wonder of the thing. How unutterably good was Ail Shaddai who had made promise that day. And

---

21 In a similar manner and spirit of care, he would later plead for Lot (Genesis 18:23,32).

what was this? The child was to be named in honour of his laughter, the mirth of the man of faith who believed in the promise of God. Through this child, whose name would ever remind the patriarch of this joyous day, God would establish the everlasting covenant.

Nor was Ishmael to be excluded from the blessings of God. For in response to Abraham's plea that he be remembered in some way, an honour was reserved for Ishmael according to his capacity. The blessings of fruitfulness and growth, of nationhood and prosperity, would all be his, and God's promise would not fail despite the subsequent history of the lad and his departure from Abraham's household. For his father's sake, Ishmael would be blessed and provided for in the wisdom of God. But his greatness would never lie in being the channel of God's blessing to others. That signal honour would belong to Isaac, and God confirmed His sovereign right to choose the one and reject the other when planning the workings of His purpose.

A precious son for Sarah at last

Three times now the angel had said that Sarah should be the bearer of the seed. First she was mentioned when affirming his birth, then when giving his name, and now when confirming the exact time of his coming. Next year! A child for Sarah next year! A promise thrice declared was surely beyond doubt, and Abraham felt more certain of the promise than he had ever felt before.

The angel departed and the man called Abraham arose. His face shone with the light of joy at the revelation he had received through this divine theophany. With characteristic enthusiasm he ran to the encampment, his flapping robes and flailing arms betraying his excitement. 'Sarah', he called as he reached their tent, 'Sarah!' Sarai appeared with a welcoming smile, but the expression in her eyes showed puzzlement as to why he pronounced her name so strangely. 'Sarah', he said, still breathless from his run, 'the angel has come and promised that next year our son will come. His name is Isaac and you, my dearest, are to bear him'.

Her heart leapt and then stood still. She searched the expression on his face, trying to read how earnest he was, and could see only the shining of certainty. She wanted to believe him, wanted desperately to believe him, but something held her back. Spiritual perception told her that the promise was possible, and womanly intuition told her that it could not be so. And for fear of a pain more grievous than that which she had already felt, her mind and heart cried in unison to deny the chance of the promise being true through her. She would not suggest that God could not fulfil the promise, for both of them believed in His power. But that it might be fulfilled through her was a possibility she had already dismissed with bitter lamentations, and she could not open her heart to that hope again. Abraham's entreaties for her to believe could not move his wife. Her eyes filled with tears, and unable to speak she merely shook her head against his gentle pleadings.

He realised that more time would be needed with Sarah to talk the matter through and began immediately to think how best this might be done. If he could only quicken her mind, then he knew that God could quicken her body. This then was his task as husband and head, and this he would do as best he might. But first, there was something else he must do, with greater urgency.

Circumcising all his household

"In the selfsame day was Abraham circumcised, and Ishmael his son. And all the men of his house, born in the house, and bought with money of the stranger, were circumcised with him."

(Genesis 17:26,27)

Word had gone around the servants that an angel had spoken with the master and the tents of the household were abuzz with excited conversation as to what the angel might have said. Those who had seen Abraham running along the path, reported that the master's

88

face was aglow with happiness, and that the news was therefore good. One had overheard the word 'covenant' in his conversation, and it was rumoured that he had called his wife not Sarai, but Sarah.

There was no need, however, for prolonged and comfortable speculation within their families as to what had happened at the encounter. For a messenger now came from tent to tent, bidding that all males gather together, that Abraham might speak to them all. When they had assembled, he told them with rejoicing that God had indeed made covenant promises with him, but that He had also demanded of his household a special token of the covenant. Abraham requested all his men to join him in this act of cutting off the flesh. And the proof that although they were not all his sons, they still shared his faith, is that they all obeyed him. The devoted servant and the hired stranger, he that was born in the house, and he that was bought with money, the child of eight days old and the man of ninety-nine. It was a rite that bound the family of faith together, not just the descendants of his blood, but all these who were the companions of his spirit. So important to Abraham was the greatness of this promise that he was insistent that his part, their part, be performed without delay, and so it was, on that very day.[22] When finally the sun sank behind the oak tree and washed the sky with ochre tints and auburn gold, it crowned and closed a day that Abraham would never forget.

Embracing the covenant blessing together

Abraham's determination to fulfil God's requirement affected Sarah. She knew this much, that everything Abraham had reported, he believed. He would not have asked the menfolk to perform this embarrassing and painful operation, unless the divine commandment was so. And if he was determined to fulfil the angelic command with such speed and diligence, it was obvious that he believed the promise with all his heart. She

---

22 Genesis 17:23,26 – note the expression, the 'selfsame' day.

knew from the remarkable events of this day that he was convinced, and she yearned to share his conviction with all her heart. But Sarah was not yet ready to join him on the top of the mountain. She still stood with leaden feet in the valley below and knew not how to climb.

Abraham understood his wife's dilemma. He had heard the angel speak, and she had not. His spirit of faith helped him to see the end in view, but Sarah could only see the way and the enormous difficulties that lay strewn along the path. His own faith had soared when the angel had spoken, but beyond the entreaties he had already made, he knew not how to lift her thinking to see the impossible and dare to believe that it could be done. How could he transport her into the heights he had known and warm her heart to the certainty of the son who would come?

He had indeed understood great things this day, for he had learned that he and Sarah were equal in the sight of God when it came to the fulfilment of this promise. But there was so much to do, to bring them both to equality of faith, and he had learned most of all that this was now his special, personal responsibility. He needed to be appreciative of her complete involvement in the promise, and to convince her of the truth of this. He needed to be sympathetic of her fears, and to spend time with her in order to build and nourish that faith which casts out fear. He needed to be considerate of her needs in this matter, which were vastly different from his. He needed to give honour unto his wife, to help her overcome her personal feelings of inadequacy. In short, he needed to show the spirit of loving sacrifice in care for her state, so that they might truly embrace this covenant blessing together. All this would require patience and love and time.

He had leapt to the conviction of faith, in joyous disregard of the physical impossibilities that confronted them. He had simply believed, but she was not ready. She would match him yet, but she would come to faith by a different way. With Sarah, the practicalities were not so easily set aside. A man might brush them off as obstacles of little moment, but she was a woman and she knew how real the difficulties were. Only when her heart was won and her feelings of doubt assuaged, could her mind be centred firmly on the promise and the prospect of its fulfilment. There was much for Abraham to do indeed, that he might 'dwell with her according to knowledge, and as being heirs together of the grace of life'.[23]

Abraham gave earnest thought to the matter over the days that followed the angelic visitation. He had time to do so, for all the men abode in the camp for several days until they were made whole again.[24] Yet he need not have been concerned. For even as he pondered on how to help his wife, help was at hand. Ail Shaddai would not provide this promise without also providing the means for its fulfilment. The Angel of the Name manifest to Abraham, was even now travelling near their very encampment, and would appear shortly. Did Sarah need the proof that Abraham already had? Then the angel of God's love would visit them again, and this time she herself would hear his glorious voice.

---

23 1 Peter 3:7: there is much in this passage that is singularly apposite to the situation in which Abraham now found himself. The recognition that his wife was indeed the heir together with him of the promise of the "grace of life" was the very circumstance of the moment, and may have been the basis for the apostle's comment. See further comments in Chapter 9.

24 After the manner of Joshua 5:8.

5

ENTERTAINING THREE ANGELIC VISITORS TOGETHER
(Genesis 18:1-33)

IT was but a few weeks since the great pronouncement had been made of the birth of Isaac. The angel had confirmed the moment of his coming, for the child was to be born at this same set time next year. Already then, the timetable of heaven was in motion, and Sarah needed to be gathered into the embrace of the promise, and nurtured into hope just as soon as might be possible. The angel therefore appeared again unto the man, but he had come for the woman; for this visitation, although conducted through Abraham as head of his household, was expressly for the benefit of Sarah his wife, that she might be brought to faith. And this time the angel did not appear alone, but came with two companions from the holy ones. Whatever would be said to Sarah this day would be established in the ears of two or three witnesses, who could vouch in heaven that the woman had heard the vital words. If she accepted them, they would lead her to the joy of conception, for the thought they contained was life-giving indeed.

Three strange and unexpected travellers

"And the LORD appeared unto him in the plains of Mamre: and he sat in the tent door in the heat of the day: and he lift up his eyes and looked, and, lo, three men stood by him: and when he saw them, he ran to meet them from the tent door, and bowed himself toward the ground." (Genesis 18:1,2)

Now the appearance of the three was on this wise. The man of God sat at the entrance of his tent, beneath the shade of a mighty tree. The dwellings of Abraham had long been pitched among the sturdy oaks of Mamre, which lay northwards of Hebron through the valley of Eshcol. There the patriarch lived, canopied by the guardian arms of the ancient oak, which overhung the curtains of their tent. The leafy branches cast their dappled shade across the dwelling, and their shadow was welcome.

Each morning, in the hot months, the tent flap was opened and fastened back to encourage every little breeze, no matter how slight or shy or soft, to waft its freshness through the rooms. Abraham sat then in his tent opening in meditation and prayer, for the heat of the day[1] was especially fierce at noon, and noon[2] was thus a time for petition and rest. The heat told not only the time of day, but the time of year also. For these were the months of harvest, when the maturing sun with gentle but irresistible power commanded the fruitful season.

The time of reaping had already passed and the garners were full of wheaten mounds of glistening grain. The vines of the valley had been gleaned and pressed, and the pure blood of the grape stored in earthen jars. The heat of harvest, which lay heavy upon the land, would soon make ready the olives for shaking and warm to mellow sweetness the dusky dates and last ripe figs, those precious fruits of the sun. The days were hot, but this was the warmth that would swell the gourds and plump the nuts, and 'fill all fruit with ripeness to the core'. Summer was the season when all nature proclaimed God's power to nourish the conception of spring unto the birth of harvest. He was Ail Shaddai indeed, who made all the land to be exceeding fruitful, by the outstretching of His hands. Surely, thought Abraham, if but one finger of God could touch his wife, she might be likewise blessed with this fruitful season. It was while thus he thought, and had perchance prayed, that a movement through the oaks caught his eye.

He was certainly startled to see these three men who stood almost beside his tent, travellers on a journey. For

---

1   2 Samuel 4:5; Job 24:19; Isaiah 18:4; Jeremiah 17:8.

2   Psalm 55:17.

herein was a strange thing. Abraham's tent was in the very centre of the camp, and around him on every side were the places of loyal men who could be trusted quickly to detain any strangers who wandered without authority through a camp that was not theirs. How, then, the men had managed to arrive unopposed and unannounced before his own dwelling, was a mystery to the patriarch.

Yet despite the dramatic suddenness of their appearance before his tent, there was nothing remarkable about the men themselves that excited either curiosity or caution. They appeared footsore and travel stained from the dust of the road on which they marched, but apart from this they seemed quite ordinary, even to the patriarch's practiced eye. He looked, but did not know them, of that he was certain. They were in fact perfect strangers, although just how perfect Abraham would only realize a little later. Abraham had always been a hospitable man, and to him every stranger was to be treated as an invited guest. When therefore he espied these visitors his face lit up with genuine pleasure, and with the enthusiasm for which he was justly famed, he ran out to welcome them, wincing only a little when he stopped and bowed.[3]

Be not forgetful to entertain strangers

One of the men was evidently the leader and spokesman, and it was to him that Abraham addressed his words. The patriarch's discourse was a masterpiece of warmth and friendliness. There was a proper order for the extending of hospitality, and Abraham's gracious words, measured and genuine, missed nothing in the expansiveness of his kind and generous offer:

"My Lord, if now I have found favour in thy sight, pass not away, I pray thee, from thy servant: let a little water, I pray you, be fetched, and wash your feet, and rest yourselves under the tree: and I will fetch a morsel of bread, and comfort ye your hearts; after

---

3 This episode must have occurred very shortly after his circumcision in Genesis 17:24.

that ye shall pass on: for therefore are ye come to your
servant." (Genesis 18:3-5)

"My Lord", he said with characteristic humility, "pass
not away, I pray thee, from thy servant". Here then
was the offer of sanctuary, given by beseeching them to
stay and not to leave. His fervent welcome assured the
men that he counted their visit as an honour, and that
it would be his privilege to serve them. Even now, his
concern was for their care after the rigours of whatever
journey had brought them here. "Let a little water, I
pray you, be fetched, and wash your feet". When the way
was dusty, and the journey hot, travellers shod only in
sandals experienced the greatest comfort in bathing tired
feet. The water cooled and soothed, and left the whole
body feeling refreshed and cleansed. When the pleasure
of washing was done, there would be time enough to
sit in peace, and Abraham urged the men therefore to
"rest yourselves under the tree". Every faithful host was
concerned to see that guests had time to recover their
strength, to rest tired limbs and to enjoy the blessing
of shade, which gave respite from the merciless glare
and relentless heat of the noonday sun. Only when rest
had brought its restorative power would sustenance
be offered, but Abraham was quick to promise that he
would fetch their needs, even as they rested. The portion
he would bring before them, despite his own modest
assessment of it as but "a morsel of bread", would fill the
hungry soul, and 'comfort their hearts'.

A meal spent in the patriarch's company would, he
promised, restore their vital powers and send them on
their way with rejoicing of heart. And, lest his guests
should demur at this unwonted generosity on his part,
Abraham, with the lovely gentleness of persuasive tact,
insisted that their very appearance in the midst of the
camp was a providential opportunity, a heaven-sent
chance that allowed him to refresh them this day. "For
therefore are ye come to your servant" he said – and what
he said, he meant. This was hospitality in all its gracious
fulness: to promise safety, to bring water, to offer rest, to

provide food and drink, to extend care, and to do all this with no regard for the inconvenience of the moment, the heat of the day, or the tiredness of his age. He smiled at his visitors earnestly and solemnly they accepted his words, "So do, as thou hast said", they replied. Abraham called for water, that his guests might wash away the dust of Hebron that reddened their sandals and their feet.

Entertaining three angelic visitors together

"And Abraham hastened into the tent unto Sarah, and said, Make ready quickly three measures of fine meal, knead it, and make cakes upon the hearth." (Genesis 18:6)

Whilst his visitors rested after the waters of washing, Abraham hastened into the tent, and besought Sarah to prepare the bread of fellowship, which was the foundation of all meals. Three things he asked of her, yea four in the fulfilment of this task.

The first was that only the best flour should be used in honour of their guests. The threshing and winnowing of the season was over, and the household had stores of the grain that would be baked as daily bread. But they also had fresh supplies of meal, ground only from the 'kidneys of wheat', the finest flour that would in aftertimes be used in the sacrifices of Israel. From this source alone[4] were the round hearth cakes of unleavened bread to be fashioned.

The second was that excellence of quality was to be matched by an abundance of provision. Three men had come and three measures would be prepared. Yet each of these was sufficient to feed and satisfy all three

---

4   Genesis 18:6: the expression "fine meal" is a combination of the two words – *coleth* (fine) and *qemach* (flour). *The Theological Wordbook of the Old Testament* states that whereas *qemach* was ground from whole kernels, *coleth* was ground exclusively from the inner kernels of the wheat. This finest of the wheat was the required standard for the *mincah* offering under the law (Leviticus 2:1). One Rabbinical commentary (Vajikra Rabba) describes *coleth* as the *qemach* of *qemachs*.

men,[5] and even then the fragments that remained would constitute an abundance. Abraham's measure would err on the side of that generosity which is the partner of true and joyful hospitality. Enough and more than enough[6] was the spirit of this household that entertained angels unawares this day.

The third was that the cakes needed to be made with haste, so that the visitors might be provided for as soon as possible. The embers of the hearth needed to be raked clean, and the bread put to bake among the hot cinders of the fire, where it would quickly brown into the flat bread beloved throughout the east. A sense of urgency and concern that none should be kept unduly waiting was part of the spirit of service that strove to render the best of care, in seeing to the comfort and welfare of their guests. If hospitality were to be shown, then it would be shown with open and willing hearts that rejoiced to serve to the uttermost.

How best might all this be done? Abraham knew the answer and had entered the tent for this very reason, for there within, was the one who was his boon companion in spiritual things. This then was his fourth request. It was Abraham's desire that Sarah herself should ready the meal, for she would do so after his spirit. It was, after all, a strange request to make. There were hundreds of menservants who lived under the banner and charge of Abraham the Hebrew, and hundreds of maidservants, who might at his word have been commanded to bake

---

5   The term "measures" used in Genesis 18:6 is *seah*, three measures of which constituted an *ephah*. An *ephah* was ten *omers*, one of which provided a daily ration sufficient for sustenance (Exodus 16:16,36). Each *seah* measure therefore would have fed all three men for the entire day. Yet Abraham expended three times this amount in preparation to feed but three men for one meal. This was truly a copious provision.

6   This idea, enough and more than enough, is the spirit of the expression, "Give a portion to seven, and also to eight" (Ecclesiastes 11:2).

bread for hundreds more of his household besides.[7] Yet Abraham asked Sarah herself to take the mixture and knead the dough, to blow upon the coals and stir the fire, to bake the bread and bring the cakes.

It was the token of his appreciation of the covenant promise so recently given to them. They were, by divine proclamation, solemnly bound together in the matter, and in honour and respect to his wife therefore, he bade her join him in the privilege of this service. Hospitality was a solemn duty and the honour lay in the performing of it personally. Abraham therefore would wait upon his guests himself, and he invited Sarah to join him in an act of generosity that would come from their own loving hands. They would labour as one in the preparation of this fellowship meal for their unknown visitors. Were they indeed heirs together? Then they would extend hospitality together, and the warmth and alacrity of their service would show just how united they were.

Sarah smiled at him in his urgent haste and bent readily to the task of stirring the coals. She had always loved his spiritual enthusiasm and his ardour for the way of the truth, which never dimmed, vigorous now even in his old age. She took up flour of the best sort, and in ample measure, just as Abraham had instructed her, and soon she was busy with the part she would play in this mutual labour of love and service for others.

Their spirit of dedication would become an example to all their offspring. The work of hospitality is one of the few practical ways in which husband and wife can labour together in the truth, and it is a thing of joy that they can do so. True hospitality springs more easily from a happily married couple, and for these two, as for others, it would be a measure of the unity of their household.

---

7   Given that he had 318 trained servants capable of fighting, it is estimated that Abraham's whole encampment may have been almost 1,000 in number (Genesis 14:14).

Hastening to render the honour of hospitality

"And Abraham ran unto the herd, and fetcht a calf tender and good, and gave it unto a young man; and he hasted to dress it. And he took butter, and milk, and the calf which he had dressed, and set it before them; and he stood by them under the tree, and they did eat." (Genesis 18:7,8)

Leaving his visitors, their visitors, resting beneath the great oak, Abraham ran again, this time to the herd. Despite the fact that he had herdsmen aplenty, he was anxious to select the animal himself.[8] His keen eye, alert and shining with the joy of service, sought and found a fine calf of the season. The young animal still drank of its mother's milk, and Abraham knew that the meat would be succulent and moist. The calf was separated from the herd and given to a young man with instructions to slay the animal, to drain the blood, and to bring a portion dressed for cooking to the fire. The young man worked with deft speed, conscious of Abraham's spirit of urgency. Abraham ran again to the tent, and soon maidservants were bustling to do his bidding. The meal was prepared swiftly, because the servants all hurried to their tasks. An old man commanded his household by the spirit of his own example and, imbued with his enthusiasm, they ran with haste to match the master, if they could![9]

The visitors, washed and rested, were ready to dine, and Abraham brought forth the fruits of the labours of his household. Flat wheaten cakes still warm were piled high in small woven baskets. A wooden platter, heaped with meat cooked in thin strips, was set down

---

8   The phrase in Genesis 18:7, "and *Abraham* ran unto the herd, and fetcht a calf tender and good" suddenly assumes greater significance concerning the patriarch's own spirit of service, when the size of his encampment is considered.

9   Note that this becomes a key aspect of this episode. Abraham hastened to Sarah (Genesis 18:6), he asked her to hasten the cooking of the cakes (verse 6), the young man hastened to dress the calf (verse 7). It was all Abraham's spirit!

before the men, and with it came bowls of leben,[10] sour but refreshing to the palate. Lastly, Abraham offered the milk of the flock that they might drink their fill of its nourishing goodness. It was a lordly repast indeed, greatly exceeding the morsel of bread he had promised them. To give beyond expectation is part of the wonder of true service.

All this then was set before the visitors, but it was in a sense, set before another as well. The food was given to the men, but the gladness of its giving was an offering unto God. The unleavened bread was the consecrated gift of their own labours, the works of their own hands. The butter and milk betokened the richness of their generosity, and that choicest part of their service, the goodness of a willing heart. The savoury meat, tender and good, came from the slain offering of their own personal dedication. Strangers cannot repay the kindness that is shown to them, but Abraham and Sarah sought no requital in kind, for this was their free will offering to God. Their hospitality was a sacrifice and one that pleased the Father well, for that which His messengers consumed, God Himself had indeed accepted.

Abraham did not partake with the three, for he had already eaten before the men arrived. Besides, it was his pleasure to stand on their attendance, observant of their needs, ready to step forward and remove an empty bowl, or add to their drinking vessel. His position as chief of his clan did not stop him from serving in humility, and herein lay a part of his greatness.[11]

The word of promise and of power

The meal was ended and the guests reclined at ease. The remnants of the meal had been collected and removed. Abraham still stood beneath his oaken bower, contented in the care they had shown to entertain these strangers.

---

10 Genesis 18:8: the term for butter, *chemah*, is descriptive of a sour milk culture similar to modern Jewish *leben*. It follows a similar procedure to yoghurt but uses a different microbiological culture.

11 Such also is the spirit and character of Christ (Luke 12:37).

Sarah likewise stood within the tent, satisfied in their service, but curious as to who the men might be and why they had come. But now with the meal ended, came the time for conversation. The placid calm of the domestic scene gave no hint of the surprising words that were about to come. For the men suddenly asked of Abraham, "Where is Sarah thy wife?" The question was direct and simple, and uttered without guile, yet its force struck the patriarch with visible effect. His eyes narrowed as he gazed afresh upon his visitors. Sarai had been Sarah for but a few weeks, yet this was the name they used. How could these men, whom he had never set eyes on before, know his wife's new name? Who were these unknown travellers?

"Behold, in the tent", he replied, and Abraham's surprised and cautious tone told the angel that he had the patriarch's full and undistracted attention. But the question had intrigued not only Abraham, for Sarah herself stood in the tent door behind, quietly interested in the proceedings, yet discreetly hidden from view. Despite her loving contribution to the meal, she was content for her husband to lead the conversation as the spiritual head of their household, and for herself to remain unobtrusive in her supportive role. Yet the voice of the angel had spoken with just sufficient power, exquisite in its precision, so as to carry clear into the tent. It was just loud enough for Sarah to hear his words and to stiffen into alert watchfulness. Her hands stole up unconsciously to smooth her hair, then down to smooth her robe. Why did these men want to know especially where she was? What could they say that might possibly involve her? Who were these unknown travellers? Husband and wife were united in their curiosity. And, truth be known, the angelic query was designed to be also heard by Sarah and to quicken her interest, since the words to follow were uttered for her benefit.

Yet before the words came, Abraham, ever perceptive, had suddenly guessed the true identity of their visitors. He knew them by the strange unfolding of events this day, and he trembled with anticipation as he realized why the angels had come again, and why they had asked concerning his wife. Sarah herself had not as yet discerned the men, but, intrigued by the calling of her name aloud, was anxious enough to hear the words that would follow. Aware that their eyes were fastened upon him, the angel spoke the "word of promise"[12] to them both.

"And he said, I will certainly return unto thee according to the time of life; and, lo, Sarah thy wife shall have a son." (Genesis 18:10)

There could be nothing plainer or clearer than these simple powerful words. They contained within themselves the vital proof of their certain fulfilment, for the guarantee of accomplishment lay not with them but with God. "I will return" was the promise made, and hidden within this declaration, so definite and sure, was the promise of the outpouring of spirit power that would quicken both the man and his wife, and make possible the birth of the son of their love.

How glorious had been their hospitality this day, offered to angels unawares.[13] They had welcomed strangers without any thought of personal reward, but had, in fact, entertained heaven's immortal and illustrious ambassadors. And how gloriously were they blessed with heaven's repayment. For here was a recompense of their kindness, which so far exceeded their own generosity as to eclipse it in glory.

The laughter of anguished inadequacy

Sarah, listening at the tent door, could not see the face of the angel, but she could hear the tone of his voice. There was nothing doubtful about his words, for they rang with

---

12 For so it is described by the apostle (Romans 9:9).

13 The apostolic admonitions to hospitality seem almost certainly to have Abraham and Sarah's example as their foundation (Romans 12:13; 1 Timothy 3:2; 1 Peter 4:9,10). In particular the famous passage of Paul is clearly an inspired commentary on this very episode (Hebrews 13:2).

an assurance and conviction that stirred her. But the practicalities of her position were inescapable, and she knew it. For all her married life, year after year, she had experienced the normal signs of ability to bear children. Many moons had passed before she had realized that perhaps she was barren, yet even then hope had not been extinguished entirely. For these were the years of her youthfulness, when flesh was firm and eyes sparkled, when hair glowed lustrous and shining, and still the bloom of vital freshness clung to her person like a rare fragrance. There was still time enough to give birth. But early years gave way to the seasons of maturity that rolled across their lives, and Sarah had known them all, as only a woman is aware of them. Each season was unique, yet similar in this one thing, that despite the continuing cycle of her womanhood, the joyous hope of bearing a child had gradually, inexorably, faded further away.

And now old age had come and settled like a mantle upon her, and her silver hair was the sign of a woman old enough to care for grandchildren, but far too old for motherhood itself. Her body told her so, for now the final proof had come. She had been brought to the point where fruitfulness was no longer possible, for "it ceased to be with Sarah after the manner of women". Faced with the indisputable evidence of her own body, she could not see beyond its incapacity. She yearned to accept the promise of life, but her own feelings of inadequacy and weakness were a barrier that prevented the conception of faith.

> "And it ceased to be with Sarah after the manner of women. Therefore Sarah laughed within herself, saying, After I am waxed old shall I have pleasure, my lord being old also?" (Genesis 18:11,12)

Such was her situation that some time had now elapsed since they had come together as one flesh. They were one in mind and heart, but to be one in body was no longer their experience. And if the joy of this had passed, then the unutterable pleasure of bearing a child as a result of their

103

union was a thing not even to be contemplated.[14] Alone with her thoughts, she laughed within herself, but her laughter was the emotion of personal doubt and fear. She was neither bitter nor sarcastic, for her careful and loving tone in speaking of Abraham told otherwise. This woman who reverenced her husband, and that in her heart, was not of a scornful spirit. Her laughter, self-deprecating and wry, was instead the measure of her painful hurt, for had she not laughed, she would have wept.

At once the angel spoke with the woman's lord. "Wherefore did Sarah laugh, saying, Shall I of a surety bear a child, which am old?" The question, immediate and pointed, surprised both husband and wife. Abraham, unable to read his wife's thoughts and unaware of her reaction, was disturbed at what the angel had suggested. As for Sarah, she was amazed beyond words. She had laughed within herself, and yet the man had heard her. Surely it was not possible. And yet his words, with uncanny and uncomfortable accuracy, had focused on the one thing that she had dwelt upon, her inability to bear through oldness of age. Could it be that the man really had read her mind so plainly? She was suddenly smitten with the uneasy thought that this stranger was no earthly visitor, but the messenger, perhaps, of heaven itself.

With God all things are possible

The angel, without pausing for a spoken answer, continued his words, and Sarah knew with that swift and sudden rush of certainty, that here was the angel of God. She looked at her husband, and knew from his countenance that it was so.

---

14 The matter of pleasure here must reach beyond the mere restoration of physical intimacy. The promise was specifically – "Sarah shall have *a son*", and this is the immediate context for the reference to the pleasure or delight she did not dare to contemplate. Similarly, the angel's reiteration afterwards is not to the experience of mere pleasure in being one flesh with her husband, but again to the promise that she shall indeed bear a son.

"Is any thing too hard for the LORD? At the time appointed I will return unto thee, according to the time of life, and Sarah shall have a son."

(Genesis 18:14)

The angel's challenge concerning the omnipotent power of God was searching, and they both knew the answer. There was nothing wrong with Sarah's distrust of the flesh, but distrust of God was a matter altogether different. To be so filled with our own inabilities that we consider God Himself to be incapable of solving them, is not humility but secret pride. To believe that our problems loom so large that even Ail Shaddai cannot lift and bear away their burden, is to vaunt our weakness above His strength. Sarah's old age had extinguished all natural hope, but she had not replaced it with spiritual faith. Yet she was halfway there in dealing with her problem. She already knew that it was beyond her power to solve. All that was needed was for her to believe that it was not beyond God's.

The angel's words, spoken to a woman's heart, were echoed again and again in later testimonies on the divine omnipotence.[15] Truly there was nothing too hard for the Lord, for with God all things are possible. Abraham, the man of God, already believed this. It was time that his wife joined him, and the angel's words would lead her there. "I will return unto thee, according to the time of life, and Sarah shall have a son". The very repetition of the words was a gentle admonition to believe them. But one thing more was added for Sarah to ponder upon. The visitation would be "at the time appointed". So this man knew the time of her conception, and if he knew the time, then he must also know the means. But if he knew the means, then surely he must be the angel of the Lord who

---

15 Indeed, the spirit of this expostulation would reverberate throughout Scripture, as God repeatedly declared His power to perform anything He has promised (Numbers 11:23; Jeremiah 32:27; Zechariah 8:6; Luke 1:37). Such declarations culminate in the glorious statement of Ephesians 3:20.

had spoken with her husband, and promised that she would indeed bear a child at God's set time.

Sarah was suddenly afraid. She could but see his back parts and not his face, but she felt overwhelmed with the knowledge that the angel of God was here present in the midst. She was embarrassed and ashamed that she had laughed at his words, and anxious to cover her mistake.

Sarah's denial because of fear

Caught in a situation that was made awkward by its public nature, Sarah tried to cover her embarrassment by a little lie. Certain in herself that she had made no sound, she sought to deny the laughter of which the man accused her. Her disavowal was wrong. Yet even godly men and women can sometimes utter foolish and untruthful things, especially when confused, or embarrassed, or afraid. All three were true of Sarah at this very moment, but especially was she afraid.

She was afraid of her own uncertainty and doubt that had prompted her reaction in the first place. She was afraid of how Abraham might perceive her, especially after his efforts over the last few weeks to lift her mind to the possibilities of faith. She was afraid of her own inability to move in joy towards the promise. Her husband had run in gladness beyond the tent door when he saw the men who brought such hope. But she stood, immobile in the opening, and knew not how to pass beyond. She was afraid at this public revelation of her inner thoughts, which hitherto she had imagined were secret only to herself. She was afraid of one who knew things about her which none ought to know, and afraid of what else such an one might say. She was afraid of the knowledge that she stood behind an angel, and perhaps most of all, afraid of the thought that his promise might be true. Yet this fear, which had led her to utter unwise words, might be turned to good account if it could be converted into the fear of the Lord that leadeth to life. This the angel intended, and his mercy therefore would not allow her to escape from her own denial quite so easily. He would rebuke her, so that she might learn to fear the omniscient God who seest the reins and the heart.

The conversation of mortals can be confirmed beyond dispute by the earnest declaration of a 'nay, nay'.[16] Yet a single nay from the lips of one of the Elohim is even more absolute in its decisiveness. "Nay", said the angel, "but thou didst laugh". The words were not uttered in stern judgement or condemnation, but they were unequivocal all the same in calling her to account. The angel was insistent that Sarah consider her reaction. He wanted to impress upon her not only that he knew with certainty that she had laughed, but that he also knew why she had laughed. He wanted her to appreciate that just as he could hear the grieving anguish of her heart that caused her to laugh within herself, so also could he see the doubtful thoughts of her mind which prompted such painful mirth. He would make her to understand that he, the angel of God, knew of her personal feelings of weakness, and yet was unwavering in the word of promise towards her.[17] Sarah knew of her own inadequacy with excruciating exactness, but the angel's purpose in speaking directly with her was to quicken her belief in the all sufficient, all surpassing greatness of the Lord, who alone could supply her deficiency.

The discussion was ended, and the men arose to take again their journey. At once Abraham was astir and seeking their intended direction, began to walk with them, moving beyond the camp on a path that travelled eastward. He

---

16 Matthew 5:37; James 5:12.

17 It is true that the expression, "I will return unto *thee* ... and *Sarah* shall have a son", uttered by the angel in both Genesis 18:10 and 14 would seem to embrace both the man and the woman in the promise of quickening. It is also true that both stood in need of this physical renewal (Romans 4:19). Yet the emphasis of the record, and of this angelic visitation, is clearly for the purpose of bringing Sarah rather than Abraham to faith. The apostolic comment would seem to support this, for there the emphasis is on the divine intervention that would take place in her life rather than Abraham's. So, "For *this is the word* of promise, At this time *will I come*, and *Sara* shall have a son" (Romans 9:9).

knew, of course, that his guests were angels, but he would have done this anyway, for it was typical of the man that he would help to bring them forward on their journey. From the first moment of greeting to the last moment of farewell, Abraham and Sarah's spirit of hospitality was a gracious offering of spiritual conversation, generous provision, and attentive care. Their hospitality extended even to the point of seeing their visitors safely on their way.[18]

The primary purpose of these three was to visit God's wrath upon the grievous sin of Sodom, in an outpouring of fiery judgement that would destroy all who lived there. Yet in the marvellous economy of God's way, mercy had rejoiced against judgement this day, for before these ministers of flaming fire unleashed the mighty cataclysm, they had made this glad detour to the oaks of Mamre to ignite Sarah to the promise of life. They left behind a subdued but thoughtful woman, who was now at least uncertain of her certainty, unsure of her earlier conviction that she could not bear. She was not alive to the fulness of faith as yet, but the first stirrings of thought had been kindled in her heart that would warm and heal the dreadful cold of her doubt. Her problem lay within herself. It would need to be overcome there.[19] But the secret to overcoming was to surrender herself entirely, first to thought, and then to belief in the wondrous and omnipotent power of God.

The friend of God and his family of faith

Whilst Sarah reflected to herself and Abraham walked the path with angels, the spokesman of this threefold company spoke as if in soliloquy:

---

18 The Abrahamic standard of farewell would likewise become the basis for apostolic custom and practice (Acts 15:3; Romans 15:24; 3 John 6).

19 The apostle with Spirit insight makes comment on the one vital word in this episode. Genesis 18:12 spoke truly in stating where the problem lay, "Sarah laughed within *herself*". From this place must needs come first the quickening of faith that would lead to childbearing "through faith Sara *herself* received strength to conceive seed" (Hebrews 11:11). See also Appendix 7 – "Did Sarah herself receive strength?"

"Shall I hide from Abraham that thing which I do; seeing that Abraham shall surely become a great and mighty nation, and all the nations of the earth shall be blessed in him? For I know him, that he will command his children and his household after him, and they shall keep the way of the LORD, to do justice and judgment; that the LORD may bring upon Abraham that which he hath spoken of him." (Genesis 18:17-19)

The answer was self-evident. He was about to tell the patriarch the reason why they looked with such stern mien against the city where his nephew dwelt. He alone would be told of the impending catastrophe, but then he after all, was the Friend of God. There are many who might claim a friendship for God, based upon their love of His principles and their obedience of His ways. But to claim a friendship from God is not the prerogative of any man. Only God Himself can declare whether He reciprocates the affections of earthly beings. Yet the Deity held this man in such esteem that he was counted as bearing a special and unique relationship with the Lord. He would, for this very reason, enjoy the finest privilege that friendship brings, the mutual sharing of thoughts and intentions.[20] Abraham was by divine admission the friend of God,[21] and God's purpose would not be hidden from His friend.

That friendship, moreover, was one that the Lord Himself initiated. He had chosen Abraham, and singled him out by an abundance of revelations which He vouchsafed unto him. The very reason for these heavenly visitations was to open Abraham's wondering mind to the glorious magnitude of the divine plan. When the revelations were ended, God had truly chosen and inspired His friend[22] to walk in the way of truth. But He

---

20 John 15:15.

21 This is an astounding title for a mortal to be given, yet the patriarch is described in this way three times: 2 Chronicles 20:7; Isaiah 41:8; James 2:23.

22 That this is the sense of the text is evidenced by most translations (cp. RSV, NIV, NASB, GLT etc.). In fact Rotherham's translation

had also moved him so powerfully that Abraham would command his children and his house, that they also should keep the way of the Lord. So deeply was Abraham affected by his relationship with the Almighty that he, in turn, etched the divine principles that guided his life on the minds of his household.

The great and mighty nation, which finally would spring from him, would be more than his natural descendants. They would be his spiritual offspring who, following their father, would know the Lord through the practice of His principles in justice and judgement. They would show the likeness of their father, inasmuch as they would also walk in the footsteps of his faith. Abraham's household would indeed become the guardians of the truth in their successive generations, those that would "keep the way of the LORD".

Impending judgement and earnest intercession

Beyond Hebron, northward across the Judaean plateau, yet also eastward by way of the sun's rising, there stood a notable height. When the summit was reached the hills stretching beyond seemed suddenly parted in the midst, and through the cleft northwards again the circle of Jordan could be seen. The plain was well watered but its inhabitants were wicked. It was to this vantage point that Abraham led the men, as the day began to wear away. It was to here again, early on the morrow, that he would hasten in anxiety to view their handiwork. When the men reached the place of which Abraham had spoken, they stopped and looked toward Sodom, down through the great ravine. The cities of the plain lay there far beyond, and far below the angelic gaze. Abraham felt thankful that he and his household were far removed from what went on below. The people of the plain revelled in their wealth and fulness, but theirs was a world of

---

says, "For *I have become his intimate friend to the end* that he may command his sons and his house after him", thereby suggesting (and probably rightly so) that this very passage is the basis for the later inspired comments which call the patriarch by that special epithet, the *Friend* of God.

depravity and sin, which destroyed all spiritual thought and life. Abraham, however, the Friend of God trod the mountain heights above, and offered prayers at his own altar, alone in the isolated fastness of Mamre's stony hills. He was separate from the evil, but close to the One whom he worshipped, close enough in fact for God to take him into His confidence.

But Abraham was not advised of Sodom's fate for friendship's sake. Nor was he warned in order that he might intercede for others, although he sought to do so. He was told so that he might know God's attitude towards ungodliness. He was informed before the event, so that he could witness the destruction and know that it was the righteous judgement of God. It was a tremendous lesson for the man, and an even greater one for the nation that would spring from him. For God, in the omniscience of His foreknowledge, had already decided on the man who was to be the father of the faithful. Without removing any of the man's free will, God knew the greatness of his heart to rise to spiritual things, and to manifest faith's response. Having therefore selected him according to His sovereign will, He appeared unto the man and made known unto him His mind, His character, and His purpose by the mouth of the Angel of the Name.

And it was characteristic of the spirit of this man, that having heard of the judgement to come, his immediate concern was for the care of his brethren. Down in the plain were members of the household of faith, and Abraham sought by petition with the angel that the whole should be spared for the sake of the righteous. It was typical of the generous spirit of the man that he should so petition. He did not countenance the sin of Sodom,[23] but he did seek that they should be spared for the sake of those who were known of the Lord in that place. He knew at least that Lot was a righteous man, and perhaps also that he was truly vexed by the ungodly behaviour of those he dwelt among.[24]

---

23 As Genesis 14:22,23 witnesses.
24 2 Peter 2:6-9.

Abraham's intercession for the righteous in Sodom began with a number that might reasonably have represented an ecclesia within the city.[25] It ended with the ten who formed Lot's immediate family,[26] and Abraham was hopeful that his intercession had thereby spared his relative, his family and his city.

"And he said, Oh let not the Lord be angry, and I will speak yet but this once: peradventure ten shall be found there. And he said, I will not destroy it for ten's sake." (Genesis 18:32)

With this assurance the patriarch had to be content, and with his pleadings ended, and the response received, the angel was gone.

The patriarch returned to his place, to his wife, and to the household of which he was the head. He needed not to convince Sarah that they had spoken with angels, for she had also realized this. Her awareness had come at a different time from his, but she knew that he who had promised the gift of a son was God's angelic messenger. It had been a strange yet memorable episode in their lives. On this day they were united as one by the shared experience of this heavenly visitation. Truly, they were heirs together of the promise, and Abraham was intent on dwelling with her according to the knowledge that had been so wonderfully imparted to them on this day. The "time of life" of which the angel had spoken, the quickening powers which were to come upon them, must be but a short period away, for already they were within a year of the birth.[27] Isaac was about to be conceived,

---

25 An appropriate number for an ecclesia (cp: 1 Kings 18:4; 2 Kings 2:7; Luke 9:14)?

26 Abraham must have been truly hopeful that his solicitation on Lot's behalf had saved his family, for he would have known the details of the family circle. There was Lot himself (Genesis 19:1), two sons (verse 12), two married daughters and therefore also two sons-in-law (verse 14), his wife and two unmarried daughters (verse 15). This made ten. Surely at the least all these were faithful!

27 The angel had previously intimated that Isaac was to be born within twelve months of the proclamation of Genesis 17:21. Given

and the power of God was about to begin the invisible renewal of their bodies that it might be so.

---

the nine months needed from conception to birth, the events of Genesis 18-20 must all fall within three months.

6

EXPERIENCING THE TRIUMPH OF FAITH TOGETHER
(Genesis 20:1-18)

ABRAHAM arose early on the morrow, and hastened to the spot where he had but yesterday seen the lush verdure of the plain. Early though he was, the angels were ahead of him, for the sun had no sooner risen upon the earth than their judgement began. The thunder and lightning of heaven, and the tumultuous reverberations of the earth, brought the patriarch running with trembling heart and anxious eye desperately to scan the eastward horizon. He was shocked at what he saw. He was too late to see the catastrophe itself, but he beheld the horror of its aftermath. The cities of the plain were but smoking holes, blackened to extinction. Sodom, Gomorrah, Admah, Zeboim were gone.[1] Every living thing must surely have perished in the blast of brimstone that had overthrown all the land and these cities of the plain. As far as the eye could see, there was nothing but desolation and ruin and everywhere arose the smoke of its burning, like the smoke of a furnace. The vastness of the destruction overwhelmed the Friend of God, for this was a calamity such as he had never witnessed before. As he looked, he was awestruck with fear at the unimaginably vast power of the angels who had eaten bread at his own table.[2] But he was desolated also at the thought that Sodom was bereft of even ten righteous in the city,[3] and that Lot was probably dead.

---

1 Genesis 19:29 indicates that "God destroyed the cities of the plain", which were afterwards enumerated as these four in Deuteronomy 29:23.

2 Here is the destructive aspect of the title Ail Shaddai – the strength of the nourishers or destroyers. The context, as always, determines the usage.

3 For so his pleadings had ended in Genesis 18:32.

114

South in sadness to sojourn in Gerar

God in truth had remembered the patriarch and his pleadings, and his "brother"[4] had been graciously delivered through the spirit of his entreaty. Lot had been gathered up by the angelic messengers and sent forth out of the midst of the overthrow.[5] But on the day that Abraham looked and lamented with astonishment and horror, he knew not that Lot was safe. The message of destruction he brought back to Sarah was dreadful indeed, for Lot was her brother[6] and the thought of his death filled her with despair. Sick with grief at the apparent failure of intercession, distressed at the magnitude of the divine judgement that evil men had made necessary, and saddened by the folly that had led a righteous man to dwell among such evil, Abraham and Sarah felt a desperate urge to move away. The awfulness of the destruction created an overwhelming desire to escape from this place with such vivid memories of the holocaust.[7]

The tents were packed and the household assembled for marching. The settled existence of nigh on twenty years in this place of fellowship and peace was terminated with abrupt suddenness, and the ground beneath the oak of Mamre lay bare again. The rugs of their tents lay rolled and strapped to the sides of the camels, swinging to the peculiar gait of the lurching beasts as they trod the path away from the plateau heights that overlooked

---

4   Genesis 14:14.

5   Genesis 19:29.

6   See Appendix 2 – "Who was Iscah?"

7   We are not told in the record why this migration occurred, although the phrase "*from thence*" in Genesis 20:1 is suggestive of a desire to get away. The suggestions made here, however, are consistent with the context of the events just recorded in Genesis 18-19, since Genesis 20:1 is the very next mention of Abraham after he beheld the holocaust of the plain in 19:27,28. In addition, there may have been pressure on the highland's pasturelands from those fleeing from the Jordan valley upwards into the hill country. "From *thence*" would be from the place of Abraham's abode in Mamre (cp. 18:1,33).

the circle of the cities of the plain. Their flight took them southwards through the mountains, as the Judaean hills eased their way down by degrees to the flatness of the Negeb.[8] The road along the plateau also took them to the west, but it was not far enough for the grieving man and his wife. When they reached Beersheba they did not continue south into the Negeb itself, but instead turned sharply west again, moving up into the lowlands of the Philistines, until behind them the wall of hills finally blocked out completely the scene of Sodom's overthrow.

Abraham and Sarah arrived in Gerar bewildered, apprehensive, unsettled and afraid. They had not even thought about the consequences of their move. They had been settled in Hebron for so many years, that the question of their identity was a problem long forgotten. Yet no sooner had they arrived than the matter of how to present themselves arose again in a strange land, with unfamiliar people and uncertain customs. Faced with a sudden urgent problem for which they were ill-prepared in mind, they fell back upon old ways.[9] And unsurprisingly, a repetition of their old practice led to a repetition of an old crisis.

When deceit brings danger and distress

"And Abraham said of Sarah his wife, She is my sister: and Abimelech king of Gerar sent, and took Sarah." (Genesis 20:2)

---

8 The word for "south" in Genesis 20:1 is *negeb* and indicates the lowland areas south of Beersheba into the highlands of the Sinai Peninsula. That it was a territory is indicated by the use of the term in 13:1.

9 Reading the episode in Genesis 20 we feel surprised that Abraham would have used a stratagem that had brought such calamity upon them previously. But two details help. The first is that many of us have habits, weaknesses, besetting sins that we have been unable to conquer in many years. Abraham and Sarah were no different. The second is that this episode is separated from that of Genesis 12 and the journey into Egypt by over twenty years, enough time certainly for memory to fade. In addition, the sudden nature of their arrival in Gerar had helped precipitate this crisis of decision.

There must have been something extraordinary about Sarah to cause Abimelech to act thus in adding her to his household. It may have been a political alliance, which bound him to Abraham in a pact that secured their mutual safety. After all, the patriarch presided over a large household in his own right, and commanded a formidable army from within his own encampment, one that had already achieved success in battle.[10] Such an alliance by marriage was a common means to prevent war and preserve amity.

But Abimelech, whose depth of character will unfold throughout this story, may also have found Sarah to be a woman with a personality, mind and character that he appreciated and enjoyed. Being both in name and status the princess of Abraham's tribe, Sarah was certainly of acceptable social standing for Abimelech to contemplate marriage, and, unaware of her present condition[11] he simply saw in Sarah a woman who was still attractive, and that there could be decided advantage in the association.

No sooner had the woman been taken into his household however, than a strange and debilitating affliction fell upon him. God had moved swiftly to safeguard the promise. Nothing would happen to this woman within the house of Abimelech. Only then did God appear to Abimelech to inform him of the circumstances.

> "But God came to Abimelech in a dream by night, and said to him, Behold, thou art but a dead man, for the woman which thou hast taken; for she is a man's wife. But Abimelech had not come near her: and he said, Lord, wilt thou slay also a righteous nation? Said he not unto me, She is my sister? And she, even she herself said, He is my brother: in the integrity of my heart and innocency of my hands have I done this."
>
> (Genesis 20:3-5)

Abimelech must have been shocked to learn that his life was in danger because of this event. The affliction

---

10 Genesis 14:14,15.

11 Genesis 18:11.

that had befallen him had already brought unease. To learn that it might be life-threatening brought fear. He protested that he had not touched Sarah. It was true that he had not come near her, but Abimelech could not claim this as a matter of virtue on his part, for it was of God that he had been prevented from doing so. It was true, however, to say that he acted in the integrity of his heart and innocency of his hands. Abimelech had believed the testimony of Abraham, and felt that his actions were righteous by the custom of the day. This travelling chieftain recently arrived, had clearly indicated that the woman was but his relative, and Abimelech had no reason to doubt what Abraham had affirmed.

But he had also believed Sarah's words, for she had told him personally that Abraham was indeed her brother. Here was a matter of mutual deceit. Whatever Abraham might have said, Sarah had joined in the subterfuge.[12] She, no less than he, had assured Abimelech of her position, complicit in the matter of misinforming the king.[13] The anxiety of the holocaust upon Sodom, and the stress of their hasty relocation to Gerar, had put both of them under strain. Sarah was distressed by the thought that Lot her brother was probably dead. With the memory of the catastrophe still so fresh, the last thing she wanted was the death of her husband also at this moment of uncertainty and fear. Faced yet

---

12 Abimelech's words clearly indicate his ire and disappointment with both of them, and perhaps with Sarah in particular – "*Said he not* unto me, She is my sister? And *she, even she herself said*, He is my brother*" (Genesis 20:5).

13 The phrase, "for she is a man's wife" in Genesis 20:3 is unusual in the Hebrew (*baal, baal*), indicating that she was 'married to a husband'. The only other occurrence of the phrase is in Deuteronomy 22:22 where a woman 'married to a husband' who was then found with another man was condemned with the man. The law deemed her involvement to indicate her consent, and she was therefore held equally accountable for their sin and suffered the same judgement. This expression suggests therefore that in this episode, Sarah as 'married to a husband' bore equal responsibility with Abraham for the deceit that led to her being under Abimelech's roof.

again with a dilemma for which no easy answer existed, she moved to protect her husband, trusting in God who alone could rescue them,[14] and mindful perhaps of that earlier occasion where He had indeed delivered them both from a similar predicament. But the decision was a mistake. They had not pondered this vital moment in their lives, nor where it might lead. Mutual deceit by mutual consent led to consequences that were to their mutual detriment, and to a tangle of circumstance that they would regret deeply.

Protected by the power of providential care

The reaction of the aggrieved and bewildered monarch was understandable. The king of Gerar was a man of integrity,[15] and his actions above reproach with regard to his spirit and intent. Abimelech however had to learn that he was caught up in a drama that reached well beyond his own circumstances. Both this man and this woman were the prophets of God; and both were soon to be the recipients of a divine unction as the anointed ones of the Lord.[16] Despite their error, they both sustained a closer relationship to God than he did, and Abimelech was bidden to understand this and to bow before its reality. The special providential care of God was upon husband and wife alike for the furtherance of His sovereign purpose, and for that very reason Abimelech was invited into the deeper things of God that he might

---

14 1 Peter 3:5.

15 The word "integrity" in Genesis 20:5 is *tom*, indicating an action devoid of wilful or deliberate wrong, and this ingenuous spirit of Abimelech is in marked contrast to Abraham and Sarah who had both deliberately sought to mislead him (cp. 2 Samuel 15:11; 1 Kings 22:34).

16 The Spirit's commentary on this episode is enshrined in Psalm 105:13-15. Here both the words "prophets" and "anointed" are in the plural (cp. ASV, RSV, Rotherham, etc.) indicating the providential care of God upon both Abraham and Sarah alike. Abraham is described as a prophet in Genesis 20:7. Sarah will be seen as a prophetess in 21:6,7,10. Both of them were to be anointed for the conception and birth of the miraculous child to come. Truly they were united together in this story!

119

play his part. He had become involved in a matter far greater than himself. Others also, through their contact with the people of God, have been caught up in the power of the divine purpose at work, and the experience has oftentimes been to change their lives completely, as Abimelech's would be from this episode.[17]

"And God said unto him in a dream, Yea, I know that thou didst this in the integrity of thy heart; for I also withheld thee from sinning against me: therefore suffered I thee not to touch her. Now therefore restore the man his wife; for he is a prophet, and he shall pray for thee, and thou shalt live: and if thou restore her not, know thou that thou shalt surely die, thou, and all that are thine."   (Genesis 20:6,7)

The 'rights' of men are incidental to the divine purpose. Here was a man who was absolute monarch of his realm, with the power of life and death at his command. Yet Abimelech, irrespective of his kingship, and despite his relative integrity, was to have no authority or power to influence the outcome of these events. The lives of the patriarchal couple were protected, despite their deceit. The life of Abimelech was not. The threat of death hung over him unless he complied with the divine instructions communicated to him. Whether innocent or not made no difference to his status. He was a stranger, beyond the ambit of the covenant, and utterly dependent on the mediatorial work of the very man he had just condemned. Abraham, for all his faults, would stand on behalf of Abimelech as his intercessor before God. Sarah likewise bore such a special relationship to the One who had appeared to Abimelech by dream, that he was bluntly advised that to touch her was to sin directly against God, and that only a divine smiting had prevented him from this error.

This has been the position the people of God have held in every generation. To the outward eye they appear as all others, citizens in common with their neighbours,

---

17 Cp. Rahab the Harlot in Joshua 6:25, and Simon of Cyrene in Mark 15:21 as but two illustrations.

and subject to both success and failure. To the Father however, they are the subjects of His guardian direction and care, possessing a rank before Him that exceeds in status all the sons of men. But our status in His eyes rests not on our worth but in His purpose with us. The providential care of God does not rescue and redeem and restore us because we necessarily deserve it, but because He is working in us both to will and to work His good pleasure. Sometimes we forget the greatness of this truth, and when we do, all that is weak and evil in our nature comes to the fore as we seek to master our own destinies, and forget that they are already known unto Him who sees the counsels of the heart.

Abimelech's council meeting in Gerar

"Therefore Abimelech rose early in the morning, and called all his servants, and told all these things in their ears: and the men were sore afraid. Then Abimelech called Abraham, and said unto him, What hast thou done unto us? And what have I offended thee, that thou hast brought on me and on my kingdom a great sin? Thou hast done deeds unto me that ought not to be done. And Abimelech said unto Abraham, What sawest thou, that thou hast done this thing?"

(Genesis 20:8-10)

Abimelech was given no option but to comply with the divine request. His life was forfeit otherwise and the lives of his entire household. There was no delay on his part, for he understood the crisis he was in. With the same decisive spirit the patriarch himself would later show,[18] he called his kingdom together the very next morning and placed the whole account before them. There is more than comfort in having counsellors in time of crisis.[19] There is wisdom in the collective guidance of

---

18 There is an earlier occasion in Genesis 19:27, but the episodes in 21:14 and 22:3 both illustrate the same principle as Abimelech. Burdened with a problem that needed to be resolved, Abraham faced the issue immediately, and rose up early to do so. It is a faithful virtue that all his children should emulate.

19 Proverbs 11:14; 15:22.

many minds, and Abimelech's men, in mortal fear at the report he gave, agreed as one that Abraham should be instantly called. Not only did they wish for him to give an honest account, but they also needed his complete involvement in setting the matter right before all, and especially before God whose threat hung like a sword over the city.

When Abraham received the summons, his spirit almost failed. His walk to the council of Gerar was a terrible journey of remembrance, as step by step he relived his earlier encounter with an angry monarch, and knew again the anxiety of fear and the anguish of shame. Certainly the visage of the king was sternly familiar, as were his words of retribution and blame. Abimelech was unsparing, claiming not only that Abraham had wronged his kingdom and people, but that he had also misjudged the king himself. Given that he had received a visitation from God, Abimelech only spoke what he felt he could aver with honesty, since he was aware that God watched from on high and that his life was still in the balance. But he felt certain enough to demand of Abraham an account of what he had been thinking, to bring such calamity upon the house of his benefactor and host.

Abraham's spirit of shame that sought to excuse

"And Abraham said, Because I thought, Surely the fear of God is not in this place; and they will slay me for my wife's sake. And yet indeed she is my sister; she is the daughter of my father, but not the daughter of my mother; and she became my wife. And it came to pass, when God caused me to wander from my father's house, that I said unto her, This is thy kindness which thou shalt shew unto me; at every place whither we shall come, say of me, He is my brother."

(Genesis 20:11-13)

Abraham had grievously misjudged the spirit of the king, and acted unwisely as a result. His explanation was that the fear of God was not in Abimelech or his people, but the reality was that the fear of man was

122

in Abraham. Shamed and nervous before Abimelech's righteous indignation, his words of excuse were awkward and inadequate. Aware of a previous yet similar incident of weakness in his own life of which Abimelech was unaware, Abraham felt utterly miserable at his lack of faith, and his inability even to explain matters with some semblance of reasonableness. There are times when our attempts at explanation only add to our culpability. This was one of them. To deny that we have sinned is the worst outcome of all, for it indicates a heart hardened against the truth. But to seek to justify what cannot be excused, is also a wrong that only adds sin to sin. Confession, however hard it may be, is always the best policy for dealing with sin, for it leads immediately to the cleansing powers of repentance, forgiveness and change.

"Because I thought", has been the unhappy prefix to many an excuse, where what we imagined and what we thought were quite unrelated to the truth of the matter. Subsequent events have only served to confirm that what 'we thought' was completely wrong, and that our subsequent and hasty reaction was wrong also. Discerning truth, judging righteously and deciding justly require great care that we first know all the circumstances before seeking to respond, and that even then our response is framed by the counsels of God for the purpose of good, and with the desire that we might honour Him. In Abraham's case he had made judgement prematurely, hastened by their mutual distress and anxiety at the time. And yet there was an aspect to their relationship that he now sought to explain.

Sarah, whilst not Abraham's sister, was his niece, being the daughter of Haran, Abraham's older brother, and probably by a different wife to Terah.[20] Haran was considerably older than Abraham, so much so, that his daughter was but ten years younger than the patriarch, a fact that made it easier to suggest that Sarah was his younger sister. Their common descent did probably result in some family likeness, lending support to their claim to

---

20 See Appendix 2 – "Who was Iscah?"

be siblings. Abraham therefore endeavoured to explain it as an action on their part that at least in measure was true. It was not. The final words, which at least Abraham felt compelled to admit, was that she had become his wife, and there the matter ended. It had been a lie all along, because it was uttered for the purpose of concealing their true state. His explanation, laboured and long, failed to acknowledge his misjudgement of Abimelech, sought to justify their subterfuge, and did not frankly avow his own mistake. He would not recall this day with gladness in later years, but it would yet become a turning point in their lives. Often our moments of greatest failure carry within them the seed of transformation that only awaits our humble acknowledgment to bring forth the fruit of change.

And there was one thing he had said that was both true and revealing, namely that their action in claiming kinship as siblings was not simply the decision of the moment. It had long been their settled position for any time they crossed into a new land. The patriarch, spiritually-minded and God-fearing, was not immune to the crises of life, nor was he a man of natural courage when facing adversity. Faced with a danger that the customs of the day made real,[21] and knowing that they might encounter this danger many times on their travels, had led to a decision when faith was young as to how best they might respond. Yet this arrangement was not forced upon Sarah by an autocratic and demanding husband, who expected subservience in all things. Abraham was indeed Lord in her heart,[22] but he had not won this response of love and support in his wife by

---

21 The custom of the day for kings to maintain a royal harem was widespread. In addition, the king's word was law, and any woman might be the object of his sovereign choice, whether for beauty or alliance. Against such a custom there was no defence for a stranger and a sojourner passing through the king's realm, and Abraham and Sarah were frequently in this position, wandering as they were by divine edict until the land of the promise was reached.

22 Genesis 18:12; 1 Peter 3:6.

callous disregard for her position, or by an overbearing and imperious spirit that demanded unquestioning obedience. He had asked it of her as a loving kindness,[23] and part of the marvel of this woman's spirit is that she gave it freely for the man she loved.

It is true that the stratagem had failed, but it had been devised with the objective of safeguarding them both in troublous times, since it offered the chance of moving on, if a difficulty with Sarah were to arise. It was not just a matter of an old habit unresolved. It was more a case of an old problem for which a better solution had not yet been found. Few of us have known the reality of a circumstance where to declare our faith plainly could threaten our lives, and few of us have known the emotion of fear that is almost tangible. "To him who is in fear, everything rustles."[24] Through fear we imagine outcomes that might never occur, and seek to control and manipulate events for our protection or betterment, all the while depending on ourselves and not on the Lord who is our helper. Only when we have surrendered control into the Father's hands and found that He on our side do we realise that we need not fear what man can do unto us.[25]

For both of them in this episode, their spirit had displayed a want of faith in the Almighty who had so evidently overshadowed their lives for many years now. Abraham was doubly to blame on this occasion compared to his earlier weakness in Egypt. Since then he had learned that the child must come from his loins,[26] and that it must be nourished in Sarah's womb.[27] But

---

23 The term "kindness" (as Abraham asked of Sarah in Genesis 20:13) is *chesed*, the term of God's own covenant love for His people. The phrase is indicative of the spirit that existed between Abraham and Sarah in their arrangements, and suggests not dominance but mutual agreement.

24 Sophocles.

25 Psalm 118:6; Proverbs 29:25; Hebrews 13:6.

26 Genesis 15:4.

27 Genesis 17:16.

Sarah also knew this, yet raised no demur.[28] From the beginning God had declared that their lives were under His special care, even in the midst of other peoples.[29] And was not the power of the promise so recently granted to them,[30] but to guarantee that their lives were inviolate at this very moment? Yet faith, certain in Abraham as to the birth of the child, did not extend to a realisation that since his own life was safe in God's hands, prevarication and dissembling were neither necessary nor honourable. And Sarah, aware of the fact that she would bear the promised seed, did not appear to comprehend that if her life was still under divine care, there was no need for dissimulation on her part.

This lack, however, where the knowledge of the mind was not as yet engraved as the knowledge of the heart, is distressingly common to us all. So often we assent to the principles of God, yet do not see their application in our lives, especially in moments of great difficulty and fear. We see the lesson in the life of an Abraham or Sarah, being either astonished at their strength, or puzzled by their weakness, but do not see the identical principle awaiting the obedience of faith in a matching circumstance in our own life. Part of the power of Scripture is that it is able to guide every generation of the people of God. And part of the journey of faith is to learn with painful slowness that God and His purpose are bound into everything we do, that the daily round, the common task, the ordinary things of everyday life are pregnant with our destiny.[31]

---

28 In other incidents such as Genesis 16:5 and 21:10 it is clear that Sarah was free to express her view to Abraham at any time, and that he would hear her counsel, whatever decision they might finally make. Sarah's compliance with Abraham's request on this occasion is indeed a demonstration of her loving obedience, but made her complicit in the matter.

29 Surely the words, "I will bless them that bless thee, and curse him that curseth thee" had promised this (Genesis 12:3)?

30 Genesis 18:10.

31 The phrase is drawn from Robert Roberts (*The Christadelphian*, Vol. 9, page 266): "Therefore, *now* is the time of action. Let *every man* look to what he is doing – and *every woman*. Let them

Abimelech's restoration of Sarah

"And Abimelech took sheep, and oxen, and menservants, and womanservants, and gave them unto Abraham, and restored him Sarah his wife. And Abimelech said, Behold, my land is before thee: dwell where it pleaseth thee. And unto Sarah he said, Behold, I have given thy brother a thousand pieces of silver: behold, he is to thee a covering of the eyes, unto all that are with thee, and with all other: thus was she reproved." (Genesis 20:14-16)

After Abraham had evaded, Abimelech acted. His restitution was in deed, not word, and displayed an astonishing spirit of humility, insight, courtesy and tact. Abimelech was a better man by far than the Pharaoh of their earlier encounter. Pharaoh had been pleased to bless Abraham with gifts at the time of receiving Sarah, the offerings of a man well pleased with the addition to his household, and which recognised his new relationship with Abraham.[32] Abimelech's gifts were not so given. For his were provided when restoring Sarah, an act of unexpected graciousness at a time when Abraham might have least expected such endowments. What spirit was this, which prompted the wronged one to offer presents unto he who had offended him? And if the gifts of Pharaoh had burdened Abraham's conscience, as indeed they had, how did both he and Sarah feel upon receipt of these presents of peace from Abimelech? Both of them would be humbled this day by such magnanimous conduct.

Even the king's offer for them to dwell wherever they would in his land was to experience the embarrassment of uncalled for kindness. Here was another thoughtful

remember that their present daily life – dull, uninteresting, unimportant though it may appear, is really pregnant with their destiny. All depends upon how they turn the present time to account. Future position will be determined entirely by present deportment."

32 In Genesis 12:16 the record is clear that Pharaoh's gifts were the result of having taken Sarah into his household. It was surely unheard of to receive gifts as Abraham did from Abimelech, when returning his wife!

gesture to complete the process of their separation, but without conflict or tension, as Abimelech permitted Abraham to lead his large encampment out to a place of pasture and water at Abimelech's expense. It was a thoroughly Abrahamic spirit,[33] but on this occasion the Gentile outshone the patriarch in his spirit of generosity.

More was to come. The primary difficulty had yet to be resolved, and that concerned Abimelech's return of Sarah into Abraham's care. He was of course now vitally aware of Abraham's position in the sight of God. His generous gifts were an acknowledgment of that standing, and he also knew that he still needed Abraham's prayer for his own healing. Before that could come however, the man's wife must be restored, and that with all careful diplomacy. One final gift was to come, intended for Sarah herself, and Abimelech addressed her directly in stating its purpose. A thousand pieces of silver was a lordly sum, his gift to her of personal appeasement, intended as a formal declaration on his part that she belonged unto Abraham. In offering this gift of atonement[34] and compensation, Abimelech acknowledged his wrong. If Abraham accepted it the matter was ended, and Sarah's position was put right, with all criticism precluded. But the gift,[35] which was intended for her as a covering of the eyes, was given not to her, but to Abraham her 'brother'. By this word and by this gift Abimelech both owned the error of his action, but declared the innocence of his

---

33 The very phrase, "my land is before thee: dwell where it pleaseth thee" in Genesis 20:15 is very reminiscent of Abraham's own kindness to Lot when separating from him in 13:9.

34 Compare the similar idea and expression in Genesis 32:20 where Jacob's gift to 'cover the face of Esau' was clearly intended as an offering of atonement. Although *kaphar* is used in 32:20 and *kecuwth* in 20:16, the essential idea of a covering to appease is similar.

35 Although the AV states "*he* (Abraham) is to thee a covering", other translations make it clear that it was the gift of the thousand pieces itself. Thus RSV – "*it* is your vindication in the eyes of all". GLT – "Behold, *it* is for you a covering of the eyes". Rotherham – "Lo, *that* is for thee as a covering of eyes". Rotherham, margin – "as a propitiation, making amends".

intention. Given the threat to his own life and that of his household, this was no time for sarcasm or contempt. It was finely balanced and well wrought, this declaration of the king. His speech was earnest, and every word was intended to play its part in the restoration of Sarah to her husband's side.

This, after all, was the principal reason why Abimelech had received his angelic visitation, and had been given the instructions that he had. There had been no difficulty for God to intervene in the matter to prevent a liaison between Abimelech and Sarah, but what was needed now was for Abimelech to make public renunciation. This then was no private requital. Abimelech made it clear that he wanted everyone to know. It was to be Sarah's vindication before all, and so it became. She was Abraham's. Let none doubt it. The king had spoken, and had restored in full.

Effectual fervent prayer in time of crisis

"So Abraham prayed unto God: and God healed Abimelech, and his wife, and his maidservants; and they bare children. For the LORD had fast closed up all the wombs of the house of Abimelech, because of Sarah Abraham's wife." (Genesis 20:17,18)

It was one of the most difficult prayers Abraham had ever offered. To pray for the healing of another when you are innocent is truly intercessory.[36] But to be the source of petition when another has suffered through your sin is humbling in the extreme. Abraham felt deeply unworthy of his intercessory office, and was crucially aware that Abimelech knew it also. Both men, however, were under the divine imperative, for on the very eve of the conception of the promised son, Sarah stood in close relation to both these men, and herein lay the problem. Here was Abraham – 'father of a multitude', and here also was Abimelech – 'father of a king'. The controversy of the moment was this. Which man would be the father of the seed? Why did such a delicate and complicated

---

36 Numbers 12:13.

puzzle arise? Why such a terrible dilemma, and at the worst possible moment? Why even the possibility that the origin of their special child could be called into question, given the precious promise they now guarded? Why this calamity that brought Abraham and Sarah at such a vital moment in their lives to a conundrum beyond their power to resolve? Why indeed?

They were to learn yet again that sin not only brings its consequences, unavoidable and irrevocable, but that those consequences are so often unexpected and unforeseen. Both of them were ashamed, not only that through their continued lack of faith a shadow of doubt might be cast over the son soon to be born, but more so again at the abiding love of the God who did not forsake them, even in the midst of their failure. Their own actions had brought this about, for their behaviour had been inconsistent with what they knew. And yet there must be no dispute as to the fatherhood of the promised seed. So much in the future rested on the fact that this child must be recognised beyond all cavil as being the offspring of Abraham and Sarah, and of none other. The future of the Lord's plan not only for Isaac, but also for Messiah, rested upon this boy being recognised as theirs. Despite the predicament of the moment, brought about by the deceit of both Abraham and Sarah, God moved to resolve what they could not. By decisive edict upon the two men, He intervened and made the pathway clear. He would brook no objection from either man. Abimelech must restore, Abraham must pray.[37]

Abimelech had already fulfilled his obligation, for he had restored Sarah unto Abraham completely, a restoration full and generous in its spirit and its terms. Such was the fear Abimelech had felt because of this divine visitation; he would be staunch in affirming her status as belonging unto Abraham, unequivocal in declaring that he had not touched her, resolute in forever abjuring any association with Sarah. Not from the lips

---

37 Their respective roles were first intimated to Abimelech (Genesis 20:7).

of Abimelech would there ever fall a query concerning the parentage of the child soon to be conceived and born.

Now then Abraham must perform his part in the transaction. It was the Lord, the covenant God, who had interposed for Abraham and preserved Sarah. They were in covenant relationship with Him, and He was faithful, even if they had faltered. But Abimelech did not possess such a covenant of fellowship. So Abraham's prayer ascended unto *the* God, the true God who had appeared unto Abimelech, and before whom he himself walked. Truly there was fervency and sincerity and humility in Abraham's prayer this day. Whether in the hearing of Abimelech or no, the patriarch with broken voice and contrite heart offered his plea for the healing of others in a matter where he had grievously sinned himself. On bended knee he poured out his supplication, made humble by the anguish of further personal failure, and by the tender mercy of his God.

The cry of Abraham, wrung from the heart and borne aloft with tears, came into the presence of God and healed his own soul. All prayers that lift our burdens to the Father bring this healing calm. We pray, not that God might know, for He already does, but that we ourselves might understand. When matters lie beyond our power to remedy or redeem, the prayer that relinquishes all into His hands reminds us of our inadequacy and of His complete sufficiency, and with that knowledge comes the peace that passes all understanding, and that heals. It was a pity that they had not offered such prayer as husband and wife when first stepping into the land of the Philistines. It was a blessing that they had at least offered it now.

Abraham's prayer did not bring healing for himself alone. It was effectual in its primary purpose as well, for not only did Abimelech's wife and maidservants experience a return to fertility, with joyful signs of conception in the household, but Abimelech himself was healed. Whatever disease it was that God placed upon him, the debilitation was gone and he knew it. Abraham

131

had prayed as God had commanded, and Abimelech felt his own healing, saw his family restored, and knew that here was the prophet of God.

There was perhaps no other incident that affected Abimelech more profoundly throughout his entire life. He had known the drama of God's visitation by dream, and witnessed the power of prayer in person because of this man and woman. He knew by divine revelation that illness had fallen upon his household because of Sarah, Abraham's wife. He knew by personal experience that the illness had been removed because of Abraham, Sarah's husband. What unique couple was this who could affect his life, his family, his household so directly and powerfully, even within his own kingdom! Lacking a full understanding of the divine purpose, he nevertheless perceived that here was a couple that God was with in all they did. If their God would bless them in their fall, what might he do for them in their rising? Such was the depth of this experience that he sought to enter in covenant relationship with the patriarch.[38] In the final outworking, the providential care of God for His own, and His response to their earnest prayers converted the king, and "through their fall, salvation *is come* unto the Gentiles".

Experiencing the triumph of faith together

In our weakness we sometimes fall into circumstances that jeopardise the operations of God. His strength however is perfected in our weakness, and if our spirit is right and our response sincere, we learn the wonderful and comforting truth that Almighty God is at work at all times in our lives. He is truly everywhere and there is no place, no circumstance beyond the reach of His providential care, nor is there any folly on our part that can ultimately prevent the fulfilment of His purpose. Indeed, God is able to lift us to new heights out of failure, if in our moments of crisis we turn to Him in prayerful

---

38 Genesis 21:22-24,31,32. His desire for this was based upon his utter conviction that God was at work in their lives.

supplication. The journey of faith brings us all to this realisation eventually. There is nothing too hard for the Lord, not even the worst entanglement of our own sinful weakness. Abraham and Sarah were about to know the fulness of this, and at a moment of such importance in their lives, that the outcome could only but leave them forever grateful and thankful for the Lord's interposition.

It was an astonishing thing. In the very midst of their own weakness and failure, Sarah suddenly saw that the prayers of her husband could open wombs. Yet he had been praying for twenty-five years and more that hers might be opened, and that the child of promise might be born. And if his prayers were effectual for such a result in Abimelech's household, and the Lord heard Abraham even when his petitions deserved not to be heard, why could her womb not be opened? Why not indeed? Suddenly, she knew. She understood. The only barrier, the sole impediment, was she, herself. God was waiting for her faith to reach its triumph where finally, empty of self, she trusted utterly, believed totally in Him. Well, she was there now, right beside her husband. The time had come. Different though their journeys to this moment may have been, they would experience the triumph of faith together and wondrous would that moment be. In the exquisite timing of God's care, He had brought them both by their own special paths to this point, where despite the knowledge that their bodies were dead, they each believed in God's power to perform what He had promised to them.

"And [Abraham] considered not *his own body now dead* ... but was strong in *faith*, giving glory to God ... being *fully persuaded that, what he had promised, he was able also to perform.*" (Romans 4:19-21)

"Through *faith* also Sara *herself* received strength to conceive seed, and was delivered of a child when *she was past age*, because she *judged him faithful who had promised.*"[39] (Hebrews 11:11)

---

39 See Appendix 7 – "Did Sarah herself receive strength?" for further comment on this passage.

What glorious counterparts they were to each other, these two who walked the valleys and hills of life together. At some moment then, and no doubt after the healing of Abimelech's household, an old yet anointed couple knelt within the sanctuary of their own tent and offered further prayer for the conception of the son who would seal the promises. And this time, dwelling together according to the knowledge of their mutual and triumphant faith, yearning together as one for the grace of quickening life, their prayers were not hindered. Sarah herself would experience healing power from her husband's fervent prayer. The Lord in heaven heard, and in the sublime wisdom that marks all the arrangements of God, it was now, at this moment, when they least anticipated, least expected, least deserved this son, that Almighty God to whom belong the "blessings of the breasts and of the womb" would intervene in their lives. It was indeed to be all of Him.

7

ENJOYING THE SON OF THEIR LOVE
TOGETHER
(Genesis 21:1 – 22:19)

IT was a pleasant land wherein they sojourned. Across the lowland hills the limestone, white and hard, broke into outcrops everywhere, yet there was verdure and water aplenty. Terebinth trees and evergreen oaks nestled in clusters and provided shade and refuge. As spring approached the gentle slopes were covered in a cascade of purple sage, crimson poppies, and white chamomile. Even amongst the crevices in the limestone, pink cyclamen found room to flourish, for this was the season when the flowers appeared on the earth, and the time of singing had come.[1] The flocks and herds of Abraham found tender grass and the herbs of the mountains to graze upon, and place in the peaceful pasturage where they might bring forth their young. And within the encampment of the patriarch, the springtide of new life had brought forth the greatest blessing of all. For Sarah, miraculously revived and renewed had conceived, and even now was tasting the pleasure and happiness of quickening life within her.

And Sarah brought forth her firstborn son

"And the LORD visited Sarah as he had said, and the LORD did unto Sarah as he had spoken. For Sarah conceived, and bare Abraham a son in his old age, at the set time of which God had spoken to him."

(Genesis 21:1,2)

The months of her childbearing brought a change within the encampment. Sarah would always be the mistress of the household, even when age had lined her face through the passage of time. But now the glow of happiness

---

1   For so the song delightfully describes the approach of spring (Song of Solomon 2:12).

mantled her with that pure and precious beauty which is God's special endowment upon her that is great with child. In some inscrutable way the wonder and the mystery of "how the bones do grow in the womb" was revealed in the softened and shining countenance of Abraham's wife. A lifetime of barrenness had been transformed into the promise of fruitfulness. The whole household was astir with the expectation of it, and great was the rejoicing when the time came for her to be delivered.

On a day she would never forget, Sarah brought forth her firstborn son, and Abraham breathed a prayer of special thanksgiving. Isaac, the son of their love and the focus of their hope, had been born. It was no accident that the child was born at this moment in their lives. The terrible crisis in Gerar had brought forth the climax of faith in both their hearts, and with it the glorious answer of God, that He would return unto them at the set time. Just as He had promised by the mouth of His angel, the Lord had indeed visited Sarah, and had done all that He had promised.

It is not God's power that is lacking to make things possible in our lives, but our inability to believe in Him, and to open ourselves up to the fulness of His promises. When we do, we bring forth fruit to His honour and our joy. Sarah believed with all her heart, and because she did there was "a performance of those things which were told her from the Lord".[2] The events of the past few months had convinced her that the omniscient, omnipotent, omnipresent God of all things could indeed accomplish that which He had purposed.[3]

---

2   Luke 1:45: indeed Mary would show the spirit of Sarah in her own implicit belief in the promise of God concerning the virgin birth (verse 38).

3   The angel's knowledge of her hidden thoughts convinced her of God's omniscience (Genesis 18:13). The angel's overthrow of Sodom convinced her of God's omnipotence (19:28). The angel's wonderful resolution of the crisis in Gerar convinced her of God's omnipresence (20:16). How could she not believe Him?

Not every barren wife is blessed with the answer of children. The sovereign wisdom of the Almighty works upon each of us according to our circumstances and His will for the developing of our character. Yet Sarah had reason to hope beyond most, that a child might come. For unto them both had the promise been made that God's blessings would flow through a son, the promised seed, and he moreover to be the child of their union and none other. This then was her moment of special joy. All the heartache, all the bitterness, all the grief of untold years, was assuaged in this instant of indescribable happiness. The anguish of barrenness and the sorrow of childbearing were alike remembered no more for "joy that a man is born into the world".[4]

The apparent deferring of the promise had sorely tested both Abraham and Sarah. They had carried this burden with them for many years, and had felt its weight to the point where it had become unbearable. They had both suffered from grief and doubt, as the march of life made the possibility of its fulfilment less and less likely. Yet strangely, the more remote the possibility lay, the greater and greater was the detail unfolded of what would be accomplished through the seed to come.

And when Isaac was finally born, he came at the set time that God had intended all along, and there was no delay. It is a lesson for the saints of all ages. Our view of the Lord's purposes, so constrained by the shortness of our own expectations, feels delay where there is none in the divine estimation. There is wisdom when we finally realise this and bow before God's own timetable, resting on Him to bring it to conclusion. In like manner Zion, (whose destiny is encompassed in Sarah's own story), will be favoured with restoration at the set time of God's sovereign appointment, and there will be no delay.[5]

---

4   John 16:21; Isaiah 66:7.
5   Psalm 102:13.

Abraham's rejoicing at Isaac's birth

"And Abraham called the name of his son that was born unto him, whom Sarah bare to him, Isaac. And Abraham circumcised his son Isaac being eight days old, as God had commanded him. And Abraham was an hundred years old, when his son Isaac was born unto him."   (Genesis 21:3-5)

A spirit of excitement gripped the patriarch with the birth of this beloved son. He was so anxious to do everything right with regard to the development of the child. Nothing would be left undone to give him a right beginning, this son of their love, and of their patient waiting. That he was a miracle child was undoubted, the result of divine intervention. And the mark of Messiah surely rested upon him as the eighth and final son, the son of resurrection power, and of a new beginning. Now, and in accordance with the divine commandment, he became a 'son of eight days',[6] foreshadowing again the firstborn son of Mary who would be named Jesus when the eight days for his circumcision were accomplished.[7]

Sarah's song of spiritual wonder

"And Sarah said, God hath made me to laugh, so that all that hear will laugh with me. And she said, Who would have said unto Abraham, that Sarah should have given children suck? for I have born him a son in his old age. And the child grew, and was weaned: and Abraham made a great feast the same day that Isaac was weaned."   (Genesis 21:6-8)

Gone forever was Sarah's laughter of unbelief concerning Isaac. Instead, she lovingly made allusion to her son's special name to indicate her laughter now of pure joy and gladness at God's goodness unto her.[8] Caught up in the greatness of this thought, she sang a song of wonder and

---

6 Genesis 17:12.
7 Luke 2:21.
8 The literal sense of the passage is, "God hath made me to *tsechoq* so that all who hear will *tsachaq* with me". Isaac, *yitschaq*, is derived from the same root.

happiness that this intervention of God had brought into her life. But she also apprehended that her joy would be shared, and that in the fulness of time a multitude would laugh with her in fellowship of the happiness that this divine blessing entailed. Matters that lay beyond this day were wrapped up in this moment.[9] But she dimly understood that the story of her son reached ahead, and her song was prophetic of those future things which lie unfolded only to the Father's eyes.

The wonder of his birth must have filled Sarah with an outpouring of deep rejoicing. As she held him in her arms she could be forgiven for focusing all her delighted attention upon the details of her child. How blessed to behold the perfection of his tiny features, to discern the first signs of family likeness, to count each little set of fingers and toes, to feel the warmth and softness of his little frame, to cradle his small head carefully and hold him safe. He was such a precious little bundle of joy. And having waited for so many years, it was entirely natural that she should be devoted to cherishing her treasured boy.

But she didn't just see Isaac. Her mind had clearly gone beyond the babe in her arms. Sarah understood that the basis upon which Isaac was born was the principle by which others also would come into being, literally so in his case by miraculous intervention, but they by the operation of divine power in their lives after the principle of faith. Her mind was exalted to range right forward into the future. The promise which had so recently been given, that nations and kings of people would be of her,[10] she now understood as having the hope

---

9 Both prophet and prophetess would speak inspired utterances based upon Sarah's own inspired words. Cp. "God hath made me to laugh, so that all that hear will laugh *with me*" (Genesis 21:6), and "Rejoice ye *with* Jerusalem, and be glad *with her*, all ye that love her: rejoice for joy *with her*, all ye that mourn for her" (Isaiah 66:10); and "My spirit hath rejoiced in *God* my Saviour ... for, behold, from henceforth *all generations* shall call me blessed (*makarizo* – happy)" (Luke 1:47,48).

10 Genesis 17:16.

of fulfilment through the birth of this child. She saw that her son, precious though he was this son of her love, was but the foundation seed of a whole multitude that should follow.[11]

Sarah was no ordinary woman. Smitten once with doubt and fear in her own incapacity, she ascended now to heavenly places, and her hymn of thanksgiving revealed not just a mother's love filled to overflowing, but a heart full of spiritual insight that embraced others within her own hope. How special was this woman whose thoughts were so enlarged, that she pondered within her heart the fulness of God's purpose rather than her own.

The great feast at Isaac's weaning was the first of many steps that would bring him to manhood. All Abraham's household knew that his parents held high expectations for his development, and that he was the heir, not only of their substance, but also of the promises which had been unfolded to them in many parts and many ways. There were other sons older than he, but no record is made of a feast at their weaning. Yet this one would be marked out as different from the moment of his birth, and as the family gathered to feast and rejoice, to dance and to sing, it was evident to all the household that on him lay the hopes and aspirations of the father and mother who had nurtured the promises of God for so long within their hearts. Although only three,[12] the young scion of

---

11 This is indeed the very comment of the apostle in Hebrews 11:11. Rotherham: "By faith even Sarah herself received power for *founding* a seed". The implication is not only that Isaac was this foundation, but that Sarah herself knew it.

12 Whilst we not told this expressly, the only Biblical evidence for the moment of child weaning is supportive of this age. The weaning of Samuel, and his subsequent 'lending to the LORD' was accompanied by the offering of a bullock *three years old*, which clearly represented the child (1 Samuel 1:23-25). The likelihood that among the Jews, children were weaned when three years old is also indicated by 2 Chronicles 31:16 where Hezekiah, in making provision for the Levites and priests, includes the children from *three years old* and upwards – which is a presumptive proof that previously to this age they were wholly dependent on their mother for their nourishment. A passage during the Inter-Testamental

the house was already aware that he was a special child, with the first inklings of his destiny becoming apparent.

The mocking taunt of Ishmael

Someone else was aware as well, and took his opportunity after the feast to taunt the little child. Ishmael was seventeen now, and it was not difficult to grasp the reason for his mockery. For many years he had been his father's firstborn, the beginning of many sons who roamed the encampment and considered their position secure. But at this feast that celebrated the first stage in the journey of Isaac's life, it was borne upon Ishmael with great force that his pre-eminence was ended. This youngest son, who was the object of the household's rejoicing, was a threat to his position and a blow to his pride. He did not share the family joy, and being at an age where his behaviour so often outran his self-control, he decided to taunt the boy with something hateful and hurtful.

When the feasting was over, he found a moment to spite Isaac with the idea that he was not really Abraham's son.[13] It wasn't an argument of detail or logic, for Isaac would not have understood. It was a jibe, a saying that could be repeated over and over, simple enough, short enough, sharp enough for a small child to hear and be hurt.[14] He thought that his little shaft of cruelty had been delivered in secret, but he counted not on a mother

---

period is also relevant, in that it is an historical statement concerning Jewish children as uttered by a Jewish mother. "O my son, have pity upon me that bare thee nine months in my womb, and gave thee suck *three years*, and nourished thee, and brought thee up …" (2 Maccabees 7:27).

13 See Chapter 9 – "Teaching in the temple", where the Biblical basis for this idea is expanded.

14 In fact the word for Ishmael's mocking is *tsachaq*, the very word used for Sarah's own laughter in Genesis 21:6. In Ishmael's mouth however, it was the laughter of derision intended to hurt. That it was directed against Isaac is evident from the response of Sarah that follows. Following hard on the heels of the episode in Abimelech's household, the primary point of the mocking was doubtless that Isaac was no special gift from God, but the son of an illicit union with a Gentile.

and her love, and the uncanny ability she had to see all, with the prescience that could only come from having 'eyes in the back of her head'. Sarah had seen, and Sarah had heard all that he had done. She was swift to move.

"And Sarah saw the son of Hagar the Egyptian, which she had born unto Abraham, mocking. Wherefore she said unto Abraham, Cast out this bondwoman and her son: for the son of this bondwoman shall not be heir with my son, even with Isaac." (Genesis 21:9,10)

Hagar had grievously vexed Sarah for many years now. How easy it would have been to respond in petty spitefulness and jealous revenge. But Sarah was moved by higher principles. Not for nothing was she to be known as the 'mother of the faithful'. Now that her faith had triumphed and Isaac was born, her spiritual perception had soared beyond Abraham's. With far greater clarity than he did she see the spiritual needs of the family, and how best they might be met.

Cast out the scorner and strife shall cease

She was not for one moment concerned that Ishmael might yet displace Isaac.[15] She knew the promise of God, and had pondered all these things in her heart for long enough to know that Isaac's part was assured. Sarah's strength of feeling was not motivated by human passion, but by a matter of principle and a matter of practice which both led to the same conclusion.

As to the matter of principle she was clear. Isaac was the chosen seed by the determinate counsel of God, and by the intervention of the Spirit. Anyone who did not believe this could have no part of the Abrahamic promise, nor belong to the Abrahamic household. Denial of the true son and heir was a denial of his father, and there was no room for a different view within the household on this most fundamental of all truths. In the life of this child ran the hope of the promise as the offspring of his

---

15 Note carefully Sarah's words in Genesis 21:10. At best Ishmael might have hoped to be an heir *with* Isaac, but never *instead* of him. God's previous intimation had made that clear (17:20,21).

father, and no aspersion on this truth would be tolerated. If Ishmael denied Isaac's position, then his relationship with Abraham must also be sundered.[16]

The matter of practice was even more profound. Sarah knew with certainty that to raise their son in an atmosphere of godliness required complete harmony within the household of faith. For a family that was to be governed by a reverence for holy matters, and an admiration of things divine, one evil above all others would threaten. The spirit of scornfulness is the essence of all that is hateful in the thinking of the flesh. Its tone of contempt damages spiritual life, and blasts the tender fruit of spiritual thought until it withers. The scorner is disdainful, mocking, disparaging, and it is impossible to bind a household in godly ways when such a spirit challenges and diminishes the principles that are the bedrock of the family. Sarah showed a better grasp of the practical reality of raising their son in a way where the truth could flourish in his heart from the earliest moment. She knew without hesitation what must be done. Ishmael must be cast out for the household to prosper.

Many of Abraham and Sarah's offspring have pondered the crisis of this moment in the patriarchal story. Families can be destroyed when the spirit of scorn for the truth or rebellion is permitted to remain amongst them. Parents alone have the privilege to lay the spiritual foundations and guiding principles of their household. Sometimes, however, a son or daughter whose spirit cavils at those foundations, have been kept within the home, their contrary attitude unhindered and unchecked. Yet left unchallenged, it will only do damage to the siblings of the family. Wisdom of course will always seek to find a way. But the ultimate objective for all our households is that the truth might prosper amongst us, and that our offspring might grow up within an atmosphere that supports the nurture and admonition of the Lord. Where

---

16 The principle is clearly set forth in the memorable words of 1 John 2:23: "Whosoever denieth the Son, the same hath not the Father."

that spirit and intent is compromised, God's counsel still holds true: "cast out the scorner, and contention shall go out".[17]

This counsel is at variance with a world that advocates unconditional love. Yet God, who is full of compassion and boundless in mercy, will not forgive the spirit of obstinate pride, which refuses to bow before His commandments or hearken to His counsels. In the end, those who deny the purpose of God in their lives have no claim to endless mercy, and find that there are always conditions attached to the Father's loving kindness, since all things are subordinate to His grand purpose and not theirs. The love of the Father, generous towards all His children, will forgive them whenever they repent, and seek afresh to honour Him. But His love does not extend to allowing His offspring perpetually to set aside His principles. In the end He holds His children accountable to display the family likeness, else they are not His, and cannot presume upon His love. Abraham's household was to be governed by the same principle, which commanded his children to obedience of the way of the Lord.[18]

Ishmael then must be removed, and not just Ishmael but his mother also. Sarah had judged aright.[19] It wasn't just Ishmael that was to blame. His mother, Hagar, undermined the family principles and values at every step. Despite her place within the encampment, she remained in heart and in spirit an Egyptian through and through.[20] Ishmael's mocking was doubtless the result of spiteful education by Hagar, who could not accept that her own child would not hold primacy in

---

17 Proverbs 22:10.

18 Genesis 18:19.

19 Note Sarah's words, "Cast out *this bondwoman and* her son" (Genesis 21:10).

20 Why else does the record so pointedly describe her as "Hagar the Egyptian" at this vital moment (Genesis 21:9)? And why also does the record subsequently note that she procured a wife for her son "out of Egypt" (Genesis 21:21), unless to indicate that she had never changed her thinking from the profane and heathen ways of Egypt and its gods, from whence she had come (16:1)?

the family. This son manifested the spirit of his mother, but not that of his father. He was born into Abraham's household, and yet was never touched with the goodness and wonder of the truth, which loomed so large in his father's life. It was as if he had never known the way of the Lord. His mother was largely to blame, for it was her influence that resulted in this unsatisfactory outcome. It is a thing of evil when someone who has known the way of righteousness not only turns from it, but transmits all their feelings of hostility to their offspring. This lad revealed all the bitterness, all the animosity, and all the rancour of his mother. Both of them would be harmful to the nurture of Isaac in the fear and admonition of the Lord. Both of them must be sent away. Sarah was clear in her thinking and true in her heart, and her utterance was the speaking forth of the divine testimony.

Abraham and the spirit of sacrifice

The decision, however, was not so clear for Abraham. Ishmael was his son, the beginning of his strength, and the thought of sending him away from the household tore his heart. He knew that the right of the firstborn had passed to Isaac, and delighted in the promise, but sending another son away altogether was a matter too hard for Abraham's large and generous heart. Surely there must be some other way, some other accommodation to their circumstance? There was not, but it would take the interposition of heaven to endorse his wife's wise words, and to make it clear that Sarah had spoken the truth of God in her counsel.[21]

"And God said unto Abraham, Let it not be grievous in thy sight because of the lad, and because of thy bondwoman; in all that Sarah hath said unto thee,

---

21 Perhaps the greatest endorsement of Sarah's wisdom in all that she said comes from the inspired apostolic comment, "Nevertheless *what saith the scripture*? Cast out the bondwoman and her son" (Galatians 4:30). If Sarah's words were themselves deemed to be Scripture, we might also reasonably conclude that the spirit with which she uttered them was also consistent with the divine mind.

145

hearken unto her voice; for in Isaac shall thy seed be called. And also of the son of the bondwoman will I make a nation, because he is thy seed."

(Genesis 21:12,13)

Tender though God's remonstrance with the patriarch was, at no time did he acknowledge Ishmael as Abraham's son. He was the lad, whom God would protect, and he was his seed who would be made a nation, but he was not Abraham's son through whom the promises ran. Abraham could not escape the meaning of the discourse. This one upon whom his bowels did yearn, and whom he would fain remember still, was in the succinct summary of God – the son of the bondwoman. He would never be anything else. The watchful care of the Almighty would ensure his eventual increase, but not as the heir of all that Abraham had. There was nothing wrong with Abraham holding fatherly feelings for his son. But our parental feelings ought never to override divine principles, or overlook a spirit within our children that dishonours God and sets aside His statutes. Indeed, a consequence of the promise and its proper outworking now demanded that Abraham provide the right environment for the spiritual growth and development of his true son, even if it meant the removal of Ishmael in the process.

There was no escape from Sarah's appeal, or from God's endorsement of her words. So, rising up early in the morning, Abraham sent Hagar and Ishmael away, provisioned with food and water, and subject to the providential hand of God. He watched them until the shimmering waves of the distant horizon, and the tears in his own eyes, took their forms and blurred them until they vanished, and his petition ascended that God might bless the lad[22] and his mother in their wanderings. He knew that Ishmael would not die. His casting out would result in exile from the household, but not his untimely death. God Himself had promised the safety of the child,

---

22 Notice how pointed and pervasive this epithet is in the story (Genesis 21:12,17-20).

and his ultimate nationhood.[23] Besides, the wilderness into which they now wandered was not far from where Hagar herself had travelled of her own free will, on an earlier expedition.[24] Despite the privations of the way, God did indeed sustain both child and mother, and the destiny promised to him was realised. But even then the answer of heaven came not for the weeping of Hagar, but because of the voice of the lad. It was the lad and not his mother which occasioned this providential care, as God remained faithful to all that He had promised.

And there was in this action of sending away Ishmael the spirit of sacrifice on Abraham's part towards his wife. He owed this offering to her in response to her entreaty. It was a heavier burden on him to acquiesce, for Ishmael was his child but not Sarah's. This sending away for her sake came not without cost to the man of God, but was rendered thereby more precious for its difficulty.[25] Sarah's words had been an appeal, not an order, which Abraham could decline to uphold if he chose. But God had also endorsed Sarah's words and bidden his co-operation, and Abraham's humility of spirit allowed him to hear and do what his wife had asked, to perceive her intention and understand her spirit. All her focus lay upon the great truth, which the angel had so unequivocally declared, "in Isaac shall thy seed be called". This must be their primary and overwhelming consideration, and she knew it with all the depth of her being. Abraham heard her, and a united decision was made. Blessing would come of it.

Enjoying the son of their love together

With Ishmael gone the sense of strife that had pervaded the family was removed. Now they could enjoy the son of their love together, and focus on raising their child in an

---

23 A truth thrice affirmed (Genesis 17:20; 21:13,18).

24 The wilderness of Beersheba of Genesis 21:14 was presumably not greatly distant from the wilderness between Bered and Kadesh of 16:14.

25 1 Chronicles 21:24; Isaiah 61:8.

atmosphere of complete spiritual co-operation. "Children are well reared when parents are well married",[26] and a godly seed is best nurtured in a godly environment. Sufficient then for the present, that all Abraham's care and attention be devoted now to develop in Isaac an amazing reflection of both Sarah and himself. This would be their labour together, as a mother's love and a father's guidance wove into the fabric of their son's mind and heart all that was true and honest and just and pure and lovely in God's truth. Isaac would grow to become the living embodiment of his parents. He displayed the same disposition for reverential worship as his father,[27] and the same spirit of submission under trial as his mother.[28] He revealed the same willingness to co-operate with others as his father,[29] and the same awareness of providential guidance in life as his mother.[30] He showed the same wisdom to avoid unnecessary conflict as his father,[31] and the same resolution to uphold the divine intention as his mother.[32] He was completely united with them both.[33] This boy would indeed prove to be the son of their love, the perfect expression of their image and likeness, the child of their household above all others who, being commanded, would keep the way of the Lord.

How could Abraham and Sarah know at this moment how crucial that development of Isaac would be? In the mercy of God's wisdom, they were not aware as yet how completely their own faith, and that of their son, would be tested to the uttermost as their story unfolded. The Spirit would veil these formative years of the young

---

26 The phrase is considered to come from John Thomas: "Children cannot be well reared unless parents are well married" as quoted in *Selah*, page 91; *Herald of the Kingdom*, Vol. 3, page 216.

27 Cp. Genesis 26:24,25 and 12:7,8.

28 Cp. Genesis 26:20-22 and 12:14-17.

29 Cp. Genesis 26:28-31 and 21:22-32.

30 Cp. Genesis 26:22,23 and 21:1,2,6.

31 Cp. Genesis 26:16,17 and 13:7-9.

32 Cp. Genesis 27:33 and 21:9,10.

33 Genesis 22:6; 24:67.

Isaac, in much the same way that the childhood of Christ would be shrouded in privacy, apart from his notable visit to Jerusalem when twelve. But the result was very similar. When Isaac (not mentioned since the great feast on the day of his weaning), stepped once more onto the stage of family life, he was immediately and dramatically at the point of his greatest test, and at the moment of his deepest connection with his father and mother. This child, whose delay had caused such anguish, and whose coming had brought such joy, was now to become the focus of their greatest trial.

The last and fiercest strife

"And it came to pass after these things, that God did tempt Abraham, and said unto him, Abraham: and he said, Behold, here I am. And he said, Take now thy son, thine only son Isaac, whom thou lovest, and get thee into the land of Moriah; and offer him there for a burnt offering upon one of the mountains which I will tell thee of." (Genesis 22:1,2)

The angel had come one afternoon, as the sun began to sink towards eventide. His words were quietly spoken, but would forever change their lives. He asked the old man to take Isaac, the heir of the household and offer him up for a burnt offering to God Almighty. The request was astounding, incomprehensible, shattering. But there was no mistake as to what the angel had said. Abraham shared the words of the command from heaven with Sarah. This was something they must face together. He could not possibly leave without her knowing, for this test bound them as one in the intensity of its agony. Besides, they would be gone for several days at the least in this march to Moriah, and back again. Despite the grief he knew she would feel, Sarah must know, must share, must join with him in submission to the angelic command. It was not just the trial of his faith, it was the trial of their faith, and they would face it together, as they had long since learned to do in all the circumstances of their life. A desperate prayer was offered that night, as aged parents clung to each other in fellowship of need, and implored the God of the spirits of all flesh that He would deliver them and their son from the terrible weight of this burden of obedience. The Father heard all their cries, and was not unmindful of their fears. But deliverance lay in submission to the divine will. It always has.

"And Abraham rose up early in the morning, and saddled his ass, and took two of his young men with him, and Isaac his son, and clave the wood for the burnt offering, and rose up, and went unto the place of which God had told him." (Genesis 22:3)

As the father and the son departed, the brave smile and lifted hand of Sarah's farewell, were the salute of a woman who had entered fully into this journey of faith with her husband, wherever it might lead them. The mother would remain behind, imprisoned in her own private realm of suffering for these next several days. But though absent in body, she travelled with them in spirit, and the tears of all her maternal love and yearning flowed unchecked as four distant figures vanished over the last hill northwards that her straining eye could see. For her the gladness of Isaac's birth, almost indescribable in its wonder, would now be matched by an anguish that felt almost unbearable in its pain. How could she know on the fateful morn that her own experience would cast such a long shadow over the holy writ, until it reached at last the Gospel page? There in a time far off, there would come another woman of God who rejoiced in the Bethlehem birth of her boy, but whose heart was absolutely broken at the cross, in beholding the suffering of her precious son. The sword, which would wound the soul of the woman of Nazareth, had long since pierced the heart of the woman of Beersheba, in bitter foreshadowing of a mother's agony on Golgotha's height.[34]

34 There is something especially beautiful about contemplating Sarah's role in foreshadowing the experience of Mary at the foot of the cross, just as we recognise in Abraham a cameo of the love of the Father in offering His own son. Both types are valid, and are intended for our deepest reflection and learning.

And yet if life had taught them anything, this husband and wife of the hills and valleys, it was that God's will, forever inscrutable and unfathomable, would nevertheless prove true. All their life the story of the promised seed had been the dominant theme woven into the record of their union. Throughout their life as the revelation of God's purpose unfolded, their faith had surged and wavered, risen and fallen, ebbed and flowed, and now that seed, Isaac, was a man full grown in body and mind. The fulness of all His promises to them had rested on this son. They still did. And if that was so, then God could, and would still bring them to pass. How He might do it was not for them as yet to know. Their place was to submit unto Him in unreserved obedience. Here, now, in mutual surrender, their faith would finally be seen as triumphant, proved by nothing less than their readiness to obey in the matter of the son who was 'their only one'.

Abraham found the journey distressing, because of the chaos of his thoughts and the nearness of his son. He could not know that the wood Isaac shouldered, as he marched so readily beside him, would portend across the span of time the very cross that would lie so heavy on Messiah's bruised and bleeding back.[35] But just as Sarah would know the bitterness of the Lord's own mother, so now he would begin to know the love and the pain of the Father Himself, who spared not His own Son, but delivered him up for us all.[36] No other man would be brought to the brink of such awareness. No other man would know with such depth the feelings of God Himself, when in His foreknowledge He permitted wicked hands to take and slay His Son. And Abraham's consuming pain was intensified by the spirit of Isaac, who with dawning realisation that there was no other lamb than he, marched nevertheless with his father, treading in harmony with his steps and walking in unity with his

---

35 John 19:17.
36 Romans 8:32.

purpose. To journey, both of them together,[37] to such a destination and such an outcome was for Abraham an experience at once exquisite and excruciating.

> "And they came to the place which God had told him of; and Abraham built an altar there, and laid the wood in order, and bound Isaac his son, and laid him on the altar upon the wood. And Abraham stretched forth his hand, and took the knife to slay his son."
>
> (Genesis 22:9,10)

The man prepared to die on the height of Moriah allowed himself to be taken and bound as the sacrificial victim. There was no struggle, for he did not contend. In an amazing display of loving obedience, he revealed who he was by his conduct under trial. He was the son of Abraham, the Friend of God, and the son of Sarah, the Princess of God's People. How wonderfully different their personalities were, and yet the supreme virtue that united them both was their preparedness to submit to the will of God, even when it ran contrary to their natural inclinations. This was the great characteristic which they had together bequeathed unto their child. It reached its climax in this story, as Isaac lay unresisting on the altar, bound in voluntary submission, ready to render obedience unto death with the quivering blade poised above him. Surely at that moment, he was revealed as their son!

In the mind of the patriarch, he had brought the knife down and made the offering, certain with all his heart that God would raise his son.[38] It was the commitment of faith that the angel sought, and instantly he called out to Abraham to stay his hand. The ram was found

---

37 The repetition of this phrase in the record in Genesis 22:6,8 is one of the most tender foreshadowings of the unbreakable bond between the Father Himself and His Son, who in like spirit would work together for the purpose of salvation.

38 For such is the clear intimation of Paul in Hebrews 11:17-19, made more clear by the Greek tenses for the word 'offering' used twice in the passage, and similarly in James 2:21: "when he *had offered* Isaac his son upon the altar."

and offered instead, the mount named to memorialise the future significance of that place, and the final aspect of the promise declared which would itself dwell on the triumph of Messiah's saving work.

"And in thy seed shall all the nations of the earth be blessed; because thou hast obeyed my voice. So Abraham returned unto his young men, and they rose up and went together to Beersheba; and Abraham dwelt at Beersheba." (Genesis 22:18,19)

With the testimony of heaven revealed it was a gladdened father and rejoicing son who made their way back to the waiting servants. Abraham's words, spoken in sure faith had been true. He and the lad had gone yonder and worshipped, and were now returned. Several days later, shouts from the watchers on the camp perimeter indicated that the travellers were nigh, and soon after the men were within the encampment. There was a stir between the tamarisks, and Abraham and Isaac stepped into the clearing of the tent to greet the woman who turned herself and saw them standing right there.[39] Sarah gasped, trembled with the weakness of relief and the gladness of joy that cascaded through her being, and burst into tears. They were home, they were safe, they were alive, both of them!

Abraham met his wife's eyes with a look that shone with the tears of love and understanding, as they wept together, and embraced their son. When finally they retired for the night, their evening prayer sent aloft to the Lord, the everlasting God, gave expression to depths which neither had known before. It was a moment of transcendent joy and oneness in their journey together. Faith had been made perfect, purified under the most intense of trials, and the incense of their thankfulness

---

39 We are not told how they met, but it is surely possible to contemplate that the experience of Sarah would match the moment of Mary Magdalene when she "turned herself" and saw the Lord in the garden. That first moment of greeting one thought to be dead was certainly experienced by Sarah, and it seems fitting to see another foreshadowing in this moment (John 20:15,16).

rose as the sweet savour of two made one in supplication. There would be no hindering of this prayer. They were in every respect – heirs together.

8

ENFOLDING EACH OTHER IN DEATH TOGETHER
(Genesis 23:1 – 25:10)

BEERSHEBA had been their home now for twenty years or more. The gentle tamarisks planted by Abraham[1] still thrived in the desert soil, their roots struck deep around the fertile spot where lay the 'well of the oath'. Sarah recalled the moment when they had first come to this place, for it was here that her son had been raised from infancy.[2] Every childhood memory that her boy had was nurtured in Beersheba, for his entire life had been spent here. She remembered every stage of his early years; from the moment she had first cradled him in her arms, to his first tottering steps, and his first faltering words. She remembered the celebration they had held on the day he was weaned, and the moment of his manhood some years later. She remembered the anguish of soul she had felt on the morning of their march to Moriah, and the unbelievable gladness that flooded her very being when she held him close upon his return. It was her triumph of faith as well as Abraham's that led to the marvellous blessings on the holy mount. For no less than he, did she believe with zealous certainty, that the One who could bring forth life from a body as good as dead, could also restore life to a body that was dead, and that He would do so to be faithful to His promises. The mother of Messiah would not only share with Sarah the tragedy of an impending

---

1 Genesis 21:33.
2 The assumption is made here that when Abimelech invited Abraham to move from Gerar and settle elsewhere within his kingdom (Genesis 20:15), Abraham moved immediately to Beersheba. On this reckoning, the subsequent dispute, resolution and covenant made with Abimelech in that place are indicative of Abraham being already settled there (21:25-34). This then would be the scene of Isaac's childhood years from infancy.

death, but also the joy of a son's wondrous resurrection. With the receiving back of her son from the 'dead', it seemed to Sarah that a whole chapter in their lives had come to a close, and she would fain begin the last one elsewhere.

Home at last to Hebron

Often when old age comes, there comes with it a yearning for the old things and the old places of earlier days. The journey taken by Abraham and Isaac had led them through Hebron, for it lay directly on the road to Salem, moving north as it climbed the Judaean hills. Hebron was a place already special in the minds of the patriarchal couple, and it was to here therefore that they returned in the process of time.[3] The old oak tree still stood, and beneath its canopy the master's servants pitched the household tents with familiar ease. The flocks were settled on the old lands of nearby pasture, selected by the old shepherds who remembered the sweetest grazing from twenty years before. The old altar was repaired with fresh stones from the rocky slopes, and from this place the smoke of the lamb of the peace offering rose again, as Abraham and Sarah breathed their prayers of thankfulness and praise to the Most High God. They dwelt in Hebron, in fellowship with each other, and in fellowship with God. Abraham and Sarah had come home. Although their tents still proclaimed their pilgrim spirit, they felt settled in this their old resting place. How often is life's journey a sweeping circle that returns us at the last to our old original place and position in the truth. We finally learn to value the ancient landmark, and to abide content within its boundary. Sometimes it takes a lifetime to return to Hebron, but when we do, we find fellowship with God. Here then, in this place, sanctified by its association with their earlier pilgrimage, Abraham and Sarah sojourned, content to see the son of their love grown to a strength and vigour that gladdened old hearts. Isaac was mightily affected by the blessing of

---

3   See Appendix 6 – "Why did Sarah die in Hebron?"

time spent in this place with his aged parents. Although the years of his manhood were spent in the lands of the south, he likewise returned in old age to the city of Hebron where the cave of Machpelah was.[4]

The death and burial of Sarah

"And Sarah was an hundred and seven and twenty years old: these were the years of the life of Sarah. And Sarah died in Kirjath-arba; the same is Hebron in the land of Canaan: and Abraham came to mourn for Sarah and to weep for her."   (Genesis 23:1,2)

The last chapter of their life together was about to close. The years of the life of Sarah at one hundred and seven and twenty were complete, and one day the old woman died. A handmaid found her and went, sorrowing, to inform the master. Abraham's heart turned to stone at the news, and he sat down heavily with that expression of pain and bewilderment that marks the face of the bereaved. For once he was unable to command his household, and it was left to faithful women to go quietly about the business of preparing the body for mourning. Tender hands lifted the lifeless form and carried it into a tent where the body might be anointed and arranged. Soon, the hills of Hebron reverberated with the cries and wails of a household in mourning. When the women were satisfied that their mistress lay with dignity even in death, Abraham was sent for that he might weep alone with his wife. He came to the place where they had laid her. A servant stood at attention, a solitary sentinel, charged with the honour of guarding the tent where Sarah's body lay. As Abraham approached the tabernacle of the dead, the servant bowed low in respect and moved aside to let his master pass. Abraham drew level with the man, looked, recognised him, and was thankful. It was good to know that Eliezer stood watch.

Abraham stooped, then trod forward, and letting the flap fall behind him slowly straightened. He was alone

---

4   Genesis 35:27.

with his beloved Sarah. Within the tent was a bier[5] resting on a platform of stones. The bier was a simple wooden frame, plain and unadorned, for there is no point in gilding death. On this the body lay. The curtains were thick enough to prevent the light of day, and two oil lamps placed at the two ends of the bier, lighted the tent instead. The lamps cast their steady glow, washing the tent walls with the yellow warmth of olive light. The light fell upon Sarah's face, but left it unwarmed, for drained of the blood wherein is the life, her countenance had that ghastly pallor that no light can cheer. Death's colour is a cold hue. The body lay in the utter stillness of death that alarms the living. He half expected her to stir and move, but would have jumped with fear if she had. He stood beside the bier and looked upon the woman who had shared this journey of faith with him. There was a terrible feeling within that the journey was somehow over, even though he was still alive. He remembered so many things, so many moments as he stood there, a changing, jumbled, vivid set of recollections that came without prompting or conscious thought. Looking at Sarah now, it seemed so hard to believe that all was finished, the story told. And yet her motionless form was witness to the terrible finality of death, proof that she had gone the way of all flesh. Their mortal life together was ended.

A time to weep ... a time to mourn

As Abraham stood, and looked, and thought, the sorrows of death encompassed him, and he felt the welling up of the fountain of tears that now came, an outpouring of grief and anguish that flowed unabated. He bent low over the body and groaned aloud with the pain of the bereft, and between the terrible sobs that engulfed and racked his entire body, he cried the cry of the lost one that is left. It was the cry of all those who have lost a marriage companion, and who already feel the ache of a

---

5　The bier upon which the body lay was, in effect, a funeral couch used to carry the dead to the place of their burial (cp. 2 Samuel 3:31; Luke 7:14).

new and bitter loneliness that seems as if it cannot ever be assuaged.

When Sarah died, a thousand of their secrets died with her. She would never pass them on to others, for death completely sealed her lips. But with Sarah gone, he could not share them either. No one else would really know, could really understand. He was left alone with their private, personal, precious memories, left to guard and keep the story for both of them. From this time forth he would spend long moments in personal reverie, for it is the burden and privilege of the widowed to journey in mind to places where once they walked together, to smile and weep anew at long forgotten but altogether lovely things.

Eventually his weeping ceased. For the moment the well was completely emptied and the stream run dry. They would refill quite soon enough. With a long sigh, Abraham stood upright, and took deep breath to begin life again, without his heart's companion. Only Eliezer had heard his master's mourning cry, and he would keep his own counsel.

Glancing again at Sarah, he was struck by the openness of her empty, staring eyes. Her eyes had been so expressive in life. He remembered them now, gleaming with interest, warm with love, flashing with disapproval, softened with concern. He recalled them sparkling with merriment, and clouded with grief. Her eyes had been turned towards him to warn and to plead, to laugh and to cry, for he had seen them both gleeful and sad. What secrets they had shared through the kinship of their eyes. And now her eyes gazed, open yet sightless, on the tent pole above, with not a flicker of recognition and not a trace of life. Never again would her eyes dance or smile, for her memory was forgotten.

Gently he bent and kissed her farewell, a chaste salute on alabaster lips. A single stray tear fell from his cheek to hers and he left it there. Reaching forth with a hand that shook slightly, he slowly closed her eyes.[6] Somehow the action was faintly comforting, for as he smoothed them shut her face seemed more peaceful, her stillness now the mark of sleep, as if her whole body had composed itself for undisturbed rest. She had gone to her 'long home'.[7] Abraham rose up from over the face of his dead, and withdrew from the tent blinking as his eyes adjusted again to the light of the living. It was time for others to come, for the mourners to go about the streets and weep for this woman whom he had loved. And there was something else he must attend to immediately. Sarah's body must be buried without delay,[8] and for that to occur he needed to purchase a place for her burial, right here in Hebron, where their home had been.

The purchase of a final resting place

"And Abraham stood up from before his dead, and spake unto the sons of Heth, saying, I am a stranger and a sojourner with you: give me a possession of a buryingplace with you, that I may bury my dead out of my sight."　　　　　　　　　　　　　　(Genesis 23:3,4)

The death of his help meet prompted him this day to an action that he had only performed once before. At the beginning of his journeyings in the land, he had purchased a parcel of ground.[9] Now at the end of his

---

6　It would seem that the custom was for the next of kin to close the eyes of their dead and give them a parting kiss, as a final mark of respect and affection (Genesis 46:4; 50:1).

7　Ecclesiastes 12:5: this beautiful expression is literally, *beth olahm* – the house of eternity.

8　It was the custom to bury bodies on the day of their death (John 11:17,39; Acts 5:6,9,10).

9　Acts 7:16 is to be taken as an inspired comment that adds further detail to the Genesis narrative. The most likely time for this to have occurred was in Genesis 12:6,7, Abraham buying a plot of land sufficient for the erection of his altar, and which may have included a burial cave on the site. It is a further possibility that after Abraham's death the land reverted to the Amorites, until the time of Jacob, who then claimed his grandfather's portion by force as suggested in Genesis 48:22. He subsequently enlarged his holding by purchase of the further parcel mentioned in Genesis

pilgrimage, he would buy another. He needed to provide a sure possession, so that his beloved could sleep in peace. Only with Sarah at rest in undisturbed security could he himself move on. So Abraham the pilgrim became Abraham the purchaser, and that very day sought an audience with the sons of Heth. His request was simple and clear. Despite his status as a sojourner among them, he sought permission to purchase a burying place.

For Abraham to be obliged to enter into this transaction was itself a paradox. As the rightful heir, he had been promised all this land as far as the eye could see, yet he needed permission to buy one small piece,[10] and even then to pay an exorbitant sum for it as events would prove. As the Friend of God he had been promised a seed who should possess the gate of his enemies,[11] yet his purchase needed the approval of the gate of the Hittites before it could proceed.[12] As the father of the faithful he had been promised offspring which would be multiplied as the stars of heaven, yet even now, as he came to bury Sarah, it was the people of the land who were many and their sepulchres numerous. He, as yet, had but one single star of the galaxy that had been promised. Yet Abraham was not deterred. His very statement that he was a stranger and sojourner declared plainly that he believed the promise, and that he awaited the county and city that God would prepare for him.

33:19, all this finally becoming an inheritance of the children of Joseph, as witnessed by Joshua 24:32. There will have been many actions of Abraham and Sarah which are not recorded, but which nevertheless occurred, and Acts 7:16 is but one example of several New Testament passages which add previously unknown details to the Old Testament narrative. John Carter reaches a similar conclusion in examining supposed contradictions in the speech of Stephen in Acts 7 (see *The Oracles of God*, pages 95,96).

10 This is the force of Stephen's argument in Acts 7:5. Whatever portion of the land Abraham claimed in his lifetime, it came not by inheritance but by purchase, indicating that the promise of possession still lay in the future.

11 Genesis 22:17.

12 Genesis 23:18.

In the meantime, however, his pilgrim status would continue, and so his negotiations began. From the outset he knew the very portion he desired, and would have infinitely preferred to have asked for that portion outright, and paid without further ado. But there were protocols to be observed in the purchase of land, and the process could not be hurried or foreshortened. Besides, it was by no means sure that he would be successful in his request. At question was the issue of whether a stranger such as Abraham should even be permitted to buy land at all. Behind the elaborate courtesy, which addressed him as a lord and mighty prince and offered him the choice among their own sepulchres, was a clever inducement to ensure that he remained as a landless dependant. But Abraham persevered. He could not, would not bury Sarah among the faithless and profane. This was the woman who had walked with him as heir together of the promise, the mother of all the promised seed. He would not allow her bones to be mingled with the dust of dead Canaanites.

The cave of Machpelah and its field

"If it be your mind that I should bury my dead out of my sight; hear me, and intreat for me to Ephron the son of Zohar, that he may give me the cave of Machpelah, which he hath, which is in the end of his field; for as much money as it is worth he shall give it me for a possession of a buryingplace amongst you."

(Genesis 23:8,9)

Seizing on their willingness for him at least to bury his dead, he bowed low before the elders of the gate, and entreated them to act as mediators between himself and Ephron. This immediately turned his request from the general to the specific. He obviously had a particular property in mind, and Abraham declared his interest at once in the cave of Machpelah. Ephron's offer to give Abraham the place without cost was the customary reply that began such a purchase. It was an empty gesture without honest intent or meaning, and yet it indicated at least that Ephron was prepared to negotiate, and

162

possibly to sell. And there was something else as well. In Ephron's apparent generosity, which of course was to be refused, he had carefully widened the scope of the transaction. Abraham had sought a cave, but Ephron now offered him the whole field in which the cave lay. The patriarch understood and responded in kind. He referred to the field, and hastened to assure Ephron that he would not consider anything other than paying an excellent price for the same. All this was done after the time-honoured custom of the day. Such dealings were conducted in an apparently gracious and leisurely way, but concealed nevertheless behind the pleasantries a careful determination to bargain to best advantage.

Although Abraham spoke with Ephron ben Zohar, the words were exchanged through the many who assembled to act as go-betweens. Everyone became involved in the transaction, debating its merits as if the purchase were their own. To assemble in such a way was counted not as a burden, but an enjoyable task. After all, to hear the sagacious skill of the buyer in reducing the article to a thing of naught, and the shrewd cunning of the seller in defending its supreme worth, was an exchange to be relished. And the presence of this multitude was the best evidence to make the transaction sure. These witnesses in the gate could vouch for every little detail that had been discussed and agreed, and without them the arrangement was of no legal standing. Now that the preliminaries were ended, it was time to begin the business of bargaining.

"And Abraham hearkened unto Ephron; and Abraham weighed to Ephron the silver, which he had named in the audience of the sons of Heth, four hundred shekels of silver, current money with the merchant. And the field of Ephron, which was in Machpelah, which was before Mamre, the field, and the cave which was therein, and all the trees that were in the field, that were in all the borders round about, were made sure unto Abraham for a possession

163

in the presence of the children of Heth, before all that went in at the gate of his city." (Genesis 23:16-18)

Ephron priced the land at a mere four hundred shekels, a comfortably large figure that allowed him ample room for negotiation. But he offered it with the air and flourish of a kindly benefactor intent on helping out another in distress. It was a skilful opening. Abraham however, had not become a wealthy man through indolence or ignorance. The patriarch was not deceived by Ephron's smile, or by Ephron's sum, and yet to the astonishment of all, he paid full money without discussion or debate. The sons of Heth shook their heads sadly at the patriarch's price, for it told eloquently how much he grieved. This once, the seller rejoiced.[13] For Abraham, sick at heart with the loss of his beloved, had no taste for commerce this day.

There was a deeper reason as well, which Gentiles could not understand. This purchase was his final salute of respect and affection for his wife. No cost was too great to secure a place that would be wholly hers, then his also, when he joined her. He knew that he must pay the full sum in order to feel the full cost of this final offering of dedication made on her behalf. An honourable burial demanded an honourable price, and he would pay no less. It is the spirit that all his offspring must show, as they strive to give full measure in their service.[14]

The price served also to put the matter beyond dispute. He might be a stranger among them, but Abraham now owned this field, and everyone knew it.[15] All of it was his, every flower of the field, every rock and every tree, the landmarks which declared its boundaries, and at its nether end, the cave that he desired for the possession of a burying place. And the transaction was not only made

---

13 Whereas usually the buyer did (Proverbs 20:14; Ezekiel 7:12).

14 1 Chronicles 21:24; Isaiah 61:8.

15 The very expressions in Genesis 23:17,18 convey the legal terms of this purchase, with the boundaries and contents of the land being described, and also the witnesses who could thereafter attest to the transaction having taken place.

certain for Abraham, but it stood the test of passing years, even to several generations.[16] Into this rocky sanctuary, hewn by the Almighty, and set apart within its own field, he brought the body of Sarah his wife, and laid her to rest. But although Sarah's body was interred, his pain was not buried, and Abraham still came daily to weep[17] and to grieve. Not until the days of mourning[18] were fully accomplished and his tears were finally stemmed, would he cease his visitations to the cave of Machpelah.

And Abraham gave unto Isaac all that he had

With Sarah gone, the story of Abraham was also almost ended. Theirs had been such a wondrous unity of mind and purpose that they had truly walked as heirs together. Death dissolved the union, and left the man alone in his smallness. Together they had trodden in high places, for their greatness lay in the heights they had conquered as husband and wife. Now Abraham was left alone in the valley of his old age and, bereft of his partner, ceased to be the mighty man of renown admired in earlier days. It was time for him to decrease. All his focus now needed to be on the establishment of Isaac's position in the family.

The episode on Mount Moriah had revealed the tremendous faith and obedience of Isaac, and the marvellous affinity they knew together as father and son. Isaac had shown just how excellent a man he was, and how worthy of inheriting his father's portion. The moment had come for his inheritance to be given. This was to be the first step in Abraham's closing of his own account, as he sought now to step aside and establish Isaac as the new head of the household.

"And Abraham gave all that he had unto Isaac. But unto the sons of the concubines, which Abraham had, Abraham gave gifts, and sent them away from Isaac

---

16 Genesis 49:30-32.

17 Cp. John 11:31.

18 Cp. Genesis 50:10; 1 Samuel 31:13; Job 2:13. The three days after death were called the 'days of weeping', followed by four further 'days of lamentations', making up the seven 'days of mourning'.

his son, while he yet lived, eastward, unto the east country." (Genesis 25:5,6)

The son of Hagar had already been banished before Isaac had grown to manhood. Now the sons of Abraham's other concubine were removed into the vast lands that sprawled eastwards, from where Abraham's household dwelt. Keturah's little men were all fully grown now, for Isaac was younger than them all, yet he himself was nigh on forty years old.[19] Abraham gave gifts to all these sons to help establish their own households, and they were then sent away to conquer other lands and build their own dominions. But unto his 'only begotten' son, the child of Sarah, he gave his substance, even all that he had. Isaac was left in undisputed, undisturbed possession of his father's goods to be the continuer of his father's name.

The finding of a bride for Isaac

Yet Isaac still grieved at the loss of the mother he had loved so dearly. Abraham might choose to live his remaining years in a state of singleness, but Isaac was young and his whole life, in God's good hand, still stretched out ahead of him. It was time that his life moved on. The young man needed his own help meet. When therefore Sarah had been dead for almost three years, Abraham bestirred himself to one final special enterprise. He would find a wife for Isaac, their son. The fact that God had blessed him in all things thus far, was proof to Abraham that He would bless him in this endeavour also. For if Abraham was to be blessed as the father of a multitude, and if Sarah was to be blessed as the mother of kings, then Isaac must marry a godly woman and raise a godly seed from whom these others would spring.

Abraham had already decided that marriage to the profane and pagan offspring of Ham was unacceptable. His whole life since God's calling had been spent in separation from these, and he was not about to

---

19 See Appendix 4 – "When were Keturah's children born?"

compromise his position now by sending out his son to view the daughters of the land. Godly companions are not to be deliberately sought among the Gentiles who walk in uncleanness, but amongst the people of God. It has ever been so for Abraham's family, where the search for one who is a kindred spirit in things divine does not begin with outside associations, but from within the family of God.[20]

Yet within his own household a suitable damsel was not to be found. He would have to search further afield among his own kindred, who although outside the land were nevertheless worshippers of the same God.[21] He knew that his brother had begotten a large family, and that there were maidens in the house of Nahor, any one of whom might be a suitable wife for his son.[22] It was time then to travel to Haran and visit his kindred. But the journey was great and Abraham old. He decided that it was not necessary for him to visit in person, but that he would use a family ambassador instead.

He would not (he thought), send Isaac on this journey. As the son of the promise and heir of the land, Abraham felt that it was wrong for Isaac to leave this place and return to the country out of which he himself had been called. Abraham needed another who could be trusted to act on his behalf, and he had just such a one in his household. For Eliezer was more than his master's

---

20 From time to time, someone within the bonds of the truth has met and been drawn towards someone from without. Where the truth is clearly set forth as an imperative within one's personal life, and as a prerequisite for future marriage, such a friendship may well act to stir an interest in spiritual things. Even here, however, care needs to be taken that the reason for baptism is not affected by the emotion of a friendship that prevails above becoming committed to Christ with all sincerity of heart. Biblical counsel, despite such occurrences, has never been to encourage such friendships, but rather the very reverse (Genesis 34:1,2; 2 Corinthians 6:14-18).

21 Genesis 31:53.

22 There had evidently been communication between the branches of his family for Abraham to be in receipt of this information (Genesis 22:20-24).

steward. He shared his master's mind. He could be instructed as to the qualities he should seek in searching for a bride, and could be depended upon to fulfil his charge in faithfulness. And beyond Eliezer's own careful, prayerful spirit, would be the watchful eye of another who would help in making the choice. For Abraham was convinced that the special angel who had talked with him for most of his life, would travel with his servant and guide the outcome.

When the patriarch had thought the matter through and resorted to prayer, he called his trusted retainer and gave him instructions. The thing was so important that he required an absolute assurance that his words would be followed. He received it. For by solemn oath, Eliezer pledged his part to Abraham, in this final adventure of faith that would secure a bride for Isaac. Eliezer was like a son to Abraham and might have been his heir. And now he travelled to help secure the future of the very one who had displaced him, the real son and true heir. Yet for all that, he would fulfil his task with loyalty and love, for noble and true, he would serve Abraham's son as if he were the master himself. In every way he was his master's man, and he worshipped his master's God. Abraham's household really had become his spiritual offspring, even in his lifetime. When the little cavalcade of laden camels left the camp to begin their northwards plod, an old man waved goodbye and breathed a prayer to God for the success of this journey.

When Isaac and Rebekah met at eventide

Abraham was content to wait now for Almighty God to bless this endeavour, which was moved by faith in Him. His son, however, found it more difficult to abide in patience. His father's actions had restored him from despondency, and for the first time in many moons he had thought on something other than the death of his mother.[23] In fact, he had thought more and more about the family in Haran he had never met, and wondered

---

23 Genesis 24:67.

whether their steward had arrived there, and whether he was returning, and with whom? Eliezer had been gone for many weeks now, and there was none who awaited his arrival more eagerly than Isaac. His whole being tingled with a strange sense of expectancy, and he found the waiting almost unbearable. And now another day had almost passed with no news of the travellers. He would pray about the matter when the duties of the day were done.

When the sun slipped peacefully over the distant hills, the whole landscape was subtly altered. Far horizons were washed with purple and magenta, and deepening shadows softened the sharpness of hill and valley into a pleasing gentleness. The business and bustle of the day was ceased, and even the air seemed stilled in anticipation of the hours of slumber that soon would come. Dusk was a special time for prayer, and its creeping mantle of quietness gave time for that reflection and thought which should precede the lifting up of hands. Isaac had left the encampment, and had gone out into the solitude of the countryside for prayer. He knelt in the open field and with bowed head implored God for the success of Eliezer's mission and his safe return.

He knew why he prayed thus. One of the camels returning would bear his bride. Yet for all that he prayed with sincerity and earnest zeal, and wondrously did God answer him. Never had the fervent prayer of a righteous man availed more than this eventide petition of Isaac. For when his prayer was ended, he looked up and beheld the camels afar off. He stood up to watch their approach, and shortly after one of the camels stopped and he saw a woman alight and cover herself with a veil before coming on. The sight was enough to quicken his heartbeat, and within minutes Eliezer was before him to present the daughter of Bethuel of Haran. Isaac looked upon the woman who was to be his life's companion, and they shared their first smile together. He would grow to love this Rebekah, and she him, in good time. Love after marriage, which grows by a mutual commitment

169

to divine principles, is far better than romance before marriage, where such a commitment does not exist.

It was a happy little company that journeyed back to the encampment by the well. Some of the men had ridden on ahead and the news had therefore already reached the encampment that Eliezer had returned, and that the Lord had blessed his mission. Night had fallen but the fires blazed brightly, and all were astir with eager curiosity as the camel train came near. Great were the rejoicings of the household, as they awaited the appearance of the bride from afar, and it was Isaac himself who proudly brought her into the tents of his people. He was anxious that Abraham his father should meet his bride and, if truth be told, his father was as anxious as he. He made his way to Abraham's tent without delay. 'Father, this is Rebekah', said Isaac, and drew her forward. When Rebekah bowed before the patriarch, and then straightened to smile shyly at him, she gave a gasp of surprise. For the old man before her was exactly like grandfather Nahor, with the same beard of white, the same tilt of the head, and why, the same twinkle in his eye. Abraham knew what she thought and nodded at her with a smile of understanding. 'I am indeed like him, am I not?' he asked, and she smiled and nodded in return, taken with the patriarch's shrewd reading of her thoughts.

Abraham, looking on his brother's offspring, also saw the family likeness, and strangely enough or not so strange, he caught glimpses of Sarah in this quick and lively girl.[24] It had been over threescore years since he had set sight on another woman from his family and the experience was an eerie one, conjuring up long forgotten thoughts and memories. He would enjoy spending time with Rebekah and coming to know her better, but his first impression was a joyous one. Isaac took Rebekah off to meet the women of the house, and to introduce them

24 Cp. Genesis 12:11; 26:7.

also to Deborah,[25] who would care for Rebekah in this new place. Within a short while, the women were happily engaged in discussing the preparations that would need to be made. Soon the time of feasting and laughter would come, and there was much to plan.

There was one more thing that Abraham needed to do before this day ended, one more conversation that he needed to have. He sent a young man with a message to the tent of his eldest servant who had rule over all that he had. Eliezer had but shortly returned to see his own wife and children within the encampment, but he came promptly at the patriarch's invitation, knowing that the old man would want to hear the story of his journey and the news of his brother's household. He had engaged in such conversations many times before, and it was an honoured ritual between them that he would render a full account of his dealings whenever he had fulfilled a charge on his master's behalf. No other charge, however, had been as important as this one, and he was ready when the request came. It would be a happy conversation this night, because the successful outcome of his mission was already known. But his master would receive the most detailed account, and he would take pleasure in recalling every moment of a journey that had been so wondrously overshadowed by angelic guidance and care. When he arrived Abraham arose and embraced him warmly as a friend. His thanks to Eliezer were warm and sincere, and he felt a rush of gratitude for the simple faithfulness of this special man who had served him with such self-denial. Sitting down beside the fire, he urged Eliezer to recount the whole adventure to him, and he listened and questioned with such absorbed attention and interest that his servant was proud of the patriarch's trust and esteem. 'It was just as you said, master' said Eliezer, 'the angel went with us', and he proceeded to tell to an attentive Abraham the wonderful story of a woman at a well.

---

25 She had come with Rebekah from the household of Bethuel (Genesis 24:59), and would be with her throughout her life (35:8).

Changes within Abraham's household

The day of the marriage was ended, and the feasting done. The singers were silent and the dancers stilled. Night had come and the entire household had retired for sleep, warmed and filled and tired, yet content after such a season of rejoicing. Abraham, finding himself at last alone in his tent, was satisfied but weary. He had rejoiced with Isaac on this the day of his espousals, and had truly shared in his gladness of heart. Yet now, alone and in private, he suddenly wept soft tears, grieving for the fact that his Sarah had not been standing beside him, and sorrowing that they had not been able to share this day of their son's marriage together. But he knelt and gave thanks on behalf of them both, that God had blessed their son with a suitable bride, and he sent aloft to the Most High a petition that He would guide and protect the young couple on their journey through life. Their son had come of age.

Every day Abraham looked upon Isaac and saw Sarah's likeness imprinted upon him. In a sense Sarah lived on in her son and he was glad of it, and glad also that Isaac's life was now unfolding to the fulness of its promise. Abraham nodded to himself slowly. It seemed right for the change in the household arrangements that he had now made. For at Abraham's urging, Isaac had brought his bride into Sarah's tent,[26] which was filled again with life and love and laughter. There she was established as the mistress of the house. She would be in Sarah's stead now, assuming her responsibilities and holding her authority. Hesitantly at first, but growing in confidence with Isaac's encouragement and support, she won the respect and approval of the women of her realm, who noted her capable way and her energy to accomplish things. And if the household had a new mistress, it had a new master also. It had been Abraham's decision, not Isaac's, for his son would not have presumed to usurp his role. But Abraham felt, now his son was married, that the household was best guided by a husband and wife

---

26 Genesis 24:67.

who would lead together just as he and Sarah had done. So Isaac was the one to whom the servants now deferred, in seeking instructions and taking advice.

It was left for Abraham to move quietly into the twilight shadows of his life, receding into reverie and thoughtful prayer. He was still the hoary head of the clan[27] who gave the counsel of the wise to those who asked, but the leadership of the house had been firmly passed to Isaac, and with Sarah gone, he was content to have it so. Besides, it was a joy to relinquish his charge into the hands of a son who loved his teaching and would guard their family values. Isaac, no less then he, would command his household after him to keep the way of the Lord.

The strange story of the hand and the heel

Abraham was indeed old, but Isaac was now married. His new wife was not only the occupier of Sarah's tent, but the possessor of some of her virtues also. Abraham looked upon her in the glow of her new love, and remembered Sarah in her youthful days. He looked upon his son in the contentment of having found a wife, and saw himself as a new and earnest bridegroom, more years ago now than he cared to remember. But he was glad of having sent his servant on a journey of faith to Haran, and doubted not that the angel of God had chosen the bride. The greatness of the promise to himself and Sarah had rested on the birth of their first begotten son. All the household had rejoiced on the day of his birth, but the little boy who had been dandled upon his mother's knees was a man full-

---

27 Old age in Biblical time was respected and revered because it represented the wisdom of experience (Leviticus 19:32; Proverbs 16:31). This very term *seybah* is used of Abraham himself in this final epoch of his life (Genesis 25:8). Current postmodern culture has destroyed this concept by inculcating within the young that their opinion is of equal value to everybody else's including those older and wiser than they. The children of Abraham and Sarah should however observe the Bible dictum of 'rising up before the hoary head', as this honouring of age will bring blessings to both family and ecclesial life.

grown now. With Isaac's marriage the promise could be advanced a further stage. Now the multiplication of the seed could begin. Now came the possibility of a multitude of nations with Abraham as their father, and the wider prospect of a family as numerous as the far-flung stars, shining by their myriads in glittering array. Abraham believed it all, and knew that all would come to pass. The first grandson would be proof that the promise continued, and Abraham was content to wait for his arrival. Now that old age had come and fulness of years, time itself seemed not so urgent. Each evening and morning that marked another day was to be savoured as a gift, and lived in peace as an end in itself. Whatever days were left to him were individual blessings, and he counted them in thankfulness one by one.

It was just as well that the old man had learned the spirit of patience. For the grandson that he fondly awaited took his time in coming. Isaac's wife was barren, just as his dear Sarah had been. He knew how they felt, and counselled them to patience and to prayer as they waited on God. The entreaties of Isaac, offered in the spirit of his father, were heard in heaven above, and in due time Rebekah his wife conceived.

> "And the children struggled together within her; and she said, If it be so, why am I thus? And she went to inquire of the LORD. And the LORD said unto her, Two nations are in thy womb, and two manner of people shall be separated from thy bowels."
>
> (Genesis 25:22,23)

All was well until the babes within her womb showed the first quickening signs. Those earliest movements of hands and feet are joyous signs that life resides in the unborn child. But in Rebekah's case there was neither the languid nudging of one drowsy with sleep, nor the occasional yet lusty kick of the contented. She felt instead the sharp and urgent lunges of two who fought as if in bitter rivalry, and she gasped in anguish, as within her womb the children struggled against each other for supremacy. Afflicted with such pain and perplexity, she

174

yearned for the counsel of age, and came in desperation to her father-in-law, to seek his mediatorship in prayer to God. She had come to trust his advice and knew of his special relationship with heaven.[28] The patriarch shared her anxious concern, and after special preparation and special offering, he called upon the Name of the Lord, as intercessor on Rebekah's behalf. Despite the waning of his physical strength, his prayers were still mighty and powerful, perhaps even more so, as declining confidence in self begat purer certainty in God. His prayer was answered, and this time not by the angel, but by a revelation which he spoke directly to Rebekah.

The burden of the message was one that Abraham knew well. It concerned the sovereign authority of God to choose, according to His foreknowledge, the seed in whom the promise would continue. The children were unborn and had done neither good nor evil, but God's election would stand, and His purpose be upheld in the declaration that Rebekah now received concerning the two nations which were in her womb. Abraham knew the truth of this, in his own selection over his brother, and in Isaac's over Ishmael. He counselled Rebekah to accept the answer and to bow before the divine edict, which chose one of her sons above the other. The pain she knew in carrying these children did not cease, but now at least she knew the reason for it. It was a daily reminder that their controversy was real, and that it was destined to reach into the story of their lives. When the boys were born the father gave thanks to God for the blessing of a family, the mother rejoiced and kept God's sayings in her heart, and the old man nodded sagely at the story of

---

28 The phrase, "went to enquire of the LORD" in this context frequently refers to petition made on behalf of the person enquiring by an interceding priest or prophet. Cp. Judges 20:18,23,27,28, 1 Samuel 23:9-12 (priests), and 1 Samuel 9:9, 1 Kings 22:7,8 (prophets). Abraham exercised the priestly function within his family and was also a prophet (Genesis 20:7), and it is therefore suggested that Rebekah came to Abraham to seek his special intercession on her behalf.

the hand and the heel, and waited in patience for God to vindicate His choosing.

Abraham sees the start of his multitudinous seed

Fifteen years had passed since Rebekah had been delivered of the twins that had struggled in her womb. They were growing lads now, and already their differences in character were emerging. Esau was lithe and strong, and revelled in the freedom of the field and the thrill of the hunt. Keen of eye, carefree and careless, he rejoiced in the excitement of the chase that tested his youthful skills. But he did not incline to the spiritual or the profound, for to stop and reflect would have stifled his soul, which longed to run whithersoever he would go. Jacob, his sibling, was physically capable too, but his love was not for the pursuit of the wild creature, but for the nurture and care of flock and herd. Jacob preferred the steady gain of honest toil, and the benefit of family routine. His spirit soared when mediating on things divine, which from an early age he had done.

Abraham marvelled at the correctness of the divine choice, and realised afresh the omniscient wisdom of the God whom he worshipped. It had taken many years to learn the lesson well enough, so that it was engraved upon his heart as a rule for life. But he knew it now, with the uncluttered simplicity of old age. God knows the end from the beginning, and His counsels are always truth. Abraham looked with old but happy eyes upon young Jacob, through whom the promise would be carried, and discerned the early vital signs. The lad already showed that uprightness of character in godly things, that was to be the peculiar trait of all Abraham and Sarah's true offspring. Though his eyes were dimmed with age, he still saw clearly why the promise would run through this child, and he was satisfied. He felt a deep sense of contentment that the Lord who had blessed him in all things had blessed him in this, that he could see the line of the promise stretching out before him. Here indeed was the beginning of his multitudinous seed. The desire of an old man was fulfilled. He had seen not only his children, but his children's children, and peace upon his people.[29]

The death and burial of Abraham

He realised, on reflection, that this was the most important thing of all. His life had been filled with many exciting moments, but now at the end of his days he was able to see with absolute clarity what the great cause of the truth was. It was simply this. To walk before Almighty God in humility and uprightness, and to bring forth a godly seed that also would walk before Him was the pinnacle of spiritual life. To maintain the truth in faithfulness in his own lifetime was a notable achievement. But to nurture the spirit of that truth in those that followed was to help preserve the remnant of the woman's seed. He felt privileged to have been given these special years, to watch Isaac his son mature into the head of his household, to see his little grandson grow, and to touch his mind with the wonder and beauty and holiness of God's way. A grandfather could ask for nothing more. And Jacob remembered these moments. Many years later in reflecting on the wonder of God's work in his own life, he would pronounce a blessing upon his own grandsons, in the name of "my fathers Abraham and Isaac".[30]

For one hundred years, Abraham had lived as a stranger and sojourner in the land of the promise. Despite his wealth, he had never forsaken his pilgrim tent, and never renounced his pilgrim spirit. Because he had seen the fulness of the promise afar off, and because he was persuaded of it, he was content to remain a pilgrim in his mortal life. When the one of whom the promise truly spoke was manifested in the land, then he would fold up his tent and sit down in the city of God. But he knew that this one, of whom his son, Isaac, was a type, would not appear until the fulness of time. Until then, each generation would need to preserve, as

29 Psalm 128:6.
30 Genesis 48:15,16.

177

a sacred charge, the way of truth. One night, Abraham offered his prayer to God for the preservation of that truth, and the guidance of his family. He prayed for God's care towards his offspring, for God's own sake in the advancing of His purpose in the earth. It was the prayer of all godly parents who know through personal experience how vital it is that the Father's blessing be sought every day, and who therefore plead daily for their children. It was to be the old man's last entreaty. For when his evening prayer was ended, Abraham fell into that sleep from which there is no awakening until the trump of God shall sound. Abraham, the Friend of God, was dead and the years of his pilgrimage were ended.

Enfolding each other in death together

"Then Abraham gave up the spirit, and died in a good old age, an old man, and full of years; and was gathered to his people. And his sons Isaac and Ishmael buried him in the cave of Machpelah, in the field of Ephron the son of Zohar the Hittite, which is before Mamre; the field which Abraham purchased of the sons of Heth: there was Abraham buried, and Sarah his wife." (Genesis 25:8-10)

Isaac received the news with a sorrowful heart, for there is a suddenness about death that shocks and saddens, even when old age proclaims that the day is near. In the spirit of brotherly respect he immediately sent a messenger to the wilderness of Paran to call Ishmael. Grief at their father's death brought the two together in a rare moment of brotherly fellowship. Yet Isaac's grief was not as sharp and poignant as the terrible pain he had experienced when his mother died. His own life had changed now, as he had assumed many of his father's responsibilities, and at his side was his own companion who was ready to console and comfort him in this loss.

Isaac and Ishmael carried their father's body into the cave, and laid it there in a place prepared. The days of mourning began, and the household of Abraham the

Hebrew bewailed the fall of a mighty chieftain, a man who had been their master, their mentor, their father and their friend. There was no quarrel between the two sons as to where Abraham should be buried. Abraham's purchase of the field of Machpelah had settled the matter, and although Sarah was not his mother, even Ishmael acknowledged that it was here, alongside his true companion, that his father ought to rest. Thus was buried Abraham the patriarch and Sarah his wife. They were inseparable in life, and in death they were not divided. Throughout their days they had walked together, he as her counterpart, and she as his companion. Now they were folded together in the fellowship of death,[31] their bodies lying in the united hope of a resurrection to life and light and immortality. When the mourning was ended, the cave was sealed that they might sleep in peace until their special angel came to call them forth. The account of their marriage was closed, but the fulness of their story was in another way, just beginning.

---

31 It does seem strangely beautiful that the final resting place of this couple was the cave of Machpelah (folded together so as to *double*, cp. Exodus 28:16), which itself was in Hebron (to be in union and fellowship). There could be no finer epitaph to their lives. They truly enfolded each other in the fellowship of death together.

9

ENCOURAGING THE CHILDREN OF FAITH TOGETHER

OVER four hundred years had passed since the death of the patriarchal couple,[1] yet the memory of their story remained undimmed. When their descendants returned from servitude and affliction in a land not theirs, their very resettlement was firmly linked to the history of their forbears:

> "And I took your father Abraham from the other side of the flood, and led him throughout all the land of Canaan, and multiplied his seed, and gave him Isaac. And I gave unto Isaac Jacob and Esau: and I gave unto Esau mount Seir, to possess it; but Jacob and his children went down into Egypt. I sent Moses also and Aaron, and I plagued Egypt ... and afterward I brought you out."   (Joshua 24:3-5)

Through Isaac, the son of Abraham and Sarah, sprang their connection and claim of association with God's earlier promises. As their offspring they returned to the land. Yet from the conquest and settlement in the days of Joshua, the nation quickly fell into that spirit of idolatry, which Abraham and Sarah had repudiated when first they had journeyed from Ur. Israel's spirit was not one of wholehearted obedience, but instead of spiritual unfaithfulness as they went after the gods many and lords many of all the nations round about them. God was wroth with His people.

The spirit of Abraham and Sarah lost

Generations passed where the word of God was rare, where visions were not open, and where the natural family bore little resemblance to their founding parents. These were times of spiritual darkness, broken only

---

1   Genesis 15:13,14.

180

by the occasional example of heroic faith or humble obedience, offering but scant evidence that the spirit of Abraham and Sarah lived on in their offspring. But at last came David, a man imbued with the spirit of faith, with a love of mercy, and with an appreciation of things divine that proved he was of Abraham's line. Jesse's son, ever mindful of the hand of God in his own life, was convinced of its touch upon the nation. When his kingdom was confirmed, and a place of worship established in ancient Salem, he composed a psalm of national thanksgiving:

"Be ye mindful always of his covenant; the word which he commanded to a thousand generations; even of the covenant which he made with Abraham … And when they went from nation to nation, and from one kingdom to another people; he suffered no man to do them wrong: yea, he reproved kings for their sakes, saying, Touch not mine anointed, and do my prophets no harm."   (1 Chronicles 16:15-22)

The certainty of the land given to the fathers was proved, in David's eyes, by the providential care of God towards Abraham and Sarah when first they entered the land and journeyed as pilgrims. The house of Asaph sang this psalm of David through all the generations of the nation, and bade Israel never to forget their heritage from of old. For this remembrance was not to fill them with complacency, but to urge them instead to acts of dedication and songs of reverence, offered to the God whose way this household had pledged to keep. This remembrance was to help them understand the spirit of the patriarchs and to follow, to live in faithful trust before the One who would protect and provide, and to know His greatness by drawing near in heart and mind to worship in His presence.

Under the inspiration of David's leadership, Israel for a time showed a measure of spiritual conduct that would have rejoiced the heart of Abraham had he seen his children. But their faith was not deep enough or strong enough to endure through successive generations. Fathers failed to command their children after them, and the nation, touched but briefly by the spirit of their forbears, fell to living lives of reluctant conformity to God's laws.

There were moments of earnest reformation when Israel, led by the passionate zeal of a righteous king, showed glimpses of their spiritual heritage from Abraham and Sarah. But these times of spiritual renewal were all too brief, all too short-lived, to change the course of the nation. More than a millennium had now passed since the death of the patriarch and his interment with Sarah his beloved wife. Their descendants had declined into such manifest wickedness that any thought they stood in some way related to this marvellous couple was nought but presumptuous arrogance.

Abraham was one ... but we are many

Yet sadly, the nation, even as it deteriorated spiritually, became inordinately proud of their supposed heritage. Ezekiel, writing after Israel's dissolution, and after the city of Jerusalem had been taken, summarised the spirit of overweening pride that gripped the nation:

> "Then the word of the LORD came unto me saying, Son of man, they that inhabit those wastes of the land of Israel speak, saying, Abraham was one, and he inherited the land: but we are many; the land is given us for inheritance. Wherefore say unto them, Thus saith the Lord GOD; Ye eat with the blood, and lift up your eyes toward your idols, and shed blood: and shall ye possess the land?"   (Ezekiel 33:23-25)

They imagined that their very numbers were the multiplication promised to Abraham, and that therefore as his multitudinous seed the land was theirs by right. How astonishing that they could manifest such arrogant certainty at the very time of their expulsion from the land. In the providence of God, they were removed and sent back into the very place from whence Abraham and Sarah had come.[2] This couple had left the idolatry of

---

2   Acts 7:43.

Babylon behind, in an odyssey of faith to serve the one true God. The people of the captivity had to learn that if they refused to walk in the steps of the father and mother of the faithful, if they persisted in their idolatry, then God could reverse His promises, not in their fulness, but at least to their generation. No one has claim to salvation by right, and certainly not by mere virtue of birth.

To the seat of idolatry then they were sent, to the very centre of apostate worship that had rebelled against the truth in ancient times. All the gods of the nations, which they had so eagerly sought after, were to be traced to this source of corruption, to the temple in the land of Shinar, famed since the revolt of Nimrod and his consort Queen Semiramis, the father and mother not of faith, but of apostasy itself. There in Babylon, the arch-enemy of Israel for all time, they were confronted with such religious depravity, such rebellious idolatry, that they were moved to abandon all such associations. Forced to hear the hymns which praised the gods of gold, of silver, of brass, of iron, of wood and of stone, they yearned instead for the songs of Zion,[3] and for the psalms of the temple which exalted the Lord their God.

Abraham's seed return from the exile

The shock of this divine judgement by exile was salutary and effective, for the experience of the captivity finally purged Israel of the spirit of idolatry, which had been their besetting sin. When they returned to the land in the mercy of God, they would, from this time forth, eschew the gods of the nations and worship only the Lord. At last they would manifest the spirit of patriarchal fidelity that would mark them as the household of Abraham. Indeed, in the days of Nehemiah, they entered into a solemn oath to serve God with single-minded devotion, by strict obedience to all His laws, and by careful observance of all His commandments. It was an honourable objective. But had the nation really heard the words of the national confession they had made together on that selfsame day?

---

3   Psalm 137:1-4.

"Thou art the LORD the God, who didst choose Abram, and broughtest him forth out of Ur of the Chaldees, and gavest him the name of Abraham; and foundest his heart faithful before thee, and madest a covenant with him to give the land ... to his seed."

(Nehemiah 9:7,8)

So it was Abraham's faithfulness that secured the divine approval and blessing. And their entitlement to share the promise would come, not by mechanical observance but by showing the same spirit of faith. Would they learn the lesson? Alas, it was not to be so, for when the sun went down over the prophets, and the seers became ashamed, the people of Abraham became obstinate in their pride. Truly the nation was descended from him, and they could with perfect propriety be described as Abraham's seed. But with that perverse capacity for self-aggrandisement, which is the mark of the thinking of the flesh, they foolishly imagined that entitlement to the land and to the wider blessings of the covenant, were theirs by intrinsic right. They failed to appreciate that the privilege of association with Abraham rested not so much on descent as in conduct. Their idolatry was gone, but it had been replaced instead with a system of worship that gloried in the meticulous but mindless observance of endless rules. The laws of God were multiplied into such a plethora of minutiae, that their original spirit and intent was lost. How vastly different all this was to the simple and earnest faith that brought Abraham and Sarah into a land of which they knew not, and moved them to live as one in faithful obedience and loving trust before Almighty God. This people, this nation that sprang from them, knew not their heritage, for they had never learned that righteousness which is of faith.[4]

Further generations passed where God was not in communication with His people, not by dream, neither by oracle, nor by seer. They were years that only served to deepen the nation's spirit of self-importance. Pride in

---

4   Romans 9:30.

their ancestry, innate certainty in their inalienable right to possess the land, and of their unalterable position in God's purpose, were all based upon their link to Abraham by direct descent. It was as if God Himself was unable to undo His promises to the fathers. They were the chosen seed and nothing could, in their opinion, change their choosing.

It was high time indeed to review from whence they had sprung, and more particularly to establish what constituted them as Abraham's seed. This then was the issue of the day that confronted Christ and his disciples, an issue that would be met and challenged by them, in warning a people steeped in pride and hypocrisy. And it was the Lord himself, the true seed, who would answer the nation with a simple yet powerful appeal to the story of Abraham. Christ's response to a nation grown complacent in their self-righteousness was to trace the line of the nation back, not only to its patriarchal head, but also to its matriarchal fount. He would show that the nation had not just a common father, but a common mother also. Abraham and Sarah would stand joined as one in this final appeal to Israel, heirs together just as they had always been. But they would no longer be referred to as husband and wife. Instead the focus of the Spirit would be upon their role as the founding parents of the family of faith, a family connected to both of them by a higher principle than blood descent. Their story, their united story, would be crucial to the argument that Christ would present.

Think not to say ... we have Abraham to our father

But it was not Christ who would first join issue with the nation. Instead it was John Baptist who would open the account, for it had been prophesied of him by angelic lips that he would. As the forerunner of the Lord, his work of preparation was to turn the heart of the obdurate nation to their fathers, and to bend their spirit towards the father's mode of thinking that rejoiced in that justification which comes by faith.[5] Blazing in his righteous indignation, he rebuked the rulers for their spirit of unreasoning pride in their Jewishness:

"But when he saw many of the Pharisees and Sadducees come to his baptism, he said unto them, O generation of vipers, who hath warned you to flee from the wrath to come? Bring forth therefore fruits meet for repentance. And think not to say within yourselves, We have Abraham to our father: for I say unto you, that God is able of these stones to raise up children unto Abraham." (Matthew 3:7-9)

Every word the messenger spoke was charged with significance. His blunt denunciation was not a rebuke of the public demeanour, which of course appeared outwardly righteous. He sought instead to challenge the far more insidious matter of their private reflections of self-worthiness.

Descent from Abraham meant nothing in itself, despite their confidence. The true offspring of Abraham were those who stood related to God and to His power operating in their lives. From the beginning, it had been the promise of Ail Shaddai that He would build the family of His friend, and so it was to be through all time. First and foremost then, the seed of this illustrious couple were those who knew of and responded to God at work in their lives: His power not theirs; His wisdom not theirs. This was the common bond that bound all their children together, and it was not the bond of personal merit or inherent worthiness. These children, every one of them the subject of divine power in their lives, were the true inheritors of the epithet 'children of Abraham'. And since that power which fashioned them was so evidently from God above, there were no grounds for self-

---

5   Luke 1:17: John Thomas translates the words in the AV, "to turn the hearts of the fathers to the children, and the disobedient to the wisdom of the just" as "to restore to posterity the father's dispositions, and disobedient ones to just persons' mode of thinking" (see *The Mystery of the Covenant of the Holy Land Explained*).

glory, when God might just as easily have raised such seed to Abraham from the stones of the river.

The Baptist's stern words, administered as a corrective to national pride, did not mention Sarah directly, but he might have done so. For her role was implied in the course of his argument. Sarah, no less than Abraham, had herself been the subject of divine power, and the only son of Abraham who was produced by that same divine intervention was he who all the world knew to be the only begotten of Abraham and Sarah.

Abraham's children ... do the works of Abraham

The Lord was teaching in the temple.[6] He claimed he was not alone but ministered with the endorsement of his Father, and in fact that his words and deeds enjoyed the approval of his Father. As a true Son, his life and teaching reflected the principles that his Father had inculcated in him. It was a message that many found strangely convincing. Jesus called upon his listeners to continue in his word as he had observed his Father's.

His promise was that the truth would make them free. He was not thinking of freedom from political servitude. He spoke instead of that liberation from the constraints of self-centred and fleshly thinking that only the truth can bring. 'The truth' was an expansive term, which represented the sum of the Father's entire mind and purpose, the totality of He who is the God of truth. That truth was seen in the mode of thinking and way of life of Christ, who perfectly exhibited the power of divine principles. His spirit and teaching was so completely different from Jewish thinking that focused so minutely on the detailed observance of law, that the very regulations themselves became of more importance than the principles they enshrined. Christ's commandments and the observance of them would exalt them to the glorious liberty of the spirit mind. Gone would be the zeal of works, moved by nothing more than the meticulous observance of ritual offered as an end

6   John 8:20,59.

187

in itself, and with the notion that it in some way made them righteous before God. They would discover to their joy a way of life that instead confessed before God the weakness of flesh, rested on the grace of justification by faith, yet still inspired works of faithful obedience to holy principles, moved by gratitude and love. This doctrine would free them from a yoke of bondage that had long hung heavy upon the nation.

Yet, instead of pondering the import of his words, they bridled with righteous indignation. Content in the knowledge that they were descended from Abraham, they repudiated any notion that the covenant people could ever be in bondage to anyone. They failed to see what Christ saw in their lives. They were in servitude to the fatal spirit of Judaism. They were slaves to sin in the assertion of their own will and in the living of self-centred lives.

Yet even in the more literal application they had given to his words, they showed the hateful spirit of pride in their history and ancestry. Successive conquests of the nation by Assyrian, Persian, Grecian, and Roman powers were totally ignored.[7] So imbued were they with the importance of their place and nation that they pretended to a freedom that simply was not true.

The response of Christ, puzzling at the first, was a spiritually acute answer to their pride. His reply was based upon their own assertion that they were "Abraham's seed", an assertion that Jesus turned to confound them in their own complacency. His words became a dissertation on Abraham's household, and an eloquent one at that in expounding the story of his two principal sons, and of the mothers that bore them.

"Jesus answered them, Verily, verily, I say unto you, Whosoever committeth sin is the servant of sin.

---

7   In fact their assertion, "We be Abraham's seed, and were *never in bondage* to any man" (John 8:33) was uttered within the temple courts in plain sight of the Tower of Antonio which loomed over the temple compound, the very symbol of Roman rule and authority in their land!

And the servant abideth not in the house for ever: but the Son abideth ever. If the Son therefore shall make you free, ye shall be free indeed. I know that ye are Abraham's seed; but ye seek to kill me, because my word hath no place in you ... They answered and said unto him, Abraham is our father. Jesus saith unto them, If ye were Abraham's children, ye would do the works of Abraham. But now ye seek to kill me, a man that hath told you the truth, which I have heard of God: this did not Abraham. Ye do the deeds of your father. Then said they to him. We be not born of fornication; we have one Father, even God."

(John 8:33-41)

The one son, although born to Abraham first, was the child of his mother, with all the limitations of servant mentality and behaviour that he inherited from her. His life and his actions revealed him to be a servant not a son, and his status in the patriarchal household proved to be temporary. Mere flesh descent then, did not in his case confer any lasting rights of sonship or inheritance. These were predicated on a higher principle than this boy could rise to in his thinking and disposition. In the end, his behaviour rendered him unfit for continued association with the Friend of God, and he was summarily dismissed from the house with his mother.

The second son, born to a different mother was of an altogether different spirit. This woman was Abraham's spiritual counterpart, and their child displayed the very characteristics that were the binding virtues of their own marriage union – faith, humility, and obedience. This son, the true heir and scion of the household, endorsed by the blessing of heaven, would remain within his father's house, abiding there as the rightful inheritor of the family promises, but also as the faithful preserver of the family principles. His sonship was seen in the manifestation of their family character. He declared himself to be their child by revealing the same spirit.

Christ's answer, profoundly simple in its succinctness, struck home with telling effect. Sonship, in the end, was

189

based upon spiritual oneness not physical descent, upon family likeness not family lineage. His answer was in effect – 'You may well be Abraham's seed, but you come from the wrong mother, for you are not Sarah's children'.

Indeed, their hostility towards him marked them out in type as Hagar's offspring. The mocking of Ishmael against Isaac was not just malicious but malevolent. His spirit of hatred towards his younger sibling was the threatening rivalry of one dispossessed of firstborn status, and Isaac's life may well have been in danger had not Ishmael been physically removed from the encampment of his father. Yet this murderous animosity was evident in the spirit of the rulers towards Christ.[8] These men felt only antagonism for this man who in his godly teaching, righteous character and exemplary life was evidently much closer to the Father than they.

Their answer that Abraham was their father was the unreasoning claim of those who, resting on the legacy of their birth, failed to see the need for repentance. Pride in their physical descent blinded them completely to the reality that sons who did not live and think and act like their father were no sons at all. They were Abraham's seed, but they were assuredly not Abraham's children. The words of Christ, irresistibly powerful in repudiating their claims, aroused not repentance but wrathful ire. "We be not born of fornication; we have one Father, even God." It was a hateful thing to say. Their response in the face of righteous criticism was to utter a wicked and spiteful calumny that openly scorned the circumstances surrounding the birth of the Son of God. Far from being the son of the Father, they implied that Christ was but the illegitimate progeny of some unknown man, not even of Joseph who had been kind enough to raise him in his household. It was an unjust and malignant assertion, not only against the Lord, but also against his mother. It cast doubts upon his parentage when his character and his life were a beautiful testimony as to who his

---

8   For so Christ bluntly declared to his audience: "Ye seek to kill me" (John 8:37).

parents were. Their slander was an evil retaliation, but it vindicated Christ's assessment of their line of descent.

For when Ishmael mocked Isaac there was, no doubt, a similar assertion. Sarah, at the time of her conception, had just been delivered from the harem of Abimelech. The birth of Isaac, following closely thereafter as it did, gave rise for some to question the father of her boy. Having been childless with Abraham for many years, suddenly to conceive a child just after being in another man's household certainly gave opportunity for earthly speculation. The suggestion that Isaac was no son of Abraham but the child of an infidel, was perhaps at the root of Ishmael's mocking when he laughed at Isaac, Sarah's only son. It was a casting of the same slur on both the son and his mother, as would be heard in the temple concerning Christ. Surely, their very taunt revealed them to be Hagar's children and not Sarah's.

I will come, and Sarah shall have a son

When Paul explained the doctrine of God's election, he began with evidence drawn from the family of this faithful couple:

> "Not as though the word of God hath taken none effect. For they are not all Israel, which are of Israel: neither, because they are the seed of Abraham, are they all children: but, In Isaac shall thy seed be called. That is, They which are the children of the flesh, these are not the children of God: but the children of the promise are counted for the seed. For this is the word of promise, At this time will I come, and Sara shall have a son."   (Romans 9:6-9)

The nation of Israel had been the recipients of marvellous blessings, not least of which was an association with the fathers, beginning with Abraham. But with these special privileges came a commensurate responsibility to witness to the God whom they served. Some within the nation did indeed see this sacred charge, and sought to reflect His principles. Others failed to rise to the greatness of their calling, and in them the glory of

His purpose was not seen. The nation therefore was, by character and conduct, divided into two categories. "For they are not all Israel, which are of Israel", was a clear intimation that such a distinction existed.

The one group simply expected benefits that could be appropriated by the claim of their lineal descent from Abraham. The other rejoiced in privileges granted, showing their appreciation by the proof of their spiritual descent from Abraham. Between the two groups and their respective modes of thinking there lay such a deep divide, and yet they were all from the same nation. It was truly a hopeless situation. And this sore dichotomy in the nation was, argued the apostle, the very parable contained within the patriarch's household. His argument, as he began to unfold it, would have delighted the Jew. For in their mind the evidence of Abraham's family was indisputable. "Neither, because they are the seed of Abraham, are they all children: but, In Isaac shall thy seed be called." No Jew could resist the power of Paul's argument, nor would they wish to. The story of Abraham's two primary sons gave, in their view, compelling evidence to favour the Jewish cause. Ishmael and Isaac were both sons of the patriarch, but only one was the true offspring. Ishmael, although a son of Abraham, and moreover the firstborn, was cast out even after his father had pleaded for him. Sonship in his case did not bring an entitlement to inheritance, or even the blessing of continued association in his father's house.

But the story of Isaac when examined carefully was a challenge to their own cherished claim of lineage. They supposed that merely by virtue of their Jewish blood they stood related to Isaac, and were thereby entitled to the blessings of the covenant. But the sovereign choice of God that selected Isaac was based upon a principle that negated the matter of flesh descent, and gave them no cause for complacency. To be simply the offspring of Abraham was not enough, not enough that is to be reckoned as the chosen seed. All the literal offspring of Abraham but one were children of the flesh, inasmuch as they were begotten by the natural powers of earthly procreation. Yet none of these was the subject of divine choice. God's purpose instead ran through the children of promise. Who then were these children? The answer of Scripture was that they were those who stood related to the word of promise. The quintessence of that word was centred not upon Abraham and Sarah, but upon God, and the drama of His intervention in their lives. "At this time will *I* come" was the focus of the promise. God would be at work in the bringing forth of a child, and His involvement and His empowerment were crucial.

Only one son of Abraham stood related to this principle, and he would become the foundation seed and prototype of all who would follow. That child was uniquely and exclusively the son of Sarah, born of her after the promise of God was brought to fruition. And the inference of the promise and its outworking were clear. If Isaac was the son of Abraham and Sarah by the operation of divine power, then he was also a son of God. None of this allowed for Jewish pride in their descent from Abraham. The teaching of the apostle was that they should rather be concerned as to whether they could also trace their descent from Sarah. For only her offspring were the children of promise, born of spiritual principles and of divine power, literally so in Isaac's case, and by the word of God in the case of other children. Where the word of promise could not be seen in its life-transforming power, then that person was not of the seed called through Isaac, and not a child of Sarah. If then, they were not children of Sarah, they were not true descendants of Abraham, and neither therefore were they children of God. Sarah's involvement with Abraham in the promise is again crucial to the argument, and the Spirit binds these two together, just as they had always been.

The bondwoman and the freewoman

Only once does the word allegory occur in holy writ, and this from the ready pen of the apostle who knew the story of this couple so well. Taught by the counsel of Gamaliel, he knew the place of Abraham at the foundation of

Israel. It was only later perhaps, when instructed by the wisdom of Christ, that he saw the role of Sarah also. Having identified that principle of faith by which both male and female find oneness and unity in Christ, the apostle proceeded to draw on the life of Abraham and Sarah concerning the theme of true descent:

"But he who was of the bondwoman was born after the flesh; but he of the freewoman was by promise. Which things are an allegory: for these are the two covenants; the one from the mount Sinai, which gendereth to bondage, which is Agar. For this Agar is mount Sinai in Arabia, and answereth to Jerusalem which now is, and is in bondage with her children. But Jerusalem which is above is free, which is the mother of us all. For it is written, Rejoice, thou barren that bearest not; break forth and cry, thou that travailest not: for the desolate hath many more children than she which hath an husband. Now we, brethren, as Isaac was, are the children of promise. But as then he that was born after the flesh persecuted him that was born after the Spirit, even so it is now. Nevertheless what saith the scripture? Cast out the bondwoman and her son: for the son of the bondwoman shall not be heir with the son of the freewoman. So then, brethren, we are not children of the bondwoman, but of the free."

(Galatians 4:23-31)

The allegory was immensely powerful inasmuch as it dwelt on two entirely different sons born to two entirely different women who were yet both related to the patriarch. In the apostolic unfolding of this parable, it was the pleasure of the Spirit to conceal the true secret of the Abrahamic covenant in the story of these two mothers and their vastly different boys. "For these women are two covenants", the apostle would say.[9] And such was the expansiveness of the thought, that the

9   So rendered by the RV. Although the translation is inferential, it is clearly supported by the subsequent flow of the argument in Galatians 4:25,26. Therefore the new covenant (within the terminology of the allegory) is actually the Saraic covenant.

allegory, which began with two women, would in the end encompass two sons, two births, two places, two mountains, two cities, two characters, two destinies, two covenants, and two ways.

The Jew only ever saw one covenant and that exclusively between God and Abraham's natural born race. To the Jewish mind, steeped in the thinking of the law, the Mosaic covenant was the natural expansion of the Abrahamic, the full development of God's dealings with His own people. But the inference of the allegory, clear and unmistakable, was that there were most assuredly two covenants, and that these in a sense were diametrically opposed, as utterly different as the two women who represented them. The Jew was certain that the covenants were but one, united by the key principle of circumcision. The apostle, however, was insistent that the covenants were two, and that they were divided in twain by the key principle of motherhood.

Hagar was a slave, and the son whom she bore was likened to children in bondage to the law, servants to the thraldom of sin. Sarah was a princess, and the son whom she bore was likened to the children of the house, free in the liberty of spiritual thinking. Here again were not only two mothers and two sons, but also two entirely different modes of birth. Even the order was significant on the basis of 'first that which is natural, and afterward that which is spiritual'. The first son was indeed natural born, for the flesh alone was sufficient to bring forth Ishmael. In like manner the nation continually produced offspring who were enslaved by the law. These, however, were of the mother who "gendereth to bondage", and were those therefore that were "born after the flesh", the children verily of the Mosaic covenant. With Isaac, however, there was no natural process for bringing to the birth. The freewoman was barren,[10] and her children therefore

---

10 Galatians 4:27 is a citation from Isaiah 54:1 and reinforces the principle that Sarah's barrenness was typical of the covenant she represents. Unlike the Mosaic covenant, no one is a natural born son of the Saraic covenant.

were of promise. That promise concerned the power of God to produce offspring that humanly were impossible to produce, a power that lay outside the natural. And yet, the very power that brought forth Sarah's only son was sufficient to beget a multitude. When that principle was outworked in the fulness of God's purpose, the freewoman would rejoice in "many more children", who would all be "born after the spirit", and she would be honoured as being "the mother of us all".

The Jew was thoroughly familiar with the Abrahamic covenant, but not in the way that the apostle presented. For the very key to Paul's thoughtful words was founded on Sarah's intimate and vital association with the promise to Abraham. It mattered not (in this context) whether Abraham was their father, but rather whether Sarah was their mother. Did they then understand that the secret of the Abrahamic covenant lay in its association with Sarah? Could they grasp that it was in effect the Saraic covenant also, for thus the allegory so divinely wrought would describe it.

How inseparable then were these two in the Spirit's testimony, and how eloquent was the appeal. For by the time the epistle was penned, the Jews of Judaea and Galilee were the last generation of Abraham and Sarah's race who would live and walk in the land once trodden by these two. In a short while, how little, how little, and the allegory would be brought to its own inexorable end. The children of Hagar would be cast out, and the offspring of Sarah would flee to a place of refuge, but remain as the children of that house which is a habitation of God.

Through faith Sarah conceived ... by faith Abraham offered

"Through faith also Sara herself received strength to conceive seed, and was delivered of a child when she was past age, because she judged him faithful who had promised ... By faith Abraham, when he was tried, offered up Isaac: and he that had received the promises offered up his only begotten son, of whom it was said, That in Isaac shall thy seed be called: accounting that God was able to raise him up, even from the dead; from whence also he received him in a figure." (Hebrews 11:11,17-19)

When Paul through the Spirit composed the compendium of the faithful, his list included both Abraham and Sarah. They are the only couple to be named in this honour roll of faithful ones, inseparable as always, and especially so in the matter of faith at work in their lives. As with all the examples he adduced, Paul gave an example of faith from both of them, and in each case a faith that revolved around Isaac their son. Yet the illustrations he provided could not have been more dramatically different. Of Sarah he would record her amazing faith in conceiving and bringing forth their son despite her natural weakness and insufficiency. Of Abraham he would recall his astonishing faith in offering their son against his natural instincts and understanding. The one matter pertained to life, the other to death. Yet both had a common origin. Faith, even in an invisible God, is not blind, especially when His influence has already been seen and felt in our lives. He had been at work in theirs, and so their faith was real, even at the point when it would be tested to the uttermost. Faith in God provides the motive power to overcome any circumstance in our lives, and especially those that pertain to our natural inclinations.

Sarah had struggled with the difficulty of bearing a child for all her adult life, a burden that centred on her personal inadequacy. Yet her son existed because of the triumph of her faith, which finally overcame her darkest despairs. Her faith, intensely personal, and woven from the fabric of her inward trial, was finally blessed with the power both to conceive and to bring forth a child when past age, and the wonder of it all was that her son would prove to be but the foundation stone of an entire household of children. At the last she understood that only the Lord can build the house, and surrendered to His will to let Him do so. An old woman past age, proved

197

that with God nothing is impossible. And from whence came the fulness of her surrender? She "judged him faithful who had promised".[11]

Abraham faced a decision that tested all his powers of belief and knowledge, and that left him wrestling with incredulity. The only way he could reconcile the request of the angel to put Isaac to death, and the promises whose fulfilment depended on Isaac's life, was to submit to the thought that God could move beyond the bounds of life and death themselves. Making the decision to obey was the triumph of his faith, which transcended his deepest doubts. He sacrificed Isaac in his heart,[12] and made offering of their son with the spirit of gladness[13] in God's promises. And from whence came the depth of his obedience? He accounted "that God was able to raise him up".

So finely was their faith matched and mirrored that these two examples could be the sum of the whole. Faith seen in a woman and a man, faith seen in overcoming inadequacy and in transcending incredulity, the one requiring inward surrender, the other demanding external obedience, and both gloriously outworked to the honour of the God whom they worshipped and served. It was not difficult to see how their example might be set forth as the benchmark for all their children to follow.

Even now, after countless generations have passed, we stand in awe of their faith, so simple, so total, so grand. Faced with the story of these two who confessed that they were strangers and pilgrims on the earth, and walked accordingly, we realise that our own lives do not

---

11 See Appendix 7 – "Did Sarah herself receive strength?"

12 The first word "offered" in Hebrews 11:17 is in the perfect tense and would therefore be better rendered 'had offered'. It indicates that in his heart Abraham had already committed himself fully to the sacrifice of their son in obedience to the divine command.

13 The base of the word "received" in Hebrews 11:17, *dechomai*, carries with it the notion of 'a welcoming or an appropriating reception' (Grimm-Thayer). It is rendered "gladly received" in the RV.

measure to the same standard of faith. We still stand in need of absorbing their story, and capturing their attitude. But if we can comport our lives more closely with theirs, showing the same spirit, walking the same road, and serving the same God, then their blessing will also be ours – the providential care and guidance of God who sees and knows, and who delights in the faithful submission of His servants. How completely encouraging it is to see this spirit in both the father and mother of the faithful, to know that whatever our trial of faith, whatever our burden of care, they have walked the road before us. Nothing we shall endure is likely to exceed the breadth of their experiences, and in this we can be comforted, as we follow after in the way. There is no better example for saints in general and husbands and wives in particular to emulate.

Even as Sarah obeyed Abraham, calling him lord

"Likewise, ye wives, be in subjection to your own husbands; that, if any obey not the word, they also may without the word be won by the conversation of the wives ... For after this manner in the old time the holy women also, who trusted in God, adorned themselves, being in subjection to their own husbands: even as Sara obeyed Abraham, calling him lord: whose daughters ye are, as long as ye do well, and are not afraid with any amazement. Likewise, ye husbands, dwell with them according to knowledge, giving honour unto the wife, as unto the weaker vessel, and as being heirs together of the grace of life; that your prayers be not hindered."   (1 Peter 3:1-7)

The Apostle Peter, in common with the Apostle Paul, provided counsel on the role of husbands and wives. Unlike Paul, however, who chose to make reference to the wonder of marriage enshrined in Eden,[14] and the mystery of marriage spoken of in the Song,[15] Peter drew on the lives of Abraham and Sarah to enhance his

---

14 Ephesians 5:31 which is cited from Genesis 2:24.
15 Ephesians 5:27 which is cited from Song of Solomon 4:7.

teaching. What better marriage relationship could be used as the benchmark for believers who needed to know how best to conduct their own marriages in Christ?

His words to wives were more detailed than those to husbands, yet both exhortations focused on a particular spirit that each should manifest. Both exhortations began with the word "likewise", and there can be no doubt what he means. For immediately before this section begins, the example of Christ had been set forth as the pattern above all others that we should strive to follow. Christ's character and disposition under trial revealed two special virtues. Here was the spirit of perfect sacrifice for others, and here was the spirit of perfect submission to his Father. Peter's employment of the word "likewise" therefore, lifted the realm of marriage, and the conduct of husbands and wives towards each other, into the sacred charge of following Christ. It is his spirit that should be seen in all the mundane matters of daily life together, his example that we must emulate in all our dealings with each other, as husbands and wives. And Peter was true to the lesson of our Lord. To the wives he counselled that they render submission with reverence. To the husbands he counselled that they demonstrate sacrifice with honour.

The wisdom of Peter, himself a married man,[16] lay in making the focus of his teaching to rest upon the duties of husbands and wives, and not their rights. If both were to focus on their duties towards each other, instead of demanding their rights from each other, then marriage in the Lord would be transformed into an experience that the world knew nothing about. Such a spirit would not remove life's difficulties, for they are ever present in every marriage, but it would allow husbands and wives to meet those challenges, resolve them mutually, and grow closer through their failures and their fears.

Peter knew of an outstanding example where this spirit of Christ was woven into the fabric of a marriage,

---

16 Mark 1:30; 1 Corinthians 9:5.

and yet again, Abraham and Sarah, this godly man and this holy woman would be seen together in an apostolic appeal. The counsel to wives that they decorate the "hidden man of the heart", was especially beautiful. In the context of plaiting the hair, wearing of gold, and costly apparel, his advice was that it is not the woman on the outside that matters, but the man on the inside. That man is Christ. Within the marriage bond, a wife seeks to enshrine her husband within her heart as if he were Christ, but in the event of his failure or unbelief, her desire should still be to keep the spirit of Messiah within herself as the man who governs her thinking and behaviour.

The episode Peter had especially in mind was that of their journey into Egypt where Sarah submitted to her husband's request that they conceal their true relationship.[17] Despite the terrors of the moment, it is evident that so complete was Sarah's trust in the mighty power of God to deliver her, that she remained in subjection to Abraham, and that moreover in the spirit of calling him lord. Her submission was real and complete, and rendered in a time of such crisis that a lesser woman would have wavered. Yet her conduct was exemplary, rendered the more eloquent by her silence, an amazing spirit that helped to save her household. It was possible to emulate Sarah, and the apostle gave counsel to the

17 The episode he has in mind is that of Genesis 12:11-17. It is the only place where the incident reflects fully the spirit of Sarah's confidence in time of great alarm, her deep submission to Abraham, her implicit trust in God, and her silence throughout the episode. He quotes however from 18:12 as illustrative of the spirit that Sarah showed on the earlier occasion. Peter is in good company. For in James 2:20-24, when expounding the spirit of Abraham in Genesis 22:9-12, James actually quotes from 15:6 to show the spirit which Abraham later revealed on Mount Moriah. Similarly in Romans 4:18-21, Paul, expounding the circumstances of Genesis 17:3-5 also quotes from 15:5,6 to capture the spirit of complete faith the patriarch revealed when later faced with what seemed to be an impossibly marvellous promise. In each case a specific episode was referred to, but a different passage cited to capture the spirit of the moment.

wives that they should. It was her doing well that they were to copy, and in following her precious example they would become her offspring. Not to be afraid therefore relates to Sarah's confidence in the Lord in a time of great anxiety and alarm. Here was the evidence of her "hidden man of the heart", a holy woman who trusted in God, adorned thereby with the spirit of reverential subjection. It is a characteristic that is questioned by some married sisters today, but only by those who have not grasped the paradox of victory through submission.

Husbands likewise are called to exhibit a characteristic that was marvellously shown in the patriarch's life. In an age where many women were but chattels, and where the lordship of men went unchallenged, this couple were the epitome of living together in mutual harmony and understanding. The record depicts Abraham and Sarah as dwelling together in the same tent, labouring together in love and obedience before God, and entertaining their angelic visitors together in unity.[18] Abraham accorded to his wife the deepest respect, honouring her not only in esteem, but also in the sharing of God's promises and all that they implied. They had discussed and debated all that God had promised, and how necessary this was, for not until their mutual faith had been perfected could the promised seed be born. Abraham, acutely aware of this reality, truly dwelt with his wife according to knowledge, in an intellectual kinship unparalleled in the record of holy Scripture.

Throughout the story of their life together, Abraham was seen as a man who gave honour unto his wife. In his gentle answer to her at a time of marital tension,[19] in his exclamation of delight at hearing her involvement in the promise confirmed,[20] in his hearkening unto the voice of his wife in a moment of acute personal pain,[21] this man

---

18 Genesis 18:1,6,9,10.

19 Genesis 16:6.

20 Genesis 17:17.

21 Genesis 21:14.

showed that he honoured her indeed, respectful of her part in the promises.

Husbands, says the apostle, ought to care for their wives as being the weaker vessel. Her weakness does not consist in her capacity to endure suffering, or in her ability to grasp divine principle. In these matters she has equality with the man. Her weakness springs from the very gifts with which God has endowed her for the outworking of her role. When God made them male and female, He provided in His wisdom different gifts. From the beginning the divine endowment to womankind enabled her to give support, but she would thereby also know the pain of empathy. Unto her it was also given to provide nurture, but through this she would experience the anxiety of care. Her softer nature, and more gentle physical constitution were fitted for the exercise of these responsibilities, but these very strengths would also bring an inverse weakness. For Sarah, the promise of a child tested her in these most vulnerable aspects of her womanhood, her emotions, her intuition, and her body. But Abraham, mindful of her weakness in this respect, showed care in helping to bring her to mutual faith. All wise and loving husbands will seek to do likewise in recognising their wife's precious and diverse role.

Peter's final advice was for husbands to recognise that they are heirs together of the grace of life, so that their united prayers might ascend freely to God on high. Abraham and Sarah were the pre-eminent example of this spirit. Both of them were blessed by the grace of God who had intervened in their lives. Their names, both of them, had been altered by the inclusion of the special letter from the divine Name itself, to indicate that His grace would rest upon them both in the granting of a son.[22] That quickening power resting upon an old man and an old woman, brought forth a child in their old age according to the grace of life. What better example for godly marriage could be brought forth than this one?

---

22 See Appendix 5: "Why were Abraham and Sarah's names changed?"

How vital that they be seen side by side, as so often they do in the New Testament account. Together they experienced the grace of God and together they revealed the spirit of Christ.

Look unto Abraham your father, and unto Sarah that bare you

The understanding of Christ and his disciples was not just drawn from Moses, but also from the prophets. Isaiah had already established the lesson that would be used by them in their teaching. That lesson was this. The principles of true righteousness were to be seen in the marriage relationship of Abraham and Sarah, and in the climax of their mutual faith that brought them to the fruits of parenthood:

> "Hearken to me, ye that follow after righteousness, ye that seek the LORD: look unto the rock whence ye are hewn, and to the hole of the pit whence ye are digged. Look unto Abraham your father, and unto Sarah that bare you: for I called *him* alone, and blessed *him*, and increased *him*. For the LORD shall comfort Zion: he will comfort all *her* waste places; and he will make *her* wilderness like Eden, and *her* desert like the garden of the LORD; joy and gladness shall be found therein, thanksgiving, and the voice of melody."
>
> (Isaiah 51:1-3)

They had always been together in the story of their life. The prophet's words were the seal and warrant for the teaching of the apostles. "Look unto Abraham your father, *and* unto Sarah that bare you". How could it be otherwise? For just as they both had learned to trust in God, so God had prospered them both. I *"called him … him … him"* cried the prophet and I will *"comfort her … her … her"*. They were inseparable in the record of God's involvement in their life together.

But it was not as husband and wife that the prophet presented them. It was, instead, as Abraham and Sarah, the father and mother of a special family. The prophet's emphasis was on the mysterious multiplication of their offspring in a manner that was not of themselves to accomplish. Abraham, called alone but blessed and increased when his body was now dead, had been only made so by the hand of God. Sarah, turned by the prophet into the figure of Zion whom she represents, had been transformed from the wilderness of a barren woman into the fruitful garden of childbearing, but this only by the same divine hand.

Their offspring then, were not at all the progeny of mere physical descent, but the offspring of promise, the offspring of divine begettal, the offspring of faith. Such a marvellous outcome was only possible because of the wondrous intervention of God in both their lives. They had both risen to the focus of that faith which believed implicitly in a power greater than their own. Their faith in God had been genuine and individual, but it was also mutual. Their very marriage itself was, at the last, blessed and sanctified by this common spirit of honouring the Almighty, an attitude that so delighted and pleased Him. His response was to take this man and this woman, alone in the solitary state of their union, and endow them with such fruitfulness that their seed, begotten and born by the same gracious principle, would truly become as the stars of the heaven for number. Here was a fruitfulness of unbelievable magnitude, for this was God's testimony of what He can accomplish in the lives of those who come and submit to His righteousness.

Now at last their story stood complete. Only when the fulness of God's purpose had unfolded could the importance of their life together be seen. Only with the inspired utterance of prophet and apostle, sealed by the words of Christ, could the significance of their marriage be understood. For here was the final and decisive response to the great issue which occupied Jewish thought – 'Who are the true offspring of Abraham?' The resounding answer of Scripture was – 'Those who are also the children of Sarah'. The key to being counted as a member of their family was to grasp the secret of their life of faith, and then to live by the same spirit.

How tragic was the end of a nation who, intent on their descent from father Abraham, had not grasped the truth that, unless they were also descended from mother Sarah, they were not the children of the covenant. Her children alone, of all Abraham's offspring, were the rightful heirs to all the promises of God. In the end the nation was cast out of the land, and their very expulsion was heaven's proof that God did not recognise them as Sarah's children, but instead as Hagar's.

In the family of faith, there is no room for boasting or pride. The entire story of this couple and of the family that springs from them was never the story of human ability or fleshly accomplishment. It has nothing to do with personal merit or individual achievement. These were the traits that the Jewish people gloried in, but it was not the quarry from whence Abraham and Sarah's true family are hewn. They, from beginning to end, are children who stand related to their parents by the evidence of a common characteristic – belief and trust in God, a family likeness of spiritual thought and faithful obedience.

EPILOGUE

IT was a long pilgrimage from the city of Ur to the cave of Machpelah. Abraham and Sarah began their journey as pagan idolaters, unaware of godly principles, and as yet unfruitful in their marriage. Yet by the time these travellers had reached the last milestone, their union was the model of marriage lived according to divine precepts. A child of promise had been given to them, the earnest of God's declaration that He would make them exceeding fruitful. Two outstanding people had been bound together as one, and at the end of their mortal life they lay buried together in the everlasting fellowship of hope.

Through the revelation of the Spirit we have been able to travel with them. We have seen each waymark that they passed, and have watched the maturing of their marriage and their faith. How comforting it is to know that even this couple walked in both the hills and the valleys of life's pilgrimage. Both of them experienced moments of strength and times of weakness, yet out of them all the Father shaped them for His purpose. Often, their progress was at different times and in different ways, each momentarily the foil of the other. As each episode of their life passes under review, we feel humbled yet privileged to observe the Spirit's record of their rises and their falls: Abraham stumbling in fear and compromise at a crisis in his faith, while Sarah, strong in her belief, rendered submission to the saving of her household; Sarah, consumed with emotion and anxiety seeking refuge in fleshly contrivance, while Abraham, wise in his patience, showed the spirit of consideration and tact; Sarah struggling to believe against the inclinations of her intuition and inadequacy, while Abraham, certain

207

of the promise, soared to the heights of faithful trust; Abraham suffering hesitation and doubt through the dilemma of paternal partiality, while Sarah, clear in her understanding, revealed a decisive perception of spiritual principle and practice.

Yet despite these moments of personal failure and progress, these two walked together before Almighty God. It was together as a couple that they learned, then lived, and finally loved the counsels of God that guided their steps. Their experiences were special but not unique, for the development of faith matured by trial, is the way of God with all His children. How encouraging it is to know, however, that even the father and the mother of the faithful needed to be taught their faith by God working in their lives.

Our journey with this couple has taken us not only from Ur of the Chaldees unto the heights of Hebron, but brought us through the time of king and prophet, and into the season of Christ himself. Even there in the New Testament record, the account of Abraham and Sarah played its part in shaping the answer to the great issues of the day. In fact, the fulness of their own story would only be revealed when the apostles gave testimony concerning them, and the meaning of their mutual faith. It has been our joy to share their journey, and to know with thankfulness that the story is not yet completed either for them or for ourselves.

For in the sovereign wisdom of the Lord, there is a grand circling of circumstance moving all things to the final denouement of His purpose. Events and episodes of the past, which seem either unfinished or unresolved, will all find completion and finality in the great accounting. The record of Abraham and Sarah is one such story, which awaits a final resolution. For the testimony tells that by their faith they won God's approval, yet never received the fulfilment of the promise. God had a better thing in mind, that they without us should not be made perfect. How humbling it is to know that even these two must remain asleep in the dust, until all their family have been matured by faith. Their redemption is linked to ours, and ours to theirs. If then, we are to receive the promise with them, we must live our lives moved by the same motive power, the power of faith.

Even now, they await the call that will signal the time of restitution. The voice of the Son of Man, unheard by the world at large, will whisper urgently in the ears of all those who lie asleep in his name. Stirred by the sound of his glorious call, the graves of countless hills and valleys, mountains and plains will open, and the bodies of the saints will arise. Deep in the heart of the land, in an ancient rocky field, the most illustrious of all burying places will bring forth its dead. For the grave of the cave of Machpelah will release Abraham and Sarah to the freshness of a new day, and their long sleep will be ended. Borne by the spirit they will arrive at the judgement seat to stand amidst a multitude that no man can number.

There, Abraham will rejoice to see that from him has sprung so many as the stars of heaven for multitude, and Sarah will laugh and laugh for joy that she has truly given children suck. Abraham will wonder at the way God has called him, blessed him, and increased him, and Sarah will sing that she has broken forth on the right hand and on the left, and that her seed has encompassed the Gentiles. Abraham will marvel that God has indeed made him exceeding fruitful, and Sarah will be astonished to understand that she has laid the foundation seed for a family as many as the sand which is by the sea shore innumerable. Abraham will learn that kings have come out of him, and Sarah will see that kings of people have been of her. This royal fellowship of holy ones who will stand there with them, will all know, every one of them, that they are the offspring of Abraham and Sarah through the power of faith, and that they are thereby the very children of God. And because, precisely because they are the offspring of their Father, manifesting Him in both image and likeness, this family alone, the family of Abraham and Sarah will fill the earth to the glory of His Name.

209

May it be our privilege to stand with these two, whose prayers and praises, whose trials and triumphs we have shared in this journey alongside them. May the story of their life bring hope into ours, that God might work a work with us, as He did with them, to the glory of His Name.

It must surely be a cause for joy to know that amidst the countless blessings of the kingdom, will be the pleasure of endless fellowship with all the faithful. Among the first of these, together with their greater Son will be:

Abraham and Sarah – heirs together of the grace of life.

Appendix 1

WHEN DID TERAH BEGET ABRAM?

THERE is a chronological difficulty in the narrative concerning the timing of Abram's begettal by Terah his father. Acts 7:4 states that Abram moved to Canaan after the death of his father, and Genesis 11:32 states that Terah was two hundred and five when he died. But Genesis 12:4 records that Abram was seventy-five when he entered Canaan, in which case Terah begat him at the age of one hundred and thirty. Yet Genesis 11:26 indicates that he begat Abram at the age of seventy. There is an unexplained variation between these accounts of some sixty years. There are three main alternatives for reconciling these statements:

1. Accept the Samaritan text of Genesis 11:32 which says that Terah was one hundred and forty-five when he died. This leaves Abraham as the firstborn son, but removes all chronological difficulties. The Samaritan text however does not command manuscript support, and being dependent on a single source is not a convincing solution.

2. Treat the statement of Acts 7:4 as referring not to Abram's departure from Haran to Canaan, but as his removal from Beersheba to Hebron after the offering of Isaac. On this reckoning, Terah would have been only one hundred and forty-five when Abram left Haran, and still alive for a further sixty years after Abram's departure (cp. *Elpis Israel*, page 244, fifteenth edition). Whilst reconciling Old and New Testament comments, it assumes the primacy of Genesis 11:32, but provides a doubtful reading of the Acts 7:4 passage.

3. Interpret the statement of Genesis 11:26,27 which mentions Abram first as indicating not the ordinal

211

position of his birth, but his place in the divine programme. Accepting the testimony of the related passages would lead to the conclusion that Abram was not the eldest son, but in fact the youngest, born when Terah was one hundred and thirty. Genesis 11:26,27,32 and Acts 7:4 are harmonised by reading the Genesis account this way.[1]

Of these three possibilities, we suggest therefore that the third is the most satisfactory in reconciling the Scriptural requirements of the case. Is there evidence however which supports the reading of Genesis 11:26,27 in this way? It would seem so. The record of Scripture is highly selective in the detail it provides, as well as in the detail it omits. The genealogies are notable in this respect in that they are not a simple historical account of family descent, but rather the development of the seed of the woman in successive generations. Because of this there are several instances where the son first mentioned is not actually the firstborn, but is however the son through whom the line of the truth was continued.

Genesis 5:32 indicates that Noah begat sons from the age of five hundred, and mentions Shem as being the first of these. Genesis 10:1 likewise places Shem at the head of his brothers in the order of Noah's sons. Certainly amongst these, God's work centred on Shem, in whose tabernacle the principles of true worship would be maintained, and before whose priestly and mediatorial primacy his brothers would yield (9:26,27). Yet a later passage indicates that Shem in fact was not the firstborn, but rather Japheth (10:21). The mention of Shem first therefore in the genealogy of Noah's sons, brought to the forefront the one in whom God would be revealed, and indicated that God's work would be unfolded in his branch of Noah's family.

---

1 Reconciling this difficulty by accepting Abram as the youngest of Terah's sons is also the solution proposed in *The Oracles of God*, John Carter (pages 96,97) and *Abraham: Father of the Faithful*, Harry A. Whittaker (page 11).

In the subsequent generation, the record in Genesis 11:10 mentions that Shem begat Arphaxad, and were this to be the only reference to Shem's family, we would deduce that Arphaxad was his firstborn. Genesis 10:22, however, records five sons of Shem, of whom Arphaxad appears to be the middle son. The later passage ignores all others since it is Arphaxad who will continue the story of Shem's genealogy.

The statement of Genesis 11:27 therefore that "Terah begat Abram, Nahor, and Haran" does not of itself provide proof of Abram's firstborn status. It does, however, provide evidence that in this particular son of Terah, the purpose of God would continue to be unfolded, the line of descent for the seed of the woman would be traced and the promise of Messiah would be preserved. And so indeed it came to pass.

Appendix 2

WHO WAS ISCAH?

ISCAH is mentioned in Genesis 11:29, where we learn that she was the daughter of Haran, and thereby the sister of both Milcah and Lot. But granted that she was indeed Haran's daughter, who else might she be, or what other role might she play to be mentioned at all in the record? The matter becomes even more intriguing when it is realised that she is never referred to again.

A contextual approach would suggest that the answer must lie in the immediate circumstances of Genesis 11, for there is no other reference point to assess her by. From this one brief and solitary appearance then, her identity must be discovered. There are three possibilities implicit in the story itself. These are that:

a. She was Lot's wife.

b. She was an unmarried daughter of Haran.

c. She was Abram's wife.

Of these three, the first appears unlikely. In contrast to Abram, the record does not indicate that Lot had a wife when the family migration from Ur took place (Genesis 11:31). Indeed her appearance as Haran's daughter (verse 29) would sit uncomfortably with the notion of her marriage to a man who is listed as Haran's son (verse 27).

The second alternative appears no more likely. For if she was simply a daughter of Haran who never married, then the question as to why she should appear at all remains unanswered, especially with no further recorded history concerning her. In fact this view would prompt a further question. Why should the genealogy of Milcah be given (verse 29), yet that of Sarai be ignored? Milcah is of secondary importance to Sarai, who is the mother of the promised seed, and of all the faithful down through time who would be reckoned as her offspring. To ignore her family descent in favour of noting Milcah's would seem very strange.

If, however, Iscah was Abram's wife, then this circumstance adds life and colour to the story of this couple.

It suggests firstly that verses 28,29 should be read as a consecutive narrative, and that Abram and Nahor married the daughters of Haran, both after and perhaps on account of his death.

This in turn supplies additional corroborative evidence for the chronological solution proposed in Appendix 1 – "How old was Terah?" For Abram and Nahor to marry their nieces, but with no significant disparity in age (ten years to be precise between Abram and Sarai) would suggest that Haran was their older brother by some considerable degree, and probably by a different wife of Terah.

The relationship between Abram and Sarai and Lot is also seen in a new light. Not only was he Abram's nephew, but also Sarai's brother. This close tie between Sarai and Lot helps to show why Lot chose to travel with them when they departed from Haran. With his father dead and his other sister (and mother?) still back in Ur, Sarai represented his only immediate family connection. Better to move with her and his uncle, may have been his thought, in deciding to join them (12:4). Lot being Sarai's brother also helps explain Abram's consistent spirit of concern for Lot in his troubles (14:14-16; 18:32), rescuing him from capture and interceding for him in prayer.

Identifying Sarai with Iscah also adds to the poignancy of her barrenness. For Iscah's sister, Milcah, bore eight children to Nahor (22:23), and her fertility may well have been in evidence before they left Ur. Such a circumstance between sisters would add to Sarai's tension, and give point to the studied superfluity of the text: "Haran, the father of Milcah, and the father of Iscah. But Sarai

215

(Iscah, in contrast to her sister) was barren; she had no child" (11:29,30).

The genealogy problem is also resolved, for the record of Milcah's family descent is also Iscah's, and thus Sarai's.

There are of course, other examples of Bible characters with two names:

- Solomon / Jedidiah (2 Samuel 12:24,25).
- Uzziah / Azariah (2 Kings 14:21; 2 Chronicles 26:1).
- Levi / Matthew (Matthew 9:9; Mark 2:14).
- Hadassah / Esther (Esther 2:7).
- Tabitha / Dorcas (Acts 9:36).

It is true that some of these are equivalents in other languages, but the fact remains that Sarai / Iscah would not be unique in the Bible record if she bore two names, as appears to be the case.

How then does this identification sit with Abram's declaration to Abimelech? (Genesis 20:12). For there he states that Sarai was his sister, and the daughter of his father. If, however, Sarai was Iscah, then she was really his niece and the granddaughter of his father. The terms of relationship in Hebrew however, are more expansive, more inclusive than their precise counterparts in English.

The terms 'brother' or 'sister' indicate male or female relatives, without being limited to immediate family, or immediate generation. If Abram can refer to his nephew as his "brother" (Genesis 14:14), then he can certainly refer to his niece as his "sister" (20:12). Similarly, Zedekiah was called Jehoiachin's "brother", when in fact he was his uncle (2 Chronicles 36:9,10; 2 Kings 24:17). If "brother" here can mean uncle, then "sister" can assuredly mean niece, for if the terms 'brother' and 'sister' can reach one generation back, then they can also extend one generation forward. Nebuchadnezzar is described as Belshazzar's father, when in reality he was his grandfather (Daniel 5:2,11). If "father" here can

216

mean grandfather, then "daughter" (Genesis 20:12) can mean granddaughter.

In fact the term is used exactly this way in another episode. Athaliah is described as the daughter of Omri, when in truth she was the daughter of Ahab, and therefore the granddaughter of Omri (2 Chronicles 22:2; 21:6).

Abram's defence in answering Abimelech therefore was that Sarai, whilst not his real sister, was at least his female relative, and a descendant of his father as granddaughter, although not of his (Abram's) mother. Their plan, however, had been to present Sarai as his actual, literal, younger sister, and given that she was his niece, there may well have been some family resemblance, which lent support to their claim.

With this view, that Iscah was in fact Sarai,[1] Josephus concurs. His account replaces Iscah with Sarai in recording the story of Haran's family; "Haran left a son, Lot; as also Sarai and Milcha his daughters ... These married their nieces. Nahor married Milcha and Abram married Sarai" (*Antiquities*, Book 1, Chapter 6.5).

---

1   This conclusion, that Sarai and Iscah were one and the same, is also suggested in *Abraham: Father of the Faithful*, Harry A. Whittaker (page 12).

217

Appendix 3

WHAT WAS THE FOUNDATION PROMISE?

THE promise given to Abraham in Genesis 12:1-3 is so well known that perhaps we fail to see how large and expansive it was in the scope of its commitment to bless this man. The words, at once simple and majestic, outlined a series of blessings, which only time and the unfolding of God's purpose would reveal in the fulness of their detail.

First the command:

"Get thee out of thy country, and from thy kindred, and from thy father's house, unto a land that I will shew thee." (Genesis 12:1)

Then the promise:

"And I will make of thee a great nation, and I will bless thee, and make thy name great; and thou shalt be a blessing: and I will bless them that bless thee, and curse him that curseth thee: and in thee shall all families of the earth be blessed." (Genesis 12:2,3)

Much has been written about this passage, and with good reason, since it represents the beginning of all that was offered to Abraham by Almighty God. Every subsequent revelation would serve to amplify and explain what had already been set down in this, the foundation promise that belonged to the "Friend of God". Successive manifestations of faith would lead to additional revelations of blessing, and these would occur at different moments in the patriarch's story, and at different places in the land, until his whole life was wrapped within the fabric of promises.

The suggestion has been made that this opening proclamation contains firstly a national promise, then a personal promise, a family promise and finally an

218

international promise. No doubt all of these are true, although it is doubtful whether they follow in quite as precise a sequence as this. The words do not of themselves break so readily into such subsets of thought. After all the pronouns "thee", "thy" and "thou" which occur throughout the promise indicate that all of it is personal to Abraham in some particular.

He was to be the special channel though whom the entire promise would run, even though its impact and its outworking would involve others. "I will make of *thee* a great nation", "I will bless *thee* and make *thy* name great", "I will bless them that bless *thee*", and "in *thee* shall all families of the earth be blessed", are not quite so suggestive of differing promises after all. It all relates to Abraham in its fulness, and he cannot be separated from any part of the words or phrases.

The cascade of things promised here to the patriarch however, were certainly not mere repetitions but successive statements, with each adding a layer of blessing previously not mentioned, so that in the whole there was a richness that we need to appreciate. Reviewing the promise statement by statement reveals the following ideas, each of which Abraham came to experience:

- "And I will make of thee a great nation." (**The promise of enjoying expansion and growth**; cp. Genesis 13:16; 15:5; 17:2.)
- "And I will bless thee, and make thy name great, and thou shalt be a blessing." (**The promise of achieving distinction and fame**; cp. Genesis 14:13; 23:6; 24:35.)
- "And I will bless them that bless thee, and curse him that curseth thee." (**The promise of receiving protection and care**; cp. Genesis 12:17; 14:20; 20:7.)
- "And in thee shall all families of the earth be blessed." (**The promise of providing mediation and peace**; cp. Genesis 12:5; 14:13; 21:23.)

Each aspect therefore had a direct outworking in the patriarch's life, and this initial and proximate fulfilment gave indication of what that aspect entailed. But the promise did not concern Abraham alone, for at the end of his journey of faith, it was made clear to him that his seed was inextricably linked to the fulfilment of the promise. And thus, "*In thee* shall all families of the earth be blessed", with which the promise began in Genesis 12:3 would eventually become, "*In thy seed* shall all the nations of the earth be blessed" in 22:18. This inclusion of the seed confirmed that whilst the promise in its completeness was first given to Abraham as an individual, there would indeed be further applications of its terms. An initial and first fulfilment would be seen in Abraham (singular), a second in the natural seed (plural), a third in the spiritual seed (singular), and a fourth in the spiritual seed (plural). It becomes a marvellous basis for personal enquiry to trace how each of these levels of the promise were taken up elsewhere in Scripture. How profound then was this foundation promise that concealed so much for future revelation.

Appendix 4

WHEN WERE KETURAH'S CHILDREN BORN?

KETURAH'S relationship with Abraham and the record of the birth of her sons is found in Genesis 25:1-6. The record reads as if this indeed was the next event in the patriarch's life, coming after a wife had been found for his son. It is suggested that the marriage of Isaac may have prompted Abraham to take a further partner himself, in the loneliness of his final years. There are, however, a number of reasons for suggesting that this episode may not be in chronological sequence, and that it belongs to another period in Abraham's life. There are in fact three or four periods when the birth of Keturah's offspring can be accounted for, with sufficient time available for the bringing forth of six successive sons.

Period 1 is the time between Genesis 16 and Genesis 17. This covers the time from the moment of Ishmael's birth when Abram was eighty-six, to the promise of the birth of Isaac when he was ninety-nine. There is therefore a span of thirteen years in Period 1.

Period 2 is the time between Genesis 21 and Genesis 22. It covers the epoch from the moment of Isaac's birth to his offering on Mount Moriah. The duration of this period depends on how old Isaac was at the time of his offering. For the purpose of this appendix, we have assumed that he was twenty, which creates a span of twenty years for Period 2.

Period 3 is the time between Genesis 22 and Genesis 24. It covers the interval from the offering of Isaac to his marriage at the age of forty. Based on Isaac being twenty at the time of Genesis 22, this creates a span of another twenty years for Period 3. If Isaac was thirty-three at the time of Genesis 22 (as some surmise after the antitype), then this effectively combines Periods 2 and 3 into one, which occurs substantively between Genesis 21 and 22.

Period 4 is the time between Genesis 24 and Genesis 25. It covers the epoch from the moment of Isaac's marriage, when Abraham was one hundred and forty, to his death in Genesis 25 at the age of one hundred and seventy five. This makes a span of thirty-five years for Period 4.

Moving backwards through Abraham's timeline enables us to assess each of these periods, to decide which is the more scripturally probable for the short account of this third woman in Abraham's life.

Period 4 relates to the events between Genesis 24 and 25, covering the last thirty-five years of the patriarch. Since the record itself places the event here, it has been argued that it rightly belongs here in chronological sequence. Abraham (it is suggested) took Keturah to wife in his final years, after the death of Sarah. The opening phrase of the episode, "Then again Abraham took a wife", is seen as supporting the idea that the narrative is sequential.

Abraham's physical powers, revived to bring about the birth of Isaac, evidently remained with him (like Moses) and enabled him to produce the sons of Keturah in fulfilment of the promise that he would become "the father of many nations" (Genesis 17:5). All this seems perfectly reasonable, but a closer inspection of the record reveals some difficulties which are not reconciled in this explanation.

A question that cannot with certainty be answered, but that should with certainty be asked, is whether Abraham would have wanted a further partner after the death of his beloved Sarah. She had been his special companion, the wife of his youth and the sharer in his life's experience, reaching to the climax of their mutual faith. No woman could ever replace her in his old age.

Now Keturah, it should be noted, was not Abraham's wife, but a concubine or secondary partner (cp. Genesis

25:1,6; 1 Chronicles 1:32; also Genesis 30:4; 35:22), and this particular status would instead argue that she was taken by Abraham while Sarah was still alive. The mention that Abraham (rather than Abram) took Keturah in this passage is no impediment to an earlier association. The entire narrative concerning the relationship between the two is only recorded in this one place, and as a necessary precursor to the record of the sending away of the sons of the concubines (note plural term) which will follow. But given that Abram's name has long been changed to Abraham by this point, it would have been incongruous to refer to him by his previous name at the end of the record of his life.

Furthermore, it seems improbable that Abraham would father six sons from the age of one hundred and forty onwards, when the birth of Isaac was deemed miraculous at one hundred. Abraham's body at one hundred was "old and well stricken" so as to be "now dead" (Genesis 18:11; Romans 4:19). The birth of additional sons in Genesis 25 would necessitate the revival of his natural powers for more than another forty years, yet the record again expressly tells us that Abraham at one hundred and forty was "old and well stricken" (Genesis 24:1). Given that Isaac's conception was the result of divine intervention, a further six boys produced some forty years later when he was "old and well stricken" again, surely robs the story concerning Isaac's birth of its wondrous power and special uniqueness.

In fact the opening phrase of Genesis 25:1 in its Hebrew form does not indicate any particular notion of time at all. The episode could have happened at any of the four different epochs listed earlier in the patriarch's lifetime. Indeed, the speech of Abraham's servant uttered earlier in the city of Nahor (24:36), implies that Abraham had already given all that he had to Isaac before his marriage to Rebekah. Since this detail is subsequently reiterated in 25:5, it is very likely that the action of sending away the sons of the concubines noted in verse 6, had also occurred at the same time. If correct, this would mean that Keturah's sons were sent away when Abraham was one hundred and forty, contemporaneous with the marriage of Isaac, and with the receiving of his father's inheritance. If so, they must have been born considerably earlier than the actual account of their birth in Genesis 25.

It is reasonable to assume by the time they travelled eastwards and away from Isaac, that they were all grown men in their own right, and embarking on the raising of their own families. This then was an opportune moment for Abraham both to confirm Isaac in his possession, and at the same time send forth his other sons to make their own names and establish their own territories, leaving Isaac alone in the land of promise. Abraham finally deemed this to be the best and wisest course at the time, and they departed with their father's blessing, and bearing the gifts of his affection. Despite the thirty-five years in Period 4, we conclude that Keturah's offspring were definitely not produced in this last section of Abraham's life, and that in fact they had left Abraham's household before this period even began.

Period 3 (if it was a separate epoch) comes between Genesis 22 and 23, from the offering of Isaac to his marriage. The time period appears adequate for the events to have occurred (twenty years are possible here), and a possible reason for Abraham to take a concubine and father additional sons is suggested in the narrative. Perhaps his action was prompted by the intelligence that Nahor his brother had begotten eight children through Milcah, and another four through Reumah, his concubine (Genesis 22:20-24). Yet there is still somewhat of the problem associated with Period 4, that a string of sons are produced at least twenty years after the birth of Isaac. This was a long time for Abraham's fertility to be sustained after its miraculous revival. Nor does this thought sit comfortably with the idea that with the birth of Isaac (the son of their love and of their old age), their deepest desire was now realised. What need was there for further sons, when the seed through whom the promises would be fulfilled had now come? God had answered their prayers, and now the promise could continue. All else was secondary to the consummation of the promise, which had so profoundly overshadowed their entire lives.

There is another consideration that is relevant to the circumstances of this period. If these sons were indeed born in Period 3, why did Abraham have them at all, if he then almost immediately sent them away? And why banish sons, when some were still children and unable to provide for themselves at this time? The birth of sons at this late epoch, so soon before their sending away, seems highly unlikely. For this reason we are doubtful that Keturah's children are brought forth in Period 3.

Period 2 concerns the time that falls between Genesis 21 and 22, from the birth of Isaac to his offering. Again the time is long enough for the events to occur. The period obviously commences from the conception and birth of Isaac, where we know with certainty of the restoration of Abraham's fertility. Yet this period, entirely suitable from a pragmatic view, is perhaps the least likely when the context is considered. For the theme of Genesis 21 concerns the expulsion of Hagar the concubine and her son from Abraham's household, to remove their spirit of rivalry with Sarah and her son. The angel had instructed Abraham to hearken to Sarah, and to send Hagar his concubine away and out of his life. The departure of Hagar left Abraham and Sarah alone and united, free to concentrate on the raising of Isaac as a godly seed.

These were joyous yet crucial years, when they raised the one known as their "only begotten son", with intensity of devotion after his miraculous appearance in their lives. There would be no child like this one in their lifetime. This is the son who, so imbued with the spirit of his parents, will in the very next episode be willingly offered in loving submission to his father's will as an astonishing type of Christ himself. It would certainly seem incongruous for Abraham to take another concubine at this precise moment of Isaac's spiritual education, and beget six half brothers to Isaac, brothers who although younger, would still stake their claim to the love, affection, time and attention of their father Abraham. And all these to be introduced into the household immediately after Ishmael had been sent away? It is a notion that seems inconsistent with the spirit of the whole episode.

This then leaves Period 1, which marks the thirteen years between Genesis 16 and 17. There are divergent views on whether this period is long enough for Keturah to bear six sons. It has been argued that the gestation / lactation cycle was much longer then, and many more years would be necessary for these sons to be born. The writer however believes that it is possible. Although infants were customarily not weaned until perhaps the age of three in those times, this was not an impediment to further conception within that period. It is widely accepted that breastfeeding children is highly effective in preventing further conception for the first six months after birth. Thereafter, however, the likelihood of conception increases, with full fertility generally returning to a feeding mother within fifteen months. Setting aside such other matters as wet nurses (found in the next generation with Deborah, the nurse for Isaac's own wife) and the possibility of twins, six sons could in fact have been born within a shorter period than thirteen years. Abraham's desire to produce offspring whilst he was still able, argues for a shorter period overall. The birth of Ishmael had confirmed for Abraham that he could indeed have children. But his age, and physical state brought an imperative, that if further sons were to be begotten, then they must be brought forth now. If Keturah was taken at this time, then it brings all Abraham's progeny through his concubines, into the same period. They are all his children during the years of his remaining vitality, before age rendered him impotent. Placed in this epoch these seven servant sons born in his house, represent the final and complete exhaustion of all fleshly solutions to the problem of the seed.

What then of Genesis 17:4-6? Does this promise point forward to Keturah's sons, whose births must therefore come later? By no means. Although Abraham was to become a father of many nations (verse 6) this was to be fulfilled through Sarah (verse 16), who, matched with him in the promise, was to be the mother of those same nations. This multitude of nations therefore could not include either Ishmael or the sons of Keturah, but would grow from the descendants of Isaac alone. Even if Keturah's sons had already been born, this promise would still have been made, as its fulfilment awaited the birth of Sarah's son.

This promise of nationhood in Genesis 17 is expounded by Paul to show that "a father of many nations" is the promise of the wider fatherhood of Abraham through his spiritual seed among the Gentiles, who all in symbol derive their family connection through Isaac (Romans 4:16,17). Ishmael is singled out for mention in this account (Genesis 17:18,23) because he was the firstborn of Abraham, and born to be a possible heir. The sons of Keturah however, are never once described as the sons of Abraham, but always as the sons of his concubine. (25:4,6). They were doubtless present at the time of the promise of Genesis 17, and were included in the rite of circumcision, being counted among those who were "born in the house" (17:23,27).

We conclude then, that the sons of Keturah were born after Ishmael, but before Isaac, and that the years of their infancy came in the decade of Abraham's life before the great promise of Genesis 17.[1] The last of them by this reckoning must have been born before Abraham was ninety-nine, and more likely several years before this. At the time of their sending away, when Abraham was one hundred and forty, these six men would be between the ages of forty and sixty-five. This is a much more reasonable conclusion. At the end of Abraham's life when finally granting inheritance to Isaac, he decided that the best course was to send forth his other sons

---

1 A similar conclusion concerning the timing of Keturah's children is suggested in *Abraham: Father of the Faithful*, Harry A. Whittaker (page 75).

to other lands. But the sons he sent away were men in their prime: mature, capable, fathers of young families themselves. And there is good reason to believe that the sons of Keturah took with them not only the presents of their father, but the gift of his faith as well. In the deserts of the east, the Bene Kedem of later generations including Keturah's offspring would witness to an Abrahamic standard and spirit of worship.

A final indication of when Keturah's children might have been born is to be found in the genealogies of Chronicles. There, the sons of Abraham are listed as Isaac and Ishmael, with Isaac first in rank as the promised seed. But then the lists of offspring would seem to be noted in the order of the family through the wives:

- First the son of Hagar (1 Chronicles 1:29-31).
- Then the sons of Keturah (verses 32,33).
- Lastly the son of Sarah (verse 34).

The details considered above seek to summarise all known facts within the narrative in order to arrive at a conclusion that best harmonises them all. They lead to the suggestion that Keturah's children were born considerably earlier in Abraham's life, and that this makes much better sense when reviewing the circumstances of Abraham sending these same sons away from his encampment.

Of course the final consequence of this sequence, secondary to the argument itself but relevant nonetheless, is to place Isaac as the last child, the eighth son, the child of Abraham and Sarah's resurrection revival to produce this special and "only begotten son". That the number eight will also be so beautifully inwrought into the story of God's "only begotten son" becomes a final seal that links these two children of promise. But let everyone be fully persuaded in their own mind.

Appendix 5

WHY WERE ABRAM AND SARAI'S NAMES CHANGED?

THE occasion where the covenant blessing was extended so that they might embrace it together was singular in the scope of its revelation. And equally dramatic was the fact that the monumental things promised on this day were forever commemorated by the solemn changes of name that were given to both Abram and Sarai.

There are of course, other examples of Bible characters whose names were changed as indicative of a change in the direction and purpose of their lives. The first child of David and Bathsheba died unnamed and uncircumcised when the judgement of God fell upon them. David's spirit of contrition however, and his deep repentance, were blessed by the bringing forth of another son, whom the Lord loved. The boy had been called Solomon by his parents, in itself a highly significant name reflecting the mutual desire of the father and mother for peaceful fellowship and harmony with God. And God did indeed love the child. None other than Nathan the prophet (he who was sent to convince David of his sin) was now sent to proclaim that God had called their son Jedidiah, 'beloved of the Lord'. This new name, pronounced by prophetic testimony, was symbolic of David and Bathsheba's restoration to favour in the eyes of God. A change of name, in this case of their son, signified this change of circumstance (2 Samuel 12:24,25).

Simon, son of Jona, came to the Lord at the invitation of his brother Andrew. Christ revealed that he knew his existing name but then declared that his name was to be changed, and that from thenceforth he would be known as Cephas. Peter being but the Greek for the Aramaic Cephas, his new name revealed that Christ foresaw the work he would fulfil amongst his people. Looking upon him, the Lord discerned the capabilities of this new disciple, and the journey to spiritual maturity that would lead him to become the 'stone'. His change of name was intended to indicate his future role, and was given to him under inspiration by a master who knew what was in man, and especially in his own men (John 1:42).

In the case of Abram, his name was to be changed by the addition of a letter. Abram's name had four consonants. Now a fifth would be added, the Hebrew letter *he*, which is in turn the fifth letter of the Hebrew alphabet. The letter *he* has a numerical value of five. The covenant, cut in Genesis 15:9,10, and now about to be confirmed, was ratified by the sacrifice of five animals. The "seed" who would share in this promise is mentioned in the conversation five times (17:7-10). The entire operation would be brought about by the grace of God at work in their lives. The apostolic commentary on this episode is found in Romans 4, where Paul states, "Therefore it is of faith, that *it might be by grace*; to the end the promise might be sure to all the seed; not to that only which is of the law, but to that also which is of the faith of Abraham; who is the father of us all, (as it is written, I have made thee a father of many nations,) before him whom he believed, even God, who quickeneth the dead, and calleth those things which be not as though they were" (Romans 4:16,17).

The letter *he* is the dominant consonant of the divine Tetragrammaton YHWH. Its insertion into Abram's name was a dramatic means of intimating that there would be a divine intervention in his life. God was to become involved in the bringing forth of the seed, and this was marked in the new name he gave unto His friend. Inclusion, intervention, involvement were all bound up in this astonishing alteration to Abram's name, as the record emphasises. "*I will* ... multiply thee exceedingly" states Genesis 17:2, and "*I will* make thee exceeding fruitful" states Genesis 17:6. Here was God at work in the patriarch's life.

230

This change, however, also meant that his name became three syllables instead of two. The addition of the *he* provides by elision an abbreviated form of *hamon*, which means multitude. There is an obvious connection of thought with this word in the narrative, for immediately before and immediately after his change of name, the word *hamon* is found in the phrase "a father of many (*hamon*, a multitude of) nations" (Genesis 17:4,5). So Abram, 'high father' became Abraham, 'father of a multitude', for "a father of many nations have I made thee" (verse 5). It was God's involvement that empowered Abraham's fatherhood. This was the significance of the changing of his name. The very phrase "many nations" suggests a promise reaching beyond Israel, and the use of the word *goyim* suggests the inclusion of the Gentiles in this reckoning.

If God was to be the Father, if His power was to operate in the matter, then anything might be done. His power might quicken Sarai just as easily as it could rejuvenate Abram. In like manner therefore, Sarai's name was to be crowned with that same *he* which now adorned Abram's. The involvement of God directly in her life to bring about the promise was as true for Sarai as it was of Abram, perhaps more so since she would be the actual bearer of the seed. And so "*I will bless* her" is twice affirmed in verse 16, just as it had been of Abram. Of course it must involve the Almighty, and of course her name therefore should also reflect this glorious change in their lives. And so Sarai, 'my princess' became Sarah, 'princess' to signify that the result of this divine involvement would elevate her to become the princess and queen of a multitude that extended well beyond her own family, and far beyond her own lifetime, and all because of God working with her.

God's intervention in their lives could not be symbolised more powerfully than by the placing of His Name upon theirs, a thought at once both wonderful and humbling to contemplate. Were ever a couple more closely linked in the purpose of God? For God to take this man and this woman, and amend both their names by interposition so that His Name was inwrought upon theirs, is profound in what it teaches concerning their place in His purpose, and their mutual involvement in it. Their new names were deeply significant, for they celebrated and memorialised that God was at work with them, and they with Him in the fulfilling of His promises.

It is part of the blessing of the Apocalypse that this promise reaches unto us also, for "To him that overcometh will I give to eat of the hidden manna, and will give him a white stone, and in the stone a new name written, which no man knoweth saving he that receiveth it" (Revelation 2:17).

Appendix 6

WHY DID SARAH DIE IN HEBRON?

"And Sarah was an hundred and seven and twenty years old: these were the years of the life of Sarah. And Sarah died in Kirjath-arba; the same is Hebron in the land of Canaan: and Abraham came to mourn for Sarah and to weep for her."   (Genesis 23:1,2)

IN this account of the death of Sarah, the record states that Abraham "came" to mourn for her. On the basis of this one word, it has been suggested that the episode of the offering of Isaac caused a division in the family. It is postulated that the shock of Abraham even deciding to offer Isaac was so deep that Sarah was completely estranged from her husband, and that this rift was never healed. By comparing 22:19 and 23:2 it is suggested that Abraham remained in Beersheba, but Sarah moved to Hebron and died there in isolation, and that Abraham had to journey from his own encampment to Hebron in order to pay his last respects. Such a suggestion is unwarranted, and is to be repudiated on several counts.

In the first instance, we note in the narrative of Abraham and Sarah's journeys, that their movements are generally accounted for in the singular, although the presence of both is rightly assumed. In the following places their movements are noted together: Genesis 11:31 (the beginning of their pilgrimage), 12:4,5 (their entry into the land), 13:1 (their return from Egypt). In most other instances however, the detail of the movements only mentions Abraham in the singular: 12:6,8,9,10; 13:3,12,18; 20:1; 21:33,34; 22:19. In all these instances however, it is obvious that Sarah is with him, especially in the episodes of Genesis 12 and 20 where Sarah will play a leading role. Her absence from these travel notes is never taken as indicating that she was somewhere else. Genesis 23:2 now mentions Sarah in the singular as being in Hebron when she died. Why then would we assume on this one occasion that Abraham was elsewhere? And there is of course, a perfectly good reason why the record of their location this time is linked to Sarah rather than to Abraham. Genesis 23:1 had already provided the context for this particular geographical note – the topic of the chapter will centre on the death and burial of Sarah, and immediately goes on to state that she died in Hebron. There is nothing here that warrants the conjecture of a household rupture. It is no more suggestive of such a division than the long list of geographical movements that mention only Abraham by name.

Secondly, the passage can be understood satisfactorily in quite a different way. The Hebrew word for came, *bow*, is used in a wide variety of applications, including: came in, went in, go in, entered in, etc. It is used for example in the following Genesis passages:

Genesis 7:7 – went in the ark.

Genesis 16:4 – went in unto Hagar.

Genesis 19:3 – entered into his house.

Genesis 31:33 – entered into Rachel's tent.

The term as used in Genesis 23:2 is therefore translated "went in" by Rotherham, Green, RSV, NASB etc. The *Speaker's Commentary* has a note that reads as follows on the text: "Some infer that Abraham was not with Sarah when she died. But it may mean no more than that Abraham went into Sarah's tent to mourn for her." This would certainly be the most obvious way of interpreting the passage.

Thirdly, the inference of separation suggests an action that does not match our knowledge of their lives, or of the culture and practice of the times. The thought that a wife (or husband) would simply walk away to live elsewhere if deeply unhappy might be modern conjugal practice, but it was not the custom of their day. More importantly it is not consistent with the Biblical narrative concerning these two. In 1 Peter 3:5,6, Sarah is set forth by the apostle as an example of a wife who obeyed her husband, "calling him lord", an attitude inconsistent with the idea that they separated from each other over an irreconcilable difference.

Fourthly, the whole notion is inconsistent with the force and beauty of the narrative. The offering of Isaac is clearly described as the pinnacle of faith that brought with it the last and greatest of blessings for Abraham and Sarah. Their children would be multiplied as the stars of heaven, their seed would possess the gate of his enemies, and in him (so wonderfully foreshadowed in their obedient son) all nations would be blessed.

To suggest that these promises came at the same time as a rupture between man and wife which was never to be resolved, would be a tragic end to the sequence, and utterly at variance with the promises just vouchsafed unto them by the oath of God. Of what value were such blessings when their marriage had been irrevocably sundered? It would be an empty gift for Abraham, if it also resulted in the bitter separation and permanent estrangement of his wife, who left him and died elsewhere. To make such a suggestion is to mock their faith and to cast an aspersion on their marriage which Scripture does not support. Their united faith in this trial revealed instead a wonderful type of the experiences of the mother and Father of the Lord himself. This is a much more satisfying outcome to contemplate, and one that carries with it several traces of scriptural connections which the Spirit conceals for the diligent searcher to find.

Why then was Sarah in Hebron at all when she died? There are any number of possible reasons that might relate to the ordinary circumstances of life, none of which are suggestive of estrangement. This is the view adopted by the writer, and the comments on this chapter suggest a possible reason as to their decision to move to Hebron in their old age.

Lastly, some thought needs to be given to the timing of this travel. Genesis 35:27 indicates that at some point in time Abraham and Isaac sojourned together in Hebron. The phrase (as another geographical note) in itself implies neither Sarah's presence nor absence. There are however only four periods in the Genesis record when this joint sojourning in Hebron of father and son can have taken place.

a. After Genesis 21 / before Genesis 22

The record of Genesis 22:1 however does not suggest a move to Hebron before the offering of Isaac. Genesis 21:33,34 indicates that Abraham clearly dwelt in Beersheba before this event, and the fact that Genesis 22:19 confirms they returned to Beersheba after the event supports the view that they had not moved to Hebron before Genesis 22.

b. After Genesis 22 / before Genesis 23

The only travel note that indicates that they were in Hebron at all comes in Genesis 23:2. Taken at its face value, the note suggests a move from Beersheba to Hebron after Genesis 22 but before the events unfolded in Genesis 23.

c. After Genesis 23 / before Genesis 24

Again the record of Genesis 24:1 does not indicate a move to Hebron at this point. In fact and to the contrary, Genesis 24:62 implies that the episode of finding a bride for Isaac (which is the burden of this chapter) commenced with Abraham and Isaac already dwelling in the south country near the well Lahai-Roi, since that is where the servant returned with Rebekah.

d. After Genesis 24 / before Genesis 25

But Genesis 25:11 implies that Isaac was still resident in the south country where he (and presumably Abraham) had been in the previous chapter. There is no suggestion of a move to Hebron within the context of this episode, which culminates in the death of Abraham. The implication is that both Isaac and Ishmael made special journeys from their own territories to bury their father together at Hebron, and then returned to their respective lands.

Based on the above, the clearest contextual evidence for the move to Hebron is to place it exactly where the record itself suggests, namely after Genesis 22 but before Genesis 23. This is the view taken by the writer.[1] But now the comment in Genesis 35:27 may be seen as having added significance. If Abraham and Isaac sojourned in Hebron together at the time the record suggests, and Sarah dies in Hebron at the same time period, then Genesis 23:1,2 and 35:27 form an 'undesigned coincidence' which reveals the whole family, father mother and son living together in peace and harmony in the city of fellowship. There is only unity here, and not division or estrangement.

---

1   A similar interpretation is advocated in *Abraham: Father of the Faithful*, Harry A. Whittaker (pages 112,113).

Appendix 7

DID SARAH HERSELF RECEIVE STRENGTH?

"Through faith also Sara herself received strength to conceive seed, and was delivered of a child when she was past age, because she judged him faithful who had promised." (Hebrews 11:11)

THE above is the rendering of the King James Version, which in turn follows the Received Text. It is a rendering that has been consistently followed in the vast majority of translations, both in the English and in other languages, over a long period of time. The verse was seen as referring to the miraculous power which operated upon Sarah by faith, and which led to the bringing forth of the child through whom the promises would be fulfilled.

Textual criticism arose however over the question as to whether the phrase *dunamin eis katabolhn spermatos* ought with propriety to be rendered, "received strength to conceive seed", since it was suggested that 'the deposition of seed' is exclusively a male function. By taking the reference to Sarah as a 'circumstantial clause' it was proposed to make Abraham the subject of the passage, and the one who received strength for 'the deposition of seed'.

Conformity to this approach led to the most obvious illustration of textual manipulation in the case of the NIV (1973, 1978, 1984 editions), which translated the verse, "By faith *Abraham*, even though he was past age, and Sarah herself was barren, *was enabled to become a father* because *he* considered him faithful who had made the promise". Neither the word 'Abraham' or 'father' are present in any Greek text, and were entirely driven by the bias of a textual opinion. The inconsistency of textual criticism is revealed in the fact that a subsequent printing of the NIV (2011 edition) completely reversed course on the translation, which now reads, "And by faith even *Sarah*, who was past childbearing age, *was enabled to bear children* because *she* considered him faithful who had made the promise".

Despite some inadequacy in this wording, it represents a return to the long held view. Indeed, the most recent scholarship supports the interpretation that Hebrews 11:11 should be taken to refer to Sarah as the subject, given that the words *kai auth Sarra*, "even Sarah herself", occur in the nominative case immediately after the initial words "by faith".[1]

Within our community there are few if any who can claim to be textual scholars, but we should certainly aim to be competent contextual scholars. Given our view on the inspiration of the Scriptures, we regard the call and echo of one Scripture to another as furnishing the best of arguments to determine meaning, especially where both manuscript evidence and 'textual experts' differ. There are at least two lines of direct Biblical contact that support the KJV reading of the passage, and a brief reference to these may be helpful.

The term *katabolhn* (conceive) used here in Hebrews 11:11 is certainly not the normal Greek word for conception in the New Testament, and in fact on every other occasion is translated as "foundation". Although textual critics incline to the view that the word be limited to the idea of conception, and hence their concern as to how this might be applied to Sarah, there is in fact a clear connection of thought with the Genesis record which widens our understanding of the term, and perhaps supplies the very reason for the Spirit's selection of it through the author of Hebrews. The 'laying down of a foundation', which is the primary meaning of the word, conveys the idea of the beginning of a building.

---

1   See *The Epistle to the Hebrews*, Gareth Lee Cockerill (NCINT) on Hebrews 11:11. Cockerill sets aside the argument advanced by F. F. Bruce in the previous NCINT commentary on Hebrews, and returns Sarah to being the subject of the verse in its entirety.

Immediately there is an echo of the words of Sarah, "Go in unto my maid; it may be that I may obtain children by her" (Genesis 16:2). But the phrase "obtain children" here is the Hebrew word *banah*, which literally means 'to be builded'. The word is used in Genesis to describe the building of a woman, the building of a city, the building of an altar, the building of a house, and by Sarah herself in this place for the building of a household. Ishmael would never prove to be the foundation stone of the family that Sarah had in mind. But when Isaac came the foundation stone was laid, and the household of Abraham and Sarah would indeed be built by this son. This allusion of thought passes into the Hebrews 11:11 reference, and expands our understanding of what might be conveyed by the term 'laying down a foundation'.

The focus of attention upon the phrase "conceive seed" should not detract from a similar level of attention that should be paid to the subsequent statement, *kai para kairon hlikias eteken*, meaning that Sarah "was delivered of a child when she was past age". This second affirmation of Sarah, which also came about as a result of her faith, was the real and final and purposeful climax of the Genesis account. It was manifestly not just the conception of Isaac, but his subsequent birth that illustrated the fulness of God's dealings with her. The Scriptural record is unambiguous and decisive about the supreme importance of Sarah being *delivered of this child*, as the following passages show:

"And God said, Sarah thy wife shall bear thee a son indeed." (Genesis 17:19)

"With Isaac, which Sarah shall bear unto thee." (Genesis 17:21)

"I will certainly return … and lo, Sarah thy wife shall have a son." (Genesis 18:10)

"I will return … according to the time of life, and Sarah shall have a son." (Genesis 18:14)

"And the LORD visited Sarah as he had said, and the LORD did unto Sarah as he had spoken. For

Sarah conceived, and bare Abraham a son."
(Genesis 21:1,2)

"And Abraham called the name of his son … whom Sarah bare to him, Isaac." (Genesis 21:3)

"And she said, Who would have said unto Abraham, that Sarah should have given children suck? for I have borne him a son." (Genesis 21:7)

The weight of these testimonies suggests an understanding of Hebrews 11:11 in this wider context. Evidently Sarah did not 'lay the foundation' of a seed by means of just the conception of Isaac, but also by means of his birth. It was his birth that provided the foundation seed of an entire family who would be brought forth by the operation of God. Through faith Sarah experienced the power of God for conception, gestation and birth, and when this process was fully accomplished, she herself had laid a foundation. All this is caught up in the passage. The KJV rendering captures the fulness of these Genesis echoes, and permits, we believe, a more expanded and enriched view as to its meaning, than that which textual analysis and counter analysis alone might reveal.

We are satisfied that this passage provides evidence that Sarah's faith matched Abraham's, as together they came to the triumph of faith.

SCRIPTURE INDEX

243

246